ISLAM IN AMERICAN PRISONS

The growth of Islam both worldwide and particularly in the United States is especially notable among African-American inmates incarcerated in American state and federal penitentiaries. This growth poses a powerful challenge to American penal philosophy, structured on the ideal of rehabilitating offenders through penance and appropriate penal measures. *Islam in American Prisons* argues that prisoners converting to Islam seek an alternative form of redemption, one that poses a powerful epistemological as well as ideological challenge to American penology. Meanwhile, following the events of 9/11, some prison inmates have converted to radical anti-Western Islam and have become sympathetic to the goals and tactics of the Al-Qa'ida organization. At the same time, other Islamic groups such as the Nation of Islam are working with large segments of black inmates to convert them to their own, often controversial, brands of Islam. This new study examines this multifaceted phenomenon and makes a powerful argument for the objective examination of the rehabilitative potentials of faith-based organizations in prisons, including the faith of those who convert to Islam.

Islam in American Prisons
Black Muslims' Challenge to American Penology

HAMID REZA KUSHA
East Carolina University, USA

ASHGATE

© Hamid Reza Kusha 2009

Published by
Ashgate Publishing Limited
Wey Court East
Union Road
Farnham
Surrey, GU9 7PT
England

Ashgate Publishing Company
Suite 420
101 Cherry Street
Burlington
VT 05401-4405
USA

www.ashgate.com

British Library Cataloguing in Publication Data
Kusha, Hamid Reza
   Islam in American prisons : Black Muslims' challenge to
   American penology. - (Law, justice and power series)
   1. Criminal justice, Administration of - United States
   2. African American prisoners - Religious life - United
   States 3. Muslim converts - United States - Attitudes
   4. Muslims, Black - United States - Attitudes
   5. Imprisonment - Religious aspects - Islam 6. Radicalism -
   Religious aspects - Islam
   I. Title
   365.6'088297

Library of Congress Cataloging-in-Publication Data
Kusha, Hamid R.
 Islam in American prisons : black Muslims' challenge to American penology / by Hamid Reza Kusha.
     p. cm. -- (Law, justice and power)
   Includes bibliographical references and index.
   ISBN 978-1-84014-722-3 (alk. paper) -- ISBN 978-0-7546-8865-5 (ebook) 1. Prisons--
United States--History. 2. Islam--United States. 3. Criminal justice, Administration of--United
States. I. Title.
   HV9471.K87 2009
   365'.6088297870973--dc22

                                                                        2008055529

ISBN 978-1-84014-722-3
eISBN 978-0-7546-8865-5

Mixed Sources
Product group from well-managed forests and other controlled sources
www.fsc.org Cert no. SA-COC-1565
© 1996 Forest Stewardship Council
FSC

Printed and bound in Great Britain by
MPG Books Ltd, Bodmin, Cornwall.

Contents

List of Tables

Preface

Islam is one of the fastest growing monotheistic faiths in the world, including in the United States of America. This growth is especially notable among African-American inmates incarcerated in both state and federal penitentiaries. The epistemological thrust of this book is that this growth poses a powerful challenge to American penal philosophy, which theoretically is structured on the ideal of rehabilitating offenders through penance and appropriate penal measures. From colonial times to present, American penal philosophy has been adamant that a just regime of punishment is one that applies penal measures that perform their designated penal functions. However, following its Judeo-Christian base and notion of penal fairness, this regime must allow for rehabilitation so as to give the convicts a second chance for redemption. American penologists have utilized institutional incarceration as the main vehicle for achieving this ideal. However, the general history of incarceration in both state and federal penal institutions hardly resonates harmoniously with the American penal philosophy's rehabilitative ideals. The nature of life in penal institutions is a dehumanizing experience marred with violence and exploitation. In addition, racial and ethnic minorities are being incarcerated disproportionately to their general crime and demographic rates in this country.

Thus, one argument of this book is that prison-bound conversion to Islam is an alternative form of redemption sought by the converts; this poses a powerful epistemological as well as ideological challenge to American penology. The larger epistemological base of this challenge is continuously being formed, refurbished, and enhanced among a segment of the inner-city African-American communities who do not perceive their overall social, economic and political standing improving. For this segment, Islam is an empowering alternative to reclaiming their deserved share of the American Dream. With the tragic terrorism events of 11 September, 2001, prison administrators have been warned of the possibility of terrorist recruitment from among prison inmates who convert to what is known as "radical Islam" which is being identified with Wahhabism practiced in Saudi Arabia as well as among the followers of the terror master Usam Bin Laden's Al-Qa'ida movement There are cases being documented showing that some of these converts are sympathetic to Al-Qa'ida organization and to its brand of radical, anti-Western Islam. At the same time, there is ample evidence of other Islamic groups that are working with a large segment of black inmates converting them to their brand of Islam such as for example, the Nation of Islam (NOI), and a host of other North American Islamic movements. The success of the Nation of Islam, as we shall explore in this book, is due to two interconnected factors. First, the Nation of Islam has provided an effective prison-bound mechanism of protection to those who convert to its brand of Islam. Second, the literature of the Nation of Islam claims that not only has it converted a large number of inmates to Islam, but has also successfully reintegrated them into its social and economic infrastructures thus preventing them from recidivating and being re-incarcerated. Accordingly, this transformation from a convicted-felon to a rehabilitated Muslim convert takes place through several stages as prospective convert-inmates are taken under the Nation of Islam's prison-bound protective networks to be gradually assimilated into the Nation's version of Islam based on the teachings of the Honorable Elijah Muhammad, the founder and the spiritual leader. This is another aspect of the challenge that this book covers.

However, this book does not intend, nor is it my claim, that we should replace American penal philosophy with an Islamic alternative. In fact, Islam's Sacred Law, the *Shari'a* is almost silent on incarceration as a rehabilitative venue. Until recently, in many Islamic countries, modern prisons did not exist because those found guilty within the traditional Islamic jurisprudential norms, would be subjected to execution after a short sojourn in dungeon-like detention centers. In fact, thanks to the forces of modernization operating in the Islamic world from mid 19th century to present, the traditional view of the role and the function of prison has changed in many Islamic societies. Gradually, a more modern and rehabilitative penal philosophy and institutions have replaced the traditional system. In sum, in the post 9/11 specter of international terrorism, prison-bound conversion is also being perceived as a serious post-incarceration release risk. This book will address these issues arguing that we need to objectively examine the rehabilitative potentials of faith-based organizations in prisons, including the faith of those who convert to Islam.

Acknowledgments

I am greatly indebted to all scholars and researchers whose work, research data, inferences and conclusions I have cited throughout the pages of this book. I earnestly believe that I won't be able to express my deep sense of debt and gratitude to all whose work I have utilized as I have traversed in a rather difficult subject which I hope will open up a much needed yet neglected area in American penology—Islam in American prisons and its impact on African-American inmates. I also would like to express my thanks and gratitude to members of the Department of Criminal Justice at East Carolina University, Greenville, NC, for their creative criticism of some of the important subjects and arguments raised in this book during the writing process. In particular, I would like to acknowledge my thanks to the Chair of the Department, Professor James F. Anderson, who was kind enough to meticulously edit a number of chapters. All the credit is due to these kind and considerate colleagues of mine, whereas all the pitfalls and shortcoming of this book falls on my shoulder.

I am also greatly indebted to the editorial staff and reviewers who meticulously went through the pages of the manuscript weeding out errors and correcting structural shortcomings of the manuscript suggesting ways to improve the overall quality of the text. In particular, many thanks go to Carolyn Court, Alison Kirk and Eric Levy who kindly and patiently worked with me during different stages of the writing and final production of the manuscript.

Finally, this work would not have reached the completion stage had it not been for the love, patience, and understanding of my beloved wife Farah, and our son, Armani Reza both of whom I consider as the expression of God Almighty's eternal love for me. Farah and Armani are Almighty's cherished reward to me for some spectacular thing that I must have done in my life, of which I have yet to discover.

Chapter 1

Introduction

Islam is one of the fastest growing religions in the world. Several reasons can be cited for this phenomenal growth. First, Islam is a simple yet coherent monotheistic faith professing that it is the destiny of humankind to follow one universal God, Allah, who personifies justice, law and universal compassion for humankind, especially the downtrodden. Allah, the faith professes further, is not only passionately concerned with our faith but is also watchful over human affairs. This is because it is Allah who has created the temporal world with "Its" very invisible hands. It is noteworthy that in the Qur'an Allah is depicted as one who is neither begotten nor begets, though in some verses the masculine epithet is used for Allah. The purpose of human creation is cited as one in which the Almighty wants to test human resolve against temptations caused by a wide range of individualistic as well as social, economic, political and communal factors. Crime, violence, injustice, aggression, greed and corruption are among temptations that the faith warns believers against criminogenic impacts. Allah with all Its majestic and unlimited might is on the side of the righteous, declares the Qur'an, in various verses as, for example, in cxiv, 1 through 6, whereby believers are told to seek refuge in the embrace of Allah from the temptations of evil forces which "whisper" in our hearts to us to entice us to commit evil deeds. It is the "duty" of men and women of faith to resist temptations. The faithful, instead of choosing the route of crime and evil deeds, should choose the righteous path that the Almighty has instituted.

Second, Islam, as a faith, is not overtly ritualistic. One only has to perform five daily prayers, make a one-time pilgrimage to Mecca, give a certain amount of one's wealth to charity, and observe dusk to dawn fast during the month of Ramadan. There are also three principal beliefs in Islam. These are: (1) belief in the Oneness of Allah; (2) belief in the Messengers of God (from Adam to Abraham, to Noah, to Lot, to Janus, to Moses, to Jesus to Muhammad); and (3) belief in our resurrection in the Day of Judgment. For the faithful these are empowering because by adhering to these principles, one finds communion not only with the larger Islamic communities and cultures scattered throughout the world, but also with members of both Jewish and Christian communities and cultures. This is because both Jewish and Christian faiths teach similar messages of righteousness thus putting aside ritualistic differences; a devout Muslim has no problem in his or her camaraderie with the Judeo-Christian principles of righteousness. It is noteworthy that Islam's sacred text, the Qur'an, portrays Allah, the *Howa* a term that can only be translated as 'an everlasting entity that is, has always been, and will always be.' Allah is the *sin qua non* entity that the Qur'an personifies as

The Creator whose realms of might, knowledge, and hegemonic dominance "over the earth and heavens and every thing in between" is beyond human range of cognition. This is the God of Abraham to whom Jews, Christians and Muslims give homage. Accordingly, Allah also possesses perfect sublime qualities as, for example in i, 1 through 7; ii, 1 through 19. Allah is categorically on the side of the righteous faithful who continuously struggle for good and ward off evil forces and their temptations. Thus, having faith in Allah and being righteous, are two complimentary aspects of belief in Islam as the faith seeks to instill peace and tranquility in those who embrace its message: submission to Allah; this is the message of *s.a.lm*– which stands for peace, the root word for Islam thus Islam in its essence is the religion of peace and tranquility. The Qur'an is adamant in this depiction of Islam.

Third, Islam, as a faith, admonishes believers to follow the straight path as, for example, in i,6; vi, 153; a path that is moral, righteous and uplifting. Thus, following such a path enables the faithful to opt for a rewarding and bountiful life in this world, and for salvation and eternal joy in the world to come. Once a believer opts for Islam's straight path in conjunction with sincere and consistent efforts that he or she exerts so as not to deviate from this righteous path, he or she will be guided by Allah regardless of gender, creed, race or social class. The path of righteousness is, however, arduous. To traverse it successfully, believers have to equip themselves with sublime moral qualities to ward off lowly temptations that emerge against one's progression in the righteous route. The unbelievers, on the other hand, stray from the straight path of Allah by not heeding the call to righteousness; this is because unbelievers' ears and eyes and hearts have been sealed (ii, 136, 142, 281). But again, one is given a choice between good (*khayr*) and evil (*shar*). Naturally crime, violence, corruption and succumbing to lowly inclinations are factors that reside on the side of evil. In contrast, compassion and charity towards humankind, patience, tolerance, forbearance and kindness towards the downtrodden of society are on the side of the good. The struggle between the good and the evil is not on a cosmic plane of reference as, portrayed by the Zoroastrian faith, one of the oldest monotheistic religions that appeared among ancient Iranians before Islam. Unlike the Zoroastrian view of a cosmic battle between good and evil, the Islamic view of this battle is one that is of an intrinsic nature as both factors of good and evil exists within our human core. As humans, we are responsible for deciding which will influence our daily lives. We are responsible for our social acts and consequences, be they good or evil notwithstanding a certain notion of predestination to which verse of the Qur'an alludes.

Fourth, in Islam, believers are duty bound to help one another in times of hardship that befall on their respective communities. Believers are duty bound to encourage each other to do good deeds in the same manner that enjoinment from committing wrongs is sought, a premise which finds expression in the Qur'anic formula of *al-amri bi'l-ma`ruf wa al-nahy `an al-munkar*. Islam, as a faith, and in its eschatological essence, posits the notion of salvation within the righteous disposition of the believers saying, that it is the purity of one's thoughts and deeds (*taqwaa*) that endear one to Allah and not spurious attributes of wealth, race, gender, or class.

Finally, Islam, like its Judeo-Christian counterparts, is expressively anti-criminogenic in its core teachings proposing that:

1. One who shares earnestly believes in Allah's many sublime qualities expressed in the Qur'an, not only will refrain from the commission of sins or crimes, but will also enjoin others against such socially harmful and victimizing acts.
2. One who shares wealth with others helps to immunize social groups and communities to the criminogenic impacts of absolute and/or relative depravity that modern criminology now recognizes as an important etiology of crime.
3. One who prays regularly to remind himself/herself of Allah's presence and might, will refrain from the commission of crime or sin.
4. One who is reared up in a decent and upright family, educational system and community sharing these values will refrain from committing sin or crime.
5. It is incumbent upon parents, educators, religious and community as well as civic and state leaders to inculcate these values on the individual/ community in order to combat sin-crime.
6. Islam stresses adherence to the principles of just conduct in social, economic and communal spheres, an emphasis that makes the religions in the line of Abraham (Judaism, Christianity and Islam) powerful advocates of compassion for the underprivileged and the disenfranchised social groups.

What do these premises imply for the subject matter of this book? One central premise of this book is that the faith of Islam is growing among the African-American community in the US, and, in particular, among black inmates who comprise a large percentage of the incarcerated population in both state and federal penitentiaries. This growth has much to do with the powerful social justice message of Islam, as well as with the nature of the prison life which is by and large oppressive, violent and dehumanizing. Survival is of chief concern to inmates in the prison settings despite the many rehabilitative, educational, and even recreational programs which have been instituted throughout the decades to make prison life more secure, rehabilitative and less violent. There are studies showing that different religious denominations, including Muslims and especially the Nation of Islam have created faith-based systems of protection within both state and federal penitentiaries with the stated aim of creating a more anti-criminogenic lifestyle within the prison settings. The efficacy of these programs differs. However, the fact that Islam is gaining a significant following among African-American inmates presents a powerful challenge to American penology considering that North American societies (Canada, United States of America and Mexico) have historically been part of the Christendom with a powerful Judeo-

Christian penal philosophy despite continuous efforts to secularize it. The fact that Islam is beginning to have influence on North American social and cultural spheres including penal institutions is a fascinating area that is explored in this book.

Islam on Social and Economic Justice

Islam represents a powerful message of social and economic justice because the Islamic notion of deity is of an all encompassing and universal nature; this deity has created human beings to follow the path of justice and righteousness. Thus a true believer should refrain from crime commission, and is duty bound to ward off individualistic as well as social and communal factors that are criminogenic. On the individual level, these typically include inclinations such as greed, aggression, unbridled violence, dishonest and immoral deeds, injustice as well as showing contempt towards those who are less fortunate. On the social and communal levels, these often include elements that disrupt the sanctity of institutions such as marriage, family, education, work and charity and the sense of communal responsibility towards the downtrodden.

The Qur'an's teachings on social and economic justice neither condemn the ownership of private property, nor condone the unlimited expropriation/ concentration of wealth in the hands of a few. The emphasis of the Qur'an, however, is on the importance of honest and hard work in earning that which rightly belongs to the individual, *al-rizq*, which in the vernacular of the Qur'an denotes "that which Allah has apportioned for each individual." Thus, the text encourages believers to struggle in order to better their material conditions, but it also warns them that the Almighty has allowed some believers to prosper over others thus some have been entitled to more *rizq* than others. This premise is not to be construed to mean that one should not try to improve one's lot, but that one should also be cognizant that it is the Almighty who determines our destiny, be it good or bad, rich or poor. The anti-criminogenic implications of this "philosophy of contentment with one's station in life" have been profound in many Islamic countries in the past. Unlike the crude modern materialism that has been the hallmark of many modern societies promoting greed for consumption, contentment with one's station in life has helped many Islamic countries to ward off the criminogenic mentality of economic success regardless of its social costs. For example, Freda Adler's classical study aptly titled as *Nations Not Obsessed with Crime* shows that a good number of oil producing Islamic countries did not experience excessive amounts of crime in the 1970s and 1980s. This was partially due to the steady flow of oil income and to the anti-criminogenic impacts of Islamic teachings. In other words, when economic viability is built in Islamic societies, the moral teachings of Islam serves to reduce crime as witnessed in a good number of oil-producing Persian Gulf Sheikhdoms in the past decades although the situation is changing as the

Middle East region is in a low intensity cycle of war, terrorism, and economic decline.[1]

Islam in its societal disposition does not oppose good and comfortable life, however, a good life is more than having the ability to consume, but one that has to take into consideration human dignity within the social and political structures of a consuming culture. The Qur'an warns believers that they should live as if they were endowed with eternal life when it comes to creating conditions for a good life; it however reminds believers that they should conduct themselves in such a moral way as if they were to stand trial in front of what the Qur'an has characterized as the Final Arbiter, the *Qaazi-al-quzaat*, the Judge of all judges, Allah. This implies that a good life and righteousness are not contradictory. One could build a good life on the foundations of morality, justice and righteousness. It is in such a medium that attempts to reduce crime and rehabilitate offenders are capable of bearing fruit. As is explored in this book, the Nation of Islam claims that it has created a wide net work of economically viable institutions (e.g., Muhammad Farms) to help post-release reincorporation of its convict adherents. This is a claim whose truthfulness is worth reassessing.

Islam on Crime and Punishment

The question as to why people commit crime is as old as human history. Various branches of social sciences, from criminology to political science, to psychology, to ethics, have tried to provide an answer for this question. There is no doubt that the major religions of the world have renounced crime locating its causes within a moralistic context albeit with social and economic parameters. To give an example, there is a wide Islamic literature on what is known as the *Qesas al-Qur'an* which stands for the Stories of the Qur'an. The thrust of these stories is that Allah endows people, tribes, dynasties and nations with a range of opportunities in order to test their moral resolves in the face of empowering aspects of such opportunities. The thrust of the literature is that those who use their God-given opportunities for the greatest common good, justice and righteousness will prosper and have social contentment, joy and a harmonious life. In contrast, those who arrogate themselves against the teachings of the Qur'an will go astray. Allah shows mercy to both groups with the difference being that those who fear Allah will heed the divine warnings; those who do not fear Allah will ignore such warnings, a process which accelerates their straying from the righteous path leading such individuals, tribes or nations to their ultimate demise.

This scenario, dramatically depicted in the Qur'an time and again, is supposed to have a personal implication as well for those who are in the position of power and authority, be it Muslim, or non-Muslim. The Qur'an seems to be saying that:

---

1   Adler, Freda, (1983), *Nations Not Obsessed with Crime*, Published by The Contemporary Criminal Law Projects, Fred B. Rothman & Co., Littleton, CO, 1983.

those who are in the position of power, wealth, prestige and "life chances," to borrow Max Weber's famous term, should be cognizant of the fact that such opportune factors are temporarily entrusted to them by Allah to test their resolves. Those who are wise will use such factors expediently and for the largest amount of common good for to do otherwise is to arrogate oneself against the teachings of the Qur'an. The worst course of action is to use one's endowments for a greed-based, corrupt and vile way of life inundated with anti-social acts, deviance and crime. In other words, the moral teachings of the Qur'an have both macro (social) and micro (individualistic) dimensions in relation to both etiology and epidemiology of crime and crime commission. This premise of the Qur'an is quite anti-criminogenic compared to the critical criminological view expressed by Left Realism. This may sound a bit odd considering that Left Realism comes from a Marxist perspective which is antithetical to any religiously oriented view. However, the thrust of the two approaches is based on the element of power and its utilization. The differences can be located in the nature of power and how it is attained. In the Islamic perspective that I propose here, power has both material and divine bases to its conceptualization whereas in the Marxist view, it is exclusively of a materialistic construction notwithstanding its psychosomatic dimensions.

Two contemporary Left Realist criminologists, Walter S. DeKeseredy and Martin D. Schwartz maintain that it is time to approach the causes of crime from the standpoint of the "Left Realism,"[2] an approach utilized in this book albeit within an Islamic perspective. Accordingly, predatory crime in general and that of the disenfranchised groups in particular, is a social reality that has to be seriously considered by critical criminologists. There is nothing romantic about predatory crime committed by this segment of society. DeKeseredy and Schwartz further maintain that the real challenge is to try to realistically assess those social, economic, political and psychological factors that make predatory crime an integral part of the daily realities of disenfranchised groups in North America. Approached from this perspective, albeit within the Islamic notion of moral conduct, it is this book's contention that critical criminologists should apply a social-justice based approach to both the etiology as well as the epidemiology of crime. This approach should consider the following points:

1. Predatory crime is a social reality whose etiology covers individualistic as well as social, economic, political, psychological and existential factors.
2. Predatory crime creates its own sub-culture, rationale, norms of behavior as well as creates a legitimating mechanism for explaining its commission.
3. Predatory crime also creates a dichotomous social mentality expressed in a kind of "We" the non-criminal, against "Them," the predatory criminal members of society. This mentality, in turn, allows for reactive and simplistic solutions to a complex problem such as crime causation and commission.

---

2   DeKeseredy, W.S., and Martin D. Schwartz. (1996), *Contemporary Criminology*, Wadsworth, Belmont, CA.

4. This mentality creates two different social worlds in each of which the other side is viewed as cruel, immoral, illegitimate and violent, a mentality that impacts the functional dynamics of every aspect of the criminal justice processes.
5. The challenge of critical criminologist is to bridge the gap between these two worlds by recognizing that society cannot be immunized against predatory crime by some panacea, but that it can be drastically reduced when different social strata conceive their share of the economic pie as just and in harmony with their perceived contribution to its formation. This can be expressed as giving the dues of both the prince and the pauper, but not at the expense of one another.

This book is not intended to prove the aforementioned points in the order that they are presented, but these points comprise this book's general intellectual as well as working assumptions namely, that predatory crime in modern democratic societies is a social reality that has a multifaceted base to its causation; predatory crime, in its most abstract format, relates to the manner in which the economic, legal and human capital resources are organized to serve the largest amount of common good. If this organization is generally perceived as being just functioning for the benefit of the largest amount of common good, it will produce less predatory crime. On the other hand, if this organization is perceived as being unjust, operating in a manner as to consistently exploit and/or disenfranchise a large segment of the society for the benefit of few, it will likely produce predatory crime.

With that stated, it should be reiterated that one premise of this book is that any form of crime and/or violence does have its individualistic choice dimension. In other words, the free will to commit predatory crime exists in many societies throughout the world including modern market economies, but free will does not operate within the confines of an abstract volitional mechanism that operates like an off and on switch. Barring exceptions, the will to commit predatory crime is inherently connected to and energized by the prevailing structural (economic, social, and political) and normative (individualistic and moral) factors. In general, it is this book's contention that most people in stable and functioning societies where legitimate opportunities for social mobility and economic progress exist do not commit predatory crime.

As this book will reveal, the correctional literature on the rehabilitative potentials of incarceration does not give much hope to the idea that American penal institutions have succeeded in being rehabilitative. In fact, it is very likely that inmates who convert to Islam do not consider American penal institutions corrective. Studies have shown that inmates consider penal institutions as oppressive, violent and exploitative, thus they seek prison-bound conversion as an effective means of protection. Some studies have shown that new converts believe that Islam is capable of providing a moral compass against those aspects of prison life that deprive a person of his or her moral worth and dignity. These include practices such as forced homosexuality, illicit drug use and pushing, alcoholism, or petty theft, to name but a few. Thus, conversion to Islam may be due to an inmate's expectation of functional post-release incorporation within the "community of believers," which not only provides the wherewithal for prison-bound protection, but is also capable of providing employment and housing to ex-convicts within the embracing arms of the same "community of believers" upon release.

It is noteworthy that institutionalized incarceration does not occupy any discernable space in Islam's primary sources or in what we may consider as Islam's traditional penal measures. This is due to two factors: first the Islamic notion of exculpation based on the advice from the Qur'an is not of an adversarial nature as it is understood and practiced in the Anglo-American system of criminal trial, but is geared towards a complex notion of fact-finding in which the judge plays a central investigative as well as interpretational role. Second, the exculpation process is not one of winning or losing cases, but one of ensuring that a right (*haq*) has not been turned into a wrong (*baatil*) through various stratagems that the accused and/ or the adjudicating authority may undertake (e.g., false witness, false oath, lying, counterfeiting, briary, colluding, applying inappropriate *Hadith* to the case for lesser punishment, etc.). The Qur'an is quite specific on this aspect of exculpation warning believers that the biggest harm to the Almighty is transgression against principles of justice in adjudicating cases.

The Qur'an is adamant that one should not shy away from witnessing the cause of righteousness even if such witnessing were to damage one's tangible benefits and social standing. For example, in iv: 135, the faithful are advised, "O ye who believe! Be ye staunch in justice, witness for Allah, even though it is against yourselves or (your) parents or (your) kindred, whether (the case be of) a rich man or a poor man."[3] In contrast to the Anglo-American notion of the exclusionary rule, the right against self-incrimination, scientific jury selection and all kinds of plea-bargaining schemes, Islamic system allows the convict to compensate the wronged party through monetary measures (in case of non-capital crimes). In the case of capital crimes, once the guilt is established, the judge is allowed to carry out the sentence provided that the wronged party does not forgive the convict. Thus, there has not been a history in the Islamic system of incarceration other than holding a convict on death row in a detention center for a short period of time prior to execution.

However, it is plausible to argue that modern forms of incarceration have garnered its modern Islamic rationale that may be as follows: I may be experiencing this ordeal because I did not follow the right path, thus I committed a crime that I have to face its consequence. The way I face this ordeal may indeed teach me how to face up to a temporal experience representing tribulations that the Heavens has placed on my path so as to test my resolve against all those negative aspects that the world of prison represents. The real ordeal here is not incarceration, but my ability not to give in to the temptations of survival through adaptation to prison-bred

---

3   *The Glorious Qur'an*, (1984), text and explanatory translation by Muhammad M. Pickthall, Mostazafan Foundation of New York, NY, p. 94.

violence or corrupt and unjust practices but remain true to the just and dignified standards of Islamic faith. The confessional aspect of the conversion raises one important question: what is my personal role and responsibility for being in this situation? Do I deserve it? Can I rescue myself from the criminogenic aspects of prison life? Considering the fact that I have committed crime, is there "salvation" for me in this world and in the next one to come? These are important questions that the literature of conversion depicts as operating in the pre and post conversion processes—not just to Islam, but to any other religion—that takes place within the American penal institutions.

What is peculiar about conversion to Islam is the fact that the central claim of Islam has been, from its inception to present, that Islam has perfected both Judaism and Christianity, and the fact that Islam is a supra-class, supra-race and supra-ethnicity faith in which salvation comes through repentance next to good deeds and noninvolvement in crime and deviance. In Islam, righteous deed is known as the *amal al-salih* whose range is almost limitless and whose magnitude, no matter how small, is nonetheless counted in Allah's unlimited divine sense of justice on the Day of Resurrection, the *Yaum al-Qiyamah*. In addition, there is no time limit for performing righteous deeds. One could start at any moment by repenting and promising to redress past wrongs and ill-conceived destructive and socially harmful deeds and replacing them with good and decent ones even if one is being incarcerated.

Incapacitation in the American Penology

Incapacitation of the criminal offenders in secure corrective facilities sounds like a logical punishment for those who violate society's values, mores and norms from which laws are made. The criminal codes in the United States, as in other modern and democratic societies, specify the boundaries of social norms and mores whose violations engender a punitive process based on meticulous procedure specifying a set of sanctions to be applied to offender(s). The secondary purpose of punitive process is to incapacitate convicted offenders in order to shield society from their antisocial behaviors that inflict social harm on individuals and social institutions. In the past, incapacitation took different forms such as banishment, execution, blinding, house arrest, or being thrown in dungeons until literally one rotted to death. A more humane form of incapacitation is the modern practice of incarceration in correctional institutions (jail, prison, half-way houses with electronic monitoring devices, community correctional facilities etc.). In the case of juveniles, mention could be made of juvenile correctional facilities, schools and boot camps.

In the US, incarceration has always been regarded as a humane punishment although it has also been used as a form of cheap labor exploitation. That is why it has been suggested that incarceration trends in the US have followed the economic trends. Giving an example of this exploitation from North Carolina's state prison system during 1741–1868, Dean J. Champion points out that it was the private businesses that controlled prison inmates due to the cost of confinement and maintenance of prison inmates that the state did not want to incur.[4] It was only after the Civil War that a shift in the responsibility for the maintenance of the inmate population from private to the State of North Carolina took place even though the exploitation of the inmate as a source of cheap labor was kept alive in North Carolina. Other states such as Oklahoma and Louisiana followed suit. With the passage of time, each state in the Union developed its correctional authority to deal with the administrative, management and organizational aspects of correctional institutions. Through time, incarceration provided the foundation of a colossal industry with its rationale, logic and advocates as almost a limitless field of employment locked in what the German sociologist Max Weber has characterized as the iron cage of bureaucracy. This did not happen overnight, but occurred over time, a synopsis of which is presented in the next two chapters.

In short, it could be argued that a penal philosophy has to take into consideration why crime is committed. A penal philosophy devoid of the etiology of crime becomes only punitive in nature, losing other functions that it is supposed to perform. An effective penal system has to strike a balance between deterrence and corrective processes. Oppressive, vengeful and dehumanizing penal systems, which treat offenders as disposable objects to be warehoused in a penal institution because offenders are deemed devoid of any redeemable human values, would only inculcate deep-seated anger, frustration and vengeance in the convicts, creating human time bombs behind prison bars ready to explode after being released from the clutches of such penal systems.

Islam and the American Criminal Justice System

It is a central premise of this book that prison-bound conversion to Islam presents a powerful challenge to American penology. Why? Because the general test of the fairness of any system of justice and conflict resolution depends on several factors such as:

- equity in the application of the justice process;
- the speed with which civil and criminal conflicts are resolved;
- the *de jure* and *de facto* perceptions of just, or unjust, resolution of the civil and criminal conflicts as generated by the operational dynamics of the system;
- the manner in which the socially disenfranchised members of society are treated when they commit crime and are subjected to the justice process;
- the public confidence in the fairness of the system.

---

4   Champion, Dean J. (1998), *Corrections in the United States: A Contemporary Perspective*, Upper Saddle River, NJ, Prentice Hall, second edn., p. 12.

The validity of the above premises (e.g., the general test of the fairness), can be defended in terms of both common sense, and the logic of the etiology of crime.

First, it is a matter of common sense that equity in the application of the justice process is a universal demand in four major systems of conflict resolution that operate throughout the world, and so is the demand of the speedy resolution of civil and criminal conflicts. Throughout the world, members of the disenfranchised social strata face both *de jure* and *de facto* hurdles in their attempts to resolve conflicts. This is due to unequal distribution of wealth, prestige and power among different societies and different social strata throughout the world. It is the unequal distribution of these factors that determine the social status of various strata in modern open-end class societies on the one hand. On the other hand, these factors impact the manner in which members of society resolve conflicts. For example, access to bail, pre-trial release and the ability to mount a viable defense strategy have a direct bearing on one's social and economic status. As a general rule, the higher one's socioeconomic status, the greater one's likelihood of access to these instruments as one traverses through different stages of the justice process in any part of the world. In the American adversarial system of criminal trial, the almost causal relationship between pre-trial release and a successful defense leading to acquittal, or to the imposition of lesser severe sentences, has become an undeniable reality.

Second, from the standpoint of the logic of the etiology of crime, it is also plausible to argue that the unjust resolution of civil and criminal conflicts creates dismay, resentment, and cynicism among the members of the disenfranchised groups—a process that if unchecked could seriously undermine both the social and legal legitimacy of a system of justice and conflict resolution. In its crisis stage, this anti-system attitude of the disenfranchised group turns into the status of a cynical conviction that their civil and criminal conflicts are not resolved based on the principle of social harm, justice and equity, but based on factors such as race, class, gender and ethnic affiliations. This is a crisis not because some individuals entertain negative feelings against the system, but because the perception reaches the level of general consensus among one or more social strata as, for example, in the case of the indigent White, African-American, Native, and Hispanic-American communities in the United States.

Third, from the standpoint of prison-bound Islam, the American system of justice and conflict resolution is going through a legitimacy crisis as described above. The operative phrase is the *genesis* of legitimacy crisis—rather than a full blown crisis—whose epistemic frame of reference is shaping among African-American communities throughout urban America, as well as among African-American prison inmates. By the term epistemic frame of reference, I aim to describe a certain social-legal perspective whose thrust can be described as follows:

1. The American notion of justice is undoubtedly a complex one which, ideally speaking, permeates the thrust of both substantive and procedural laws utilized in the resolution of conflicts and in the dispensing of justice;

2. The American criminal justice system is the main venue through which the justice process is applied to the resolution of conflicts;

3. Whether conceived of a system, or non-system, the constituents of the American criminal justice system responsible for the orderly resolution of conflicts and dispensing of justice (the police, courts and corrections) are complex entities employing large number of persons from all walks of life with their likes, dislikes and proclivities;

4. The constituents of the American criminal justice system handle large number of both civil and criminal cases resolving a multifaceted array of legal and social conflicts on a daily basis.

This complexity is further compounded by the fact that the each of the criminal justice constituents is locally, rather than nationally, financed and managed. There is a perception among both American lay people and intelligentsia that the American criminal justice system dispenses justice in the context of a tangible commercial commodity, rather than dispensing it on the basis of the presumed legalistic equity principle. This perception is the most prevalent among the members of socioeconomically disenfranchised groups and communities throughout the US. It is within these segments of the population that the call of legal justice finds its most receptive audience as for example, among the indigent poor and socioeconomically challenged segments of the American society.

What Does This Book Entail?

This book focuses on the role of one important factor that has played a significant impact on the formation of the genesis of the aforementioned crisis: the disproportionate and systematic incarceration of the African-American males in both state and federal correctional facilities. This book also focuses the role of the faith of Islam which is gaining adherents from among African-American community and inmates. This book outlines some of the most important aspects of this legitimating crisis by exploring: (1) the historical role of incarceration in the American penology from colonial times to the present, (2) the reasons for the disproportionate and systematic incarceration of African-American males, and (3) the paradoxical (corrective and/or radicalization) impacts of Islam on inmates. The book concludes by arguing that prison-bound conversion to Islam presents a powerful challenge to the American penal philosophy on the grounds that the faith emphasizes the role of personal responsibility, family and community in the rehabilitative processes.

Chapter 2

Judeo-Christian Foundations of American Penology

The conventional wisdom is that colonial America was deeply religious. Whether it were the Puritans of Massachusetts Bay Colony, the Quakers of Pennsylvania, or the Amish of Virginia, they all shared one common concern namely, that there existed a generic relationship between sin and crime: those who committed sin were also likely to commit crime. Thus, it was incumbent upon all God fearing members of the colony to combat against a wide range of evil forces that lurked within the colonies, facilitating the sin-crime synergy. The belief in a sin-crime synergy led to the rise of penal measures and procedures that by modern standards were cruel and unusual despite the fact that colonial penal philosophy, following its Judeo-Christian core values, adhered to the principles of justice and fairness in punishment. Exploring these issues in some details, the thrust of this chapter is that despite all modern efforts to secularize penal measures, American penal philosophy in its epistemic core has remained faithful to its Judeo-Christian thrust of fairness in punishment.

The Sin-Crime Synergy in Colonial Penology

American colonial penologists believed that a synergy existed between sin and crime that permeated through the harsh social realities of colonial life and its settings. Daily life in North American colonies was marred with uncertainties that tested one's will and dedication to colonial mandates. What were these mandates? To "civilize" the rest of the world that had not come under the control of Christendom. A look at the foundational charters of the thirteen original colonies that later united to form the United States of America, gives an idea about the spirit and the material nature of such civilizing colonial mandates. It is an established fact that during the course of the Great Explorations that led to the colonization of large segments of Africa, Asia and the Americas by the European seafaring nations (e.g., the British, the Dutch, the French, the Italians, the Portuguese, the Spaniards), colonial charters were issued by the reigning monarchs authorizing their captains and enterprising court functionaries to colonize whatever part of the globe that had not been claimed by other "Christian Princes or People".[1] An

---

1   The First Charter of Virginia; April 10, 1606 (1), The Avalon Project at Yale Law School website at: http://www.yale.edu/lawweb/avalon/states/va01.htm; pp. 1–9.

example is the colonization of Virginia whose foundational charter, dated April 10, 1606, declared that: "JAMES, by the Grace of God, King of England, Scotland, France, and Ireland, Defender of the Faith ... ," had vouchsafed unto "[his] loving and well-disposed Subjects, Sir Thorn as Gales, and Sir Georges Somers, Knights, Richard Hackluit, Clerk, Prebendary of Westminster ... [his] Licence, to make Habitation, Plantation, and to deduce a colony of sundry of our people into that part of America commonly called VIRGINIA."[2] Reading various British colonial charters, one gets the distinct impression that the colonization mandates envisioned a set of comprehensive undertakings that required: (1) the exact determination of the geographical coordinates and territorial boundaries of the colony; (2) division of the colonial territories among British companies, merchants and men of adventure so as to expedite the so-called "plantation and habitation" of each colonies; (3) undertaking Christian proselytizing activities with the stated purpose of glorifying God by spreading the one and only true faith, Christianity, among the so-called "Infidels and Savages living in those parts," which meant territories that had not been "civilized" as of yet; (4) establishing total control over all riches of the colonies, be it above or beneath the ground; and (5) procure such colonial riches and resources for both internal and overseas commerce and mercantile purposes.[3]

The First Charter of Virginia also mandated the formation of a governing council authorized, "to govern and order all Matters-and Causes, which shall arise, grow, or happen, to or within the same [or] several Colonies ...."[4] The colonization mandate necessitated a powerful spiritual rationale next to a ruthless governing body that could carry out a multitude of colonization tasks. The British royal seal of Virginia read, "*Sigillium Regis Magne Britanniae, Franciae, & Hiberniae*," on one side and, "*Pro Concilio fuo Virginiae*," on the other side.[5] The term *Sigillium Regis Magne Britanniae* certified that the bearer of the seal (i.e., the governing council) had the authority to carry out the colonization mandates in Virginia—a term that applied to a larger territory from James Town all the way to Florida and that Virginia's affairs were within the purview of the British laws. This, in effect, meant that the British colonies were to be structured as replicas of their constituent counterparts in Britain. The First Charter of Virginia also stated the fact that royal licensees had given their solemn words for carrying out the mandates of 'plantation and habitation' of the colonies along Virginia coasts; to achieve these purposes all the licensees were "... desirous to divide themselves into two several Colonies and Companies; the one consisting of certain Knights, Gentlemen, Merchants, and other Adventurers, of our City of London and elsewhere ...."[6] Thus, British royal licenses were granted to those who could financially, logistically, as well as

---

2　The First Charter of Virginia, Ibid.
3　The First Charter of Virginia, Ibid.
4　The First Charter of Virginia, Ibid.
5　The First Charter of Virginia, Ibid.
6　The First Charter of Virginia, Ibid., p. 1.

emotionally and psychosomatically undertake the wherewithal for colonization tasks in the New World; all men of capital and adventure throughout Great Britain, be it in Bristol, Exeter, or "Plimouth" as mentioned in the Charter, were allowed to avail their services for this purpose.

The Root Causes of Sin-Crime Synergy

Attempts at restructuring a New England in the face of the harsh realities of the New World gave rise to Anglo-American colonial penology that did not demarcate between sin and crime. As the new settlers tried to restructure centuries old British legal sedentary norms, mores and values along North Atlantic shores—that stretched from Newfoundland all the way to Florida—they came across a vast area that had already been populated by the North American natives who had established a relatively advanced and sophisticated agrarian social structure. The inevitable encounter between the two led to the rise of a colonial culture that was Judeo-Christian in its ideological core, but had to accommodate a set of social realities in the New World that were not in sync with its Judeo-Christian core and spirit. For example, Native Americans deeply respected the symbiotic balance and harmony that they believed existed in nature, a belief that led to natural animism prompting the worship of nature and its iconic symbols. The North American colonizers (be it the French, the British or the Spaniards), on the other hand, believed in monotheism (the Judeo-Christian version of it) that presumed that everything in the cosmos belonged to one universal God. Not only was this antithetical to the Native American's belief system, the colonial charters and mandates were also designed for the creation of a new grand socioeconomic and legal structure that was also antithetical to the Native established order along the North Atlantic shores. Thus, the sin-crime synergy was a natural outcome of this restructuring attempt. To "re-civilize" an already civilized Native America within the context of a New England, British colonizers had to: (a) proselytize in order to convert an admixture of colonial population that included African slaves as well as Native Americans; and (b) to economically restructure the North Atlantic shores in the persona of a New England, by utilizing the emerging European mercantilism epitomes. The end result was a long and continuous dislocation of human and material capital and resources from colonies to Europe and its centers of wealth and power. Thus, although structuring a New England along the Atlantic Shores was marred with acts that conflicted the very core of Judeo-Christian monotheism, the utilization of the sin-crime synergy proved functional throughout British colonies enabling British mercantilism in conjunction with Anglican Church to carry out its share of the so-called White Man's Burden, along the North Atlantic shores. However, from a purely penal perspective, this utilization was not a grand conspiracy, but one that reflected the spirit of the time: Anglo-American colonial penologists believed wholeheartedly that the sin-crime synergy had intertwined root causes that could effectively be controlled at each level. A synopsis of each is presented below.

Sin-Crime Synergy at the Individual Level

By and large, American colonial penologists believed that to effectively combat the sin-crime synergy, one had to wholeheartedly believe in the Good Book's advice that whatever one sow, one reaped; that idle hands were the tools of the Devil; that what went around came around; that the worldly affairs did not unfold haphazardly. Simply stated, the Heavens watched over human affairs with a meticulous purpose, one that not only steered cosmic affairs, but also applied to humankind's accountability in relation to whatever course of action one took. Thus, all members of the colonies, regardless of race, creed or social standing were encouraged to seek redemption against the occult power of the evil forces that roamed around enticing weak souls into the sin-crime synergy. One effective way to expel these forces was by engaging in hard work, good mannerisms, and a charitable attitude towards others. Of prime importance was the respect that every one was expected to give their parents, teachers, elders of the community as well as to those in the position of authority, be it the clergy or the members of the Colonial Magisterial System, the purveyors of law and morality. Among those negative personal attributes which facilitated the work of the Devil—thus the sin-crime synergy—the ones that had moral context were of supreme importance. It was believed that attributes such as lust, greed, gluttony, or capacity for idleness and hedonism, dishonest disposition towards work and one's fellow men, or deception and lying played important roles in the sin-crime synergy. Therefore, it was incumbent upon all responsible and God-fearing members of the colonies to combat these moral turpitudes by replacing them with positive ones. These were attributes such as honesty, discipline, foresight, hard work and perseverance, chaste and dignified mannerisms and honorable conduct at home and in public. It was also incumbent upon the church and Sunday Bible-schools to excise individuals of their negative personal attributes through proper educational and communal services. Colonial penologists earnestly believed that those who neglected their personal responsibilities towards God, self, family and community were more likely to stray from the righteous path of the Good Book than those who did not. Colonial penologists also believed that the route to the sin-crime commission sloped downward, as against the route of righteousness that sloped upwards. The former was easy to stroll through because each temptation once one gave-in to its lures, would facilitate the traveler to give-in to other ones corrupting one's soul and furthering one's immersion into the pit of sin and criminality. Again, as stated above, one powerful remedy to combat evil temptations was work, positive thoughts, submission to the teachings of the Good Book, attending church on a regular basis and showing deference to those whom, because of their high moral standings in society, were in a position to steer one's temptations in the path of righteousness.

Sin-Crime Synergy at the Family Level

At the family level, the responsibility for combating the sin-crime synergy rested on the shoulders of the parents, composed of a duly wed husband-wife duo deemed responsible, from the standpoint of both common law and God's law, of maintaining a positive home environment for themselves and their offspring. Marriage vows were considered sacred, thus one did not enter into marriage lightheartedly; it was firmly believed that marriage wows engendered solemn responsibilities for both parties. The wife was expected to be chaste, obedient to husband's wishes and commands, and to be kind and nurturing towards offspring. The husband was expected to be honest and hard working, provide for his family, and maintain a firm yet compassionate hold on household affairs. It was widely believed by many, including colonial penologists, that fathers were responsible for the general well-being and the correct conduct of the offspring at home and in public. Unruly children were allowed by both social conventions and law to be subjected to corporal punishment both at home and at school, following the Good Book's advice that to spare a rod is to spoil a child. The family was also responsible for inculcating religiously based-moral attributes such as honesty, discipline, foresight, consistency of hard and honest work, chaste and dignified conduct both within and without the household, dedication to one's family and respect for one's parents and the elderly.

Out of wedlock sex, as well as any type of inappropriate form of it, was strongly frowned upon as it was believed that unregulated sex played a central role in the genesis of the sin-crime synergy. Colonies had strict rules of conduct relating to intimacy both at home and in public. The Puritans and Non-Conformists, both off-shots of Calvinist church and later the Quakers, Pentecostals, Mormons and Shakers were renowned for their doctrinarian view of the centrality of the family in keeping individuals in check. It was a commonly-held belief that sexual urges made men vulnerable to the lures and temptation of sin and crime. Celibacy was encouraged during adolescence. For example, Shakers who appeared on the 18th century American social and political scene praised the virtues of the celibate life whose main function was to enrich one's life not by sacrificing one's lot of worldly pleasure but to enhance it. One Shaker writer, Louis Basting, maintained that:

> Shakers do not believe in the propriety of making themselves unhappy and miserable in this world for the sake of being happy in the next. A good shaker is the most thoroughly happy being in existence. Why not? The world, the flesh, and the devil have no attractions for him; he is at peace with God, himself and his neighbor ....[7]

---

7   Basting, L's (1887) "Reply," *The Manifesto* 16:91, cited in Robert H. Lauer and Jeannette C. Lauer, *Marriage and Family: The Quest for Intimacy*, third edition, Dubuque, IA, Brown and Benchmark Publishers, 1997, p. 14.

Naturally, those content with their station in life within the colony were very likely to be at peace with themselves and, if they believed in religion, it was also very likely that they felt a euphoric sense of closeness to God. Thus, it is plausible to suggest that American colonies did not suffer from what we consider today as a crime epidemic *per se*, but from acts that were deemed offensive to public morality and colonial sense of dignity. For example, studying crime data based on, "The records of the Essex County Court ... for the years 1636 to 1682,"[8] Kai T. Erikson presented an offense dynamic that included the following:

a. Crimes against the church (disturbing the congregation, absence from church, contempt of the ministry, and so on).
b. Contempt of authority (criticism of the government, contempt of court, abusing public officials).
c. Fornication (including offenses charged against married persons who delivered their first child within too short a period after wedding).
d. Disturbing the peace (drunkenness, disorderly conduct, and so on).
e. Crimes against property (largely a matter of theft).
f. Crimes against persons (assault, slander, defamation).
g. Other.[9]

The first three offenses are not part of modern crime categories *per se*, but represent acts that would fit within the colonial view of the sin-crime synergy. Although not asked directly by Erikson, but one could fathom questions such as: why would any responsible and God-fearing member of a church congregation disturb such a solemn event in the presence of God's ecclesiastic representatives on earth? Who in their rightful mind and conscience would abstain from attending church sermons? Why would a Christian be contemptuous of the clergy, the colonial authorities or the magisterial courts? Inquisition into the lives of such characters regularly showed that they were neither person of high "moral" standards, nor of good character; some were even the "agents" of the very Devil himself as alleged in the case of Salem Trials of 1692.

Sin-Crime Synergy at the Communal Level

At the community level, it was also incumbent upon the church, public schools and community-based civic organizations to help individuals in their attempts to excise themselves of their negative personal attributes so as to enable them to gradually inculcate positive ones instead. This was made possible through regular attendance to church sermons and Bible schools. Colonial penologists believed that if these activities were carried out regularly and with good intentions, they

---

8   Erikson, Kai T., (1966), *Wayward Puritans: A Study in the Sociology of Deviance*, New York, NY: John Wiley & Sons, Inc., p. 171.
9   Erikson, Ibid., p. 171.

would engender charitable attitudes and compassionate disposition towards others, especially the weaklings of the colonies. Thus, the community was deemed as a protective gear; it sheltered its members from imaginary as well as real "dangers" that lurked in the larger realm of "otherness," a constellation of mostly negative attributes that one colony or community had ascribed to on the basis of racial, ethnic, gender, creed factors, norms and proclivities. By the passage of time, the defense of the community turned into the defense of one's communal virtues; those who defended community were heroes, and those who tried to change it were villains.

This colonial view of the community as the bastion of social and moral virtuosity led North American penologists to the inevitable conclusion that it was through structured communal solidarity against sin-crime synergy that communal integrity could be preserved, enhanced and passed on from one generation to the next, thus the rationale for the application of harsh penal measures to which reference has already been made above. Shaming played a significant role as a control mechanism against the lure of sin-crime thus the rationale for penal measures whose primary purpose was public shaming. It is not ironic that in both Judeo-Christian as well as Islamic penal philosophy and vernacular, the shaming played similar roles from medieval times to present. For example, in many Middle Eastern societies, honor killings take place despite the fact that its history predated Islam's rise and the fact that it egregiously contravenes the basic tenets of Islam's sacred text, the Qur'an, that admonishes believers against unjustifiable homicide that honor killing has been from its inception to present. The same applies to stoning to death whose roots date back to the first five books of Moses, the Pentateuch. The position of the Qur'an, as I have shown elsewhere, is that the Qur'an has replaced stoning as a penal measure with that of public lashing on the grounds that stoning was never meant to kill, but to inflict shame on the culprit. By the passage of time, it turned into stoning to death, rather than to shame. The point is that from Biblical times until very recent time, in many societies communal shame has played important anti-criminogenic function against sin-crime synergy; thus American colonial penology could not have remained impervious to utilizing it against sin-crime synergy.

However, each colony acted independently in the imposition of punishment to various forms of crime, but all followed a common law perspective namely, that the community was responsible for its indigent, mentally insane, and sinner-criminals' acts. As observed by David R. Rothman:

> The colonists judged a wide range of behavior to be deviant, finding the gravest implications in even minor offenses. Their extended definition was primarily religious in origin, equating sin with crime. The criminal codes punished religious offenses, such as idolatry, blasphemy, and witchcraft, and clergymen declared infractions against persons or property to be offenses against God. Freely mixing the two categories, the colonists described an incredibly long list of activities. The identification of disorder with sin made it difficult for legislators

and ministers to distinguish carefully between major and minor infractions. Both were testimony to the natural depravity of man and the power of the devil [,] sure signs that the offender was destined to be a public menace and a damned sinner.[10]

Because of the blurred lines between sin and crime, the family, church and community were all deemed responsible in the creation and adoption of measures that would entice self-control against, and aversion to, factors that engendered sin-crime synergy. These symbiotically intertwined organs of the larger society were also charged with the responsibility of inculcating moral strength, respect for authority, and the fear of God in every member of the colony. In that regard, the American colonial crime control mechanisms, be it the formal or informal, were truly of a localized and community based nature; at the same time, these mechanisms followed the Judeo-Christian values with regard to just punishment, they were also bound by their British Common Law heritage that permeated the colonial notion of jurisprudence. This meant that punishment could not be applied without just cause based on formal trial in which all factors of *Habeas Corpus* had to be presented to an impartial judge and jury. Even in the notorious Salem witch trials that led to the burning of alleged witches, a trial based on 'real' or 'concocted' evidence had to convene for the sake of impartiality towards the accused. Steven Pfohl observes that, "Five types of evidence were accepted to identify the Salem witches."[11] Notwithstanding the absurdity such as making the accused recite the "Lord's Prayer in public," believing that because witches recite the prayer backwards in their congregations, the accused would inevitably resume to that diabolical practice in public and thereby prove that she is indeed a witch as alleged in the court indictment.[12]

In modern times, the significance of the community itself has been widely acknowledged and its various dimensions have been studied. These include, but are not limited to, factors such as ecological stability and its impacts on delinquency;[13] the relationship between housing and community crime careers;[14] and the impacts of communal economic conditions and neighborhood organization on urban crime.[15] Again, the point is that as observed by Albert J. Reiss, Jr., "[that]

---

10   Rothman, D.J., "The Discovery of Asylum" pp. 37–43 in Marquart, J.W., and Sorensen, J.R., (eds), (1997), *Correctional Context: Contemporary and Classical Readings*, Los Angeles, CA, Roxbury Publishing Company.

11   Pfohl, *Images of Deviance and Social Control*, p. 27.

12   Pfohl, *Ibid.*

13   Bursik, Robert J, Jr., "Ecological Stability and the Dynamics of Delinquency", pp. 35–66 in Albert J. Reiss and Michael Tonry (eds.), *Communities and Crime*, vol 8, Chicago, IL: The University of Chicago Press, 1986.

14   Bottoms, Anthony E and Paul Wiles "Housing Tenure and Residential Community Crime Careers in Britain" pp. 101–162 in Reiss and Tonrey, Ibid.

15   McGabey, Richard M., "Economic Conditions, Neighborhood Organization, and Urban Crime" pp. 231–270 in Reiss and Tonrey, Ibid.

our sense of personal safety and potential victimization by crime is shaped less by knowledge of specific criminals than is by knowledge of dangerous and safe places and communities."[16] According to Reiss, what determines the safe-danger dichotomy is not just the factor of crime *per se*, but the aggregate law abiding versus criminal elements in a certain neighborhood.[17] The question becomes: does this apply to penal institutions considering that a penal institution is a dichotomous institutional entity whereby convicted criminals are being guarded by correctional officers and administrators? Ideally, the good guys i.e., the warden and correctional officers and staff would want to rehabilitate the bad guys; this would succeed only if the good guys could gradually turn the inmate community into one in which good will prevails between the two sides to the effect that the convict is no longer the manifestation of dangerousness, but one that is gradually being incorporated into the side of safeness. It is in this context that penal institutions are conceived as a place of danger that has to be monitored and can be transformed into one that is also self-monitoring. This may be odd and naïve, but the thrust of faith-based rehabilitation is to inculcate in each individual inmate such a mechanism succored by appeal to a faith and morality.

Sin-Crime Synergy at the Legal and Institutional Level

At the legal and institutional level, it was the province of the Colonial Magisterial System to attend to the affairs of the sin-crime synergy as well as those who got entangled in its multifaceted web of social control through harsh punishments. The system had its organizational raison d'être in the manner in which North American colonies were founded as British commercial appendages. These colonies were created and maintained for both mercantilism and proselytizing purposes. Thus, where as each colony utilized the Good Book extensively to engendering aversion to sin-crime synergy, it excluded slaves on the grounds that the slaves were not fully developed human beings because they were "different" from non-slaves; this difference was not one of just "otherness," but one of "atavistic otherness" that had its intellectual roots in the European view of Demonology. This atavism, of course, was not of its modernist positivistic genre, but one that had a religious and cultural base to its social adumbration. As recorded in one historical letter, "Description of Charles-Town: Thoughts on Slavery; on Physical Evil; A Melancholy Scene," the letter first gave a positive picture pertaining to those who benefitted from colonization endeavors observing that:

> The three principal classes of inhabitants are, lawyers, planters, and merchants; this is the province which has afforded to the first the riches spoils, for nothing can exceed their wealth, power, and their influence. They have reached the net

---

16   Reiss, Albert J., Jr., "Why Are Communities Important in Understanding Crime?", pp. 1–33 in Reiss and Tonrey, Ibid.

17   Reiss, Ibid., p. 2.

plus ultra worldly felicity; no plantation is secured, no title is good, no will is valid, but when they dictate, regulate, and approve.[18]

This being the case, the author of the letter contrasts that state of affairs with the abject misery to which the slaves were subjected to, lamenting that:

> While all is joy, festivity, and happiness in Charles-town, would you imagine that scenes of misery overspread in the country? Their ears by habit are become deaf, their hearts are hardened; they neither see, hear, nor feel for the worse of their poor slaves, from whose painful labours all their wealth proceeds. Here the horrors of slavery, the hardship of incessant toils, are unseen; and no one thinks with compassion of those showers of sweat and of tears which from the bodies of Africans, daily drop, and moisten the ground they till. The cracks of the whip urging these miserable beings to excessive labour, are far too distant from the gay Capital to be heard. The chosen race eat, drink, and live happy, while the unfortunate one grub up the ground, raise indigo, or husks the rice …. This great contrast has often afforded me subjects of the most conflicting meditation. On the one side behold, behold a people enjoying all that life affords most bewitching Oh, Nature, where art thou?–Are not these blacks thy children as well as we?[19]

Against this state of affairs, the Colonial Magisterial System was naturally inclined to establish a mechanism of sin-crime control that next to harsh penal measures, utilized the "Fear of God" among the general populace. Thus in the Colonial Magisterial System, the Fear of God stood at the apex of an hierarchical social and legal construct of revered authority whose integrity was vouchsafed by the clergy. Following the Good Book's advice that one should give the dues of the Caesar's next to that of the Church, this hierarchy emphasized the viability of the harshness of the penal measures in garnering respect for social mores and norms without which the colony would fall to the clutches of sin, crime and anarchy. An example of that reverence was reflected in the legal documents that are known as the Colonial Charters.

Sin-Crime Synergy at the Occult/Diabolical Level

Finally, the colonial perception of sin-crime synergy had another root-cause that was of an occult/diabolical nature being engendered by a wide range of diabolical creatures under the command of the very persona of Devil. Colonial America was not just religious, it was also deeply superstitious. The settlers believed in

---

18   Letter From an American Farmer: Letter IX-Description of Charles-Town; Thoughts on Slavery; on Physical Evil; A Melancholy Scene, The Avalon Project at: http://www.yale.edu/lawweb/avalon/treatise/american_farmer/letter_09.htm.

19   Letter From an American Farmer, Ibid.

the very material existence of diabolical forces and especially of the Devil (aka Satan, Mephistopheles, and Diablo) as well as in their ability to appear in various forms and shapes to entice the sin-crime synergy, a view that was reflective of the centuries old Judeo-Christian as well as Islamic occult perspectives. Naturally, various European settlers in North American colonies brought that perspective with them. The diabolical forces not only could entice persons of weak disposition towards sin, but because they were hierarchical in terms of their demonic prowess, they could also possess men and beast alike and entice them to commit acts of unimaginable horridness. The Devil and his associates were also believed to reside in a diabolical *terra incognita* that sheltered a multitude of anti-Christian agents in its embrace; these were categorized in the prevailing demonology literature as witches, warlocks, sorcerers, goblins and lunatics. Not only were these ungodly creatures of the underworld capable of tempting humans of weak moral foundations to commit sin and/or diabolical crimes, they were also capable of possessing the souls of both humans and beasts alike to utilize them for their unholy purposes. The mentally insane, the moon-stuck lunatics, the bodily deformed hunchbacks and eunuchs, epileptics and even thieves and street beggars, were deemed as possible vessels for demonic possession. These agents of the underworld, if cited, could easily be distinguished by their bizarre physical as well as temperamental features which distinguished them from God-fearing normal persons, thanks to "The Science of the Occult," which had developed through centuries covering among others, demonology, witchcraft, sorcery, astrology, and magic. The medieval Islamic world also possessed a similar literature of occult, but the level of superstition was not as intense as in medieval Europe. Demonology, although it was a European perspective in relation to sin-crime synergy, deeply influenced American colonial society and penology to the effect even today quite a few numbers of educated Americans believe in the actual and material presence of Satan and in his ability to interfere in our daily affairs, including in the commission of sin and crime. Although we no longer prosecute those who engage in sinful acts (however one wants to interpret such acts) in modern democratic societies, The Vatican as the very eschatological bastion of world Catholicism allows for the divine rite of exorcism to be performed by Catholic priests meticulously trained in de-possessing those afflicted with demonic possession. In colonial America, these rites were performed, including others that applied to uproot diabolical practices such as witchcraft.

Colonial Witchcraft   The American colonial literature on witchcraft is voluminous showing that it was practiced by those who worshiped diabolical forces of the underworld. The practice had a definite European legacy to its intellectualism as well as technical know how. For example, writing on the subject of witchcraft, Montague Summers observes that witchcraft was widely spread in medieval Europe, in France, England and Germany. In France, it was the likes of Antoine-Louis Daugis, and Jules Garient who conducted systematic research on witchcraft and black magic.[20] Accordingly, Daguis wrote *Traite sure le magie, le sortilege, les possessions, obsessiones et maelfices* in 1732, and Garient wrote *Historie de la Magie en France depuis le commencement de la monarchie jusqu'a nos jouros*, 1818.[21] Similar works were available in German as, for instance, Ebergard Hauber's *Biblioteca Magica*. In England, Thomas Wright's *Narratives of Sorcery and Magic*, written in two volumes in 1851, and F.G. Lee's *The Other World*, written, again, in two volumes in 1875, can be mentioned.[22]

In Colonial America, similar ideas about the Devil and his agents' causal role in the propagation of sin-crime prevailed as, for example, in the case of Salem witch trials of 1692. Steven Pfohl is of the opinion that, "The 'facts' of the Salem case are clear evidence of the continued dominance of demonic theorizing up until the end of the seventeenth century."[23] The trials of the likes of Tibuta, "a mysterious kitchen-slave from Barbados ...."[24] and Martha Carrier, accused of witchcraft, shed light on the American colonial thinking of demonic possession and of its causal link to crime. In the document known as "The Trial of Martha Carrier at The Court of Oyer and Terminer, Held by Adjournment at Salem, August 2, 1692," the facts of the proceedings have been detailed in eleven items with one "Memorandum" to the document that summarizes the whole proceedings in the most bizarre format.[25] Item I, partially quoted below, give the background of the case:

> Martha Carrier was indicted for the bewitching of certain persons, according to the form usual in such cases, pleading not guilty to her indictment; there were first brought in considerable number of the bewitched persons who not only made the court sensible of an horrid witchcraft committed upon them, but also deposed that it was Martha Carrier, or her shape, that grievously tormented them, by biting, pricking, pinching and choking them. It was further deposed that while this Carrier was on her examination before the magistrates, the poor people were so tortured that every one expected their death upon the very spot, but that upon the binding of Carrier they were released.[26]

Subsequently, incriminating evidence was presented to the court, most of which were either of hearsay, or of a self-incriminating confessional, nature. Such evidence would be thrown out of the court as having no exculpatory value

---

20   Summers, Montague, (1987), *The History of Witchcraft*, New York, NY, Dorset Press, p. xii.

21   Summers, Ibid.

22   Summers, Ibid.

23   Pfohl, Steven, (1994), *Images of Deviance and Social Control: A Sociological History*, New York, McGraw-Hill, Inc., p. 26.

24   Pfohl, Ibid., p. 26.

25   For the text of the document see Lauter, P., (1994), *The Heath Anthology of American Literature*, Lexington, MA, D.C. Heath and Company, pp. 423–425.

26   Lauter, Ibid., p. 423.

in modern court proceedings. In fact, the first evidence pertaining to Carrier's children's confessions to the effect that their mother had been a witch, who had performed witchcraft, was not produced against her. The second evidence was the testimony of one Benjamin Abbot alleging that Carrier had put some curse on him leading to swelling in Abbot's feet and the appearance of some agonizing sores in his side and groin. Abbot's wife, Sarah, also testified that not only had her husband been afflicted, but so were their cattle.

Another testimony came from Allin Toothaker who reportedly had had some scuffles with Carrier's son, Richard. Toothaker testified that the mother put a curse on him and his cattle. Similar testimonies were presented to the court by John Rogger and Samuel Preston. In her testimony, Phoebe Chandler alleged that Carrier had predicted that she would be poisoned within three days after a strange question that Carrier had asked her concerning her place of residence that she had knowledge about. And yet, more incriminating evidence was presented to the court by:

> One Foster, who confessed her own share in the witchcraft for which the prisoner stood indicted, affirmed that she had seen the prisoner at some of their witch-meetings, and that it was this Carrier, who persuaded her to be a witch. She confessed that the Devil carried them on a pole to a witch meeting; but the pole broke, and she hanging about Carrier's neck, they both fell down, and she then received an hurt by the fall, whereof she was not at this very time recovered.[27]

Similar accounts were produced by two self-confessed witches both of whom were identified by the name of Lacy. There is a memorandum to the document that is quite interesting of the sexist and anti-Semitic mind set of the time. It reads:

> Memorandum: This rampant hag, Martha Carrier, was a person of whom the confessions of the witches, and of her own children among the rest, agreed that the devil had promised her she should be Queen of Hebrews.[28]

The anti-sin-crime synergic logic of witch trials was as follows: because witchcraft was an unholy and conspiratorial device of Satan against God-fearing members of the colonies, it was incumbent upon legal authorities to inquire on the bizarre and diabolical logic and inner thoughts of the witches. This was only possible through inquisition. Once understood through inquisition, the schemes of Satan could effectively be neutralized by the proper authorities who could then excise witches, and thus witchcraft, from the body and soul of the colonies. This simplistic sentiment has been variously expressed in the colonial legal and social documents as, for instance, in "The Wonders of the Invisible World." It reads:

---

27 Ibid., pp. 424–425.
28 Ibid., p. 425.

The New Englanders are a people of God settled in those, which were once the
devil's territories; and it may easily be supposed that the devil was exceedingly
disturbed, when he perceived such a people here accomplishing the promise of
old made unto our blessed Jesus, that He should have the utmost parts of the
earth for His possession …. The devil thus irritated, immediately tried all sorts
of methods to overturn this poor plantation: and so much of the church, as was
fled into this wilderness, immediately found the serpent cast out of his mouth
a flood for the carrying of it away …. We have been advised by some credible
Christians yet alive, that a malefactor, accused of witchcraft as well as murder,
and executed in this place, did then give notice of an horrible plot against the
country by witchcraft, and a foundation of witchcraft then laid, which if it were
not seasonably discovered, would probably blow up, and pull down the churches
in the country.[29]

The above document reflects partially the medievalist view that Satan,
although capable of doing *maleficia* through its own prowess, used witches and
other ungodly creatures of the underworld to spread as wide a web of deceit and
temptation as possible in order to entice weak and corrupt souls to commit sin-
crime. This ability of Satan was first discussed in length in *Malleus Maleficarum*
written in 1486 by Jakob Sprenger and Heinrich Kramer.[30] In the Salem witch
trials, as for example, in the trial of Martha Carrier documented above, some of the
main themes of *Malleus Malificarum* were utilized by the magistrates in indicting
Martha as a witch. Satan was portrayed as having had directly assisted the accused
(in the testimony of one Foster who had already been indicted of witchcraft) in her
various schemes.

The Logic of the Severity in Punishment

In both European and American colonial penal philosophies, severity of the penal
measures was deemed central to the penultimate purpose of punishment—saving
the soul of the culprit from eternal damnation. Those possessed by evil spirits—
which enticed them to sin-crime synergy—had to be excised from their demons
first and then punished for the actual infraction of the law (be it man's or God's
law). Thus, severity in punishment was not due to the popular notion that in the
eyes of medieval Christianity (be it Roman Catholic, and, later, Calvinist-Lutheran
or Anglican Church) human life and limbs had no value; severity in punishment
served an indispensable function—saving the soul by literally excising the
diabolical agents that medieval penologists believed clung on to the culprit's body.
It was only through application of severe corporal punishments that such excision
was possible. At the same time, to engender general deterrence, punishment was

---

29   Ibid., p. 421.
30   For the document see Monter, W., (1969), *European Witchcraft*, New York, NY,
John Wiley & Sons, Inc., pp. 10–27.

meted out in public with the purpose of humiliating and putting the convict to shame. However, there was a recognition among European penologist that even the most severe forms of capital punishments, such as death by quartering, crucifying, beheading and hanging the convict by neck until death occurred, could not guarantee the excising of the soul from the demonic agent(s).[31] That is why, "a variety of apotropaic rituals" were designed for that purpose, observes Pfohl.[32] Thus, pre-Enlightenment punishments were more than punitive, but also were ritualistic and excising in nature. Pfohl writes:

> Consider the apotropaic function of that particularly brutal punishment known as "breaking on the wheel." This form of purging may be traced back to the practice of *apotympanismos* in ancient Greek. After the deviant was pegged to a board with irons, an executioner proceeded to break all his or her major bones with a heavy metal bar. Later variations of the "sacred punishment" included such things as tying someone to the broad side of a wheel and then rolling it down an incline, and pegging a person to the ground and running him or her over with a spiked wheel. Why such elaborate means of death? Because in breaking the bones of a sinner, one breaks the hold that an evil spirit exercises over an earthly body.[33]

Although Colonial America of the 17th and 18th centuries was agrarian-based in social and economic organization, post-colonial America transformed itself into a dynamic nation-state in a relatively short period of time (1850–1950) thanks to its semi-continental size with huge arable land and water resources with a bourgeoning immigrant human-capital at its disposal. More importantly, post-colonial America was (and still remains) relatively receptive to new and innovative ideas and cultural traditions that different immigrant groups brought with them to the New World, including the rationale of reforming the penal system.

The Judeo-Christian Ideal of Just Punishment in Colonial Penology

The Judeo-Christian ideal of just punishment occupied a central place in the North American penal systems. However, this remained an ideal that was difficult to uniformly maintain due to the fluxing nature of colonial life. On the one hand, there were witch trials conducted by the magisterial church authorities in colonies. On the other hand, there were the likes of William Penn (1644–1718) who " ... abolished corporal punishment and gradually introduced fines and incarceration in facilities

---

31   Pfohl, *Images of Deviance and Social Control*, p. 29.
32   Pfohl, Ibid.
33   Pfohl, Ibid., p. 29.

known as jails, named after their gaols (pronounced "jails") British counterparts."[34] Cliff Roberson maintains that as the founder of the Quaker settlement that later became the State of Pennsylvania, William Penn was the precursor of both treatment and rehabilitation of offenders in the American penology.[35] Accordingly, William Penn's progressive penal ideas were instrumental in the enactment of The Quaker Code of 1682. The Code was antithetical to the prevailing British notions of punishment reflected in the codes of the Duke of York, or of Hampshire Code, argues Roberson writing:

> The Quakers advocated eliminating the harsh principles of criminal law in favor
> of more humane treatment of offenders. The Quakers, though very religious,
> eliminated most of the religious crimes and created a criminal code which was
> very secular. The Quaker Code, enacted in 1682, remained in force until its
> repeal in 1718, the day after the death of William Penn. The code was replaced
> by the English Anglican Code, which was even worse than the former codes
> of the Duke of York. The English Anglican Code restored the death penalty
> for many crimes and restored mutilations, branding, and other brutal forms of
> corporal punishment.[36]

The English Anglican Code reflected a typical pre-Beccarian view of the symbiotic relationship that the medieval penologists had theorized, one that was based on sin-crime synergy whose excision required a certain form and regime of punishment. Unlike Continental Europe, Colonial America did not possess one entrenched ancient culture of its own, therefore, the elite among the North American colonists were cognizant of the fact that for their "New" England to be truly a new entity, it had to free itself from the malaise of the European medievalist penal thoughts expressed so passionately and eloquently in the "*Magnalia Christi Americana*: or, *The Ecclesiastical History of New-England*."[37] In the document, as much as the author gave a detailed account of the Protestant Church's rise in Europe, he also detailed various events leading to the prosecution of the Protestants in Europe that caused their exodus from Europe to the New World. It was in the midst of this mixed heritage that the colonial penologists gradually developed a specifically American notion of punishment regime with its interconnected purposes namely, that an ideal penal system had to be retributive at the same time that it had to incarcerate in order to physically incapacitate the culprits in penitentiaries. However, due to the Judeo-Christian notion of fairness in punishment, the convicts

---

34   Champion, Dean. J., (1998), *Corrections in the United States: A Contemporary Perspective*, third edn, Upper Saddle River, NJ, Prentice Hall, p. 11.

35   Roberson, Cliff, (1997), *Introduction to Corrections*, Incline Village, NV, Copperhouse Publishing Co., p. 13.

36   Roberson, Ibid., p. 13.

37   For the document, see Lauter, *The Heath Anthology of American Literature*, pp. 425–427.

had to be given a chance for redemption through rehabilitation. Thus, historically speaking, the ideal of rehabilitation has occupied an important niche in the history of American penal philosophy.

Enter the Enlightenment Era

European Enlightenment thinkers and social philosophers, the likes of Voltaire, Hobbes, Montesquieu, Rousseau, to name a few, sought to explain the societal dimensions and impacts of power and free will in relation to crime and punishment. The Enlightenment thinkers did not seek the remedial role of the Providence in crime control mechanisms as they tried to posit a more anthropocentric, as against theistic, explanation as to why humans acted the way they did. Greed, for example, was no longer looked upon as one of the Seven Grand Sins among Enlightenment thinkers, but a natural outcome of the European mercantilism that emerged out of the Great Explorations and colonization of a vast part of the world that contained fabulous riches. Mercantilism did not thrive on the Judeo-Christian and/or Islamic advice of sharing the wealth with others, but by the accumulation of wealth and hording it in the hands of few. Next to Great Explorations that led to colonial schemes in the transference of unprecedented amount of wealth from colonies to Europe, the Transatlantic Slave Trade also helped the cultural uprooting and dislocation of African human capital as slaves to the European colonies in the New World. Although it was trade and commerce that Adam Smith considered as the base of the "Wealth of the Nations," in reality, it was slaves who provided the material base of such wealth through their sweat and blood, including that of New England along the Atlantic shores. In addition, Transatlantic Slavery also played a significant role as it availed to European sovereigns a worldwide market for exploitation of human capital. The most ruthless among the European sovereigns got the lion's share because he or she was no longer bound by a medieval view of propriety in action, but by the new "spirit of capitalism," as succinctly described by the German Sociologist Max Weber.

Max Weber (1864–1920) in his highly acclaimed *Protestant Ethics and the Spirit of Capitalism* argued that what differentiated the Protestant view of salvation from Catholicism was in the Protestant ability to transform religious call from its ecclesiastical base to one of worldly-material wealth garnering based on hard and honest work. This transformation took place through the application of mercantilism principles to colonization mandates legitimated by the Protestant notion that the creation of material wealth was a sure sign of one's salvation in the next world to come; those who achieved material wealth in this world could readily conceive it as a "sign" of salvation in the next world to come. Colonization of foreign lands and people was an arduous and risky venture, but if successful, the endeavor could lead to discovery of enormous sources of both human capital as well as raw material that could be transformed into material wealth. This was achieved through the Transatlantic Slavery Trade that thoroughly impacted life in Europe. As the new riches were being transferred from colonies in Africa, Asia, the Caribbean as well as the Americas to European centers of mercantile power, the emerging Protestant ethics cautioned against worldly indulgencies and instead encouraged thriftiness on the grounds that it was the only way that enabled the faithful not to flaunt his or her material wealth against the Godly virtue of humility; at the same time it allowed reinvestment in enterprising business ventures that garnered more profits. However, the creation of material wealth under Protestant Ethics was not just a monist process determined solely by hard and honest work alone, there was a deeply entrenched intellectualism as to what the role of the divine will and predestination was in relation to man's station in life. After all, Europe was gradually emerging form the millennial shackles of the Dark Ages— with its distinct hierarchical notion of God-church-man relationship. The Vatican was the base of this intellectualism thus by going outside Catholicism's main base, the post-Reformation Protestant intellectualism had to formulate the ethics of salvation in a way that did not overtly clash with the doctrine of divine providence whose logic and/or rationale was deemed beyond mortal man's ability to fathom, let alone to comprehend. Thus, rather than trying to decipher the proclivities of the divine will, the functional logic of the Post-Reformation intellectualism was to look for men's divine call that had its worldly signs and manifestations. What were these? Individual health, wealth, general contentment, good name and reputation, good family and offspring, fear of God, aversion to sin-crime and hope for salvation.

It is noteworthy that the same rationale applies to the Islamic notion of salvation and work ethics that Muslims used in their conquest/colonization of the greater Middle East, North Africa and South East Asia. The Muslim doctrine of salvation through hard and honest work has its bases in Islam's sacred text, the Qur'an, reflected in the Hadith literature; the Hadith literature was composed of the sayings and deeds that Muslim theologians and legal scholars attributed to Prophet Muhammad and his deputies– especially to the first four, known as The Four Rightly Guided Caliphs (*Khulafa al-Rashindin*). It is noteworthy that Muhammad and his deputies were all involved in trade and international commerce during Islam's formative stages (610–661 CE). In fact, the Qur'an is filled with all kinds of mercantilism doctrines and advice. For example, the text considers merchants, traders, shop-keepers and producers of wares as *al-Kaasib* (those who produce, garner, add-value to manufactured products, etc.), portraying them as *Habib-Allah* (beloved ones in the eyes of Allah). The Qur'an admonishes Muslims against usury reminding them that such practices do not endear them to the Almighty; that those who engage in usurious practices to oppress the weak will be punished dearly in the Day of Resurrection. The essence of Muslim mercantilism is premised on the notion that to please Allah, the *al-Kaasib* have to be honest and work hard in producing wealth but not hoarding it; it is better to spread one's wealth through charity, or by financing public projects (e.g., building mosques, centers of learning and especially libraries, public bath houses, hospitals and orphanages to name but a few). In particular, the Qur'an advises men of wealth to be charitable to the less fortunate and especially the needy. Like other monotheistic divine texts, the thrust of the Qur'an has been from its inception that all wealth belongs to the Almighty, be it on land, in sea or between the earth and the heavens. The rationale of this stance of the Qur'an is that it is Allah who gives, and it is Allah who reclaims that which we posses; lo and behold that all wealth belongs to Allah. The rationale is that wealth is to be enjoyed but not used to oppress others.

Within both the Protestant and the Islamic work ethics, the sin-crime synergy has historically rested on similar root causes: those who yearn for material success but do not want to achieve it through hard work based on moral and righteous path— as advised by the Bible and/or the Qur'an—inadvertently resort to dishonest and/ or immoral means and stratagems, including sin-crime. This perspective has been instrumental in the rise of two social typologies in relation to sin-crime synergy: (a) those who have equipped themselves with strong moral foundations and iron-clad will and determination to improve their lot stand up to the multifaceted challenges of success without resorting to unsavory, or immoral acts; (b) those who lack strong moral foundations, or are of weak disposition towards life's contingencies in relation to hard and honest work, succumb to alternate routes that induces sin and/or crime. That is why the colonial charters emphasized the propriety of deeds and thoughts that were expected of each colony. According to James A. Cox, these were reflected in colonial documents as, for example, in the "Articles, Laws and Orders Diuine, Politique, and Materiall for the Colony in Virginia," enunciated by the Virginia Colony of London in 1611.[38] Noting the severity of these laws, Cox writes that:

> The English-American colonies were autocratic and theocratic with a particular system of justice: magistrates and religious leaders, sometimes one and the same, made the laws, and the burden of obeying them fell on the less exalted— the tradesmen, soldiers, farmers, servants, slaves, and the young. That burden could be weighty.[39]

This colonial legal harshness noted by Cox was perhaps due to the nature of colonization process; on the one hand, the colonies were allowed to engage in a wide range of mercantile-based activities. On the other hand, the expansionist thrust of Christendom, like its counterpart, the *Dar al-Islam*, allowed for conquest—thus the term "Conquistador," that applied to the Spanish flanks' attempts to expand Christendom throughout the New World. Interestingly, among Muslims, the equivalence of the Conquistador was the Holy Warrior (*Ghaazi*); it was he who waged Islam's holy war (*ghaza*) against the infidels. During the Great Exploration era, the Muslim holy warriors, be it the Ottoman Janissary, the Egyptian Mamluk, or the Safavid Qizilbash, were deemed duty-bound to bring the "infidels" to their knees as they engaged in spreading Islam to the yonder lands. However, if the

---

38 Cox A. James, (2003), "Bilboes, Brands, and Branks" at the web page of Colonial Williamsburg at: http://www.history.org/Foundation/journal/spring03/baranks.cfm.
39 Cox, Ibid.

so-called infidels converted to Islam, they would be treated fairly as part of the Islamic Community of Believers (*Ummah*).

Among this racial and ethnic amalgamation called Muslims, any man of worldly ambition could and did rise to the highest position of sovereign power. That is why among a multitude of Muslim dynasties that rose to power from 750s CE until 1750s in different locales of the *Dar al-Islam*, one finds African Muslim convert dynasties next to Turkic, Semitic, and Caucasian. Examples include dynasties that ruled in various parts of Africa. One of these was the dynasty of the Kings of Songhay who ruled parts of Mali along the western bank of the Niger River from around 9th century CE to 1592 CE. The Songhay Dynasty was loosely composed of three branches known as: (1) the Zas or Zuwas of Gao, (2) the Sis or Sonnis, and (3) the Askiyas according to Clifford Edmund Bosworth who observes that "Al-Sa'di relates a tradition that it was the fifteenth Za, Kosoy, who in the eleventh century became the first convert to Islam being called Muslim Dam 'the voluntary Muslim'." [40] By the passage of time, the Songhay dynasty cut its umbilical cords from the original founder of Mali, the Keita household and gradually rose to socioeconomic as well as military prominence under Sonni 'Ali Great.[41]

What is significant about the Songhay is that by conversion to Islam, ambitious African Muslims affiliated with the dynasty they could now assume the position of sovereign as in the case of aforementioned Muslim Dam who voluntarily converted to Islam. It is noteworthy that the term 'Dam' is very likely the corrupted version of the term *Dhimmah*. In traditional Islam's Sacred Law, the Shari 'ah, *Dhimmah* denotes those who have sought Islam's protection without converting to Islam. The *Dhimmah* status engendered a set of obligations as well as protection that the status conferred upon those who sought it. One obligation was the payment of a yearly tax that was known as the *jaziyah* to the Islamic state that had granted the *Dhimmah* status in the first place. Another obligation on the part of the *Dhimmah* grantee was to respond to the state's call to arms during external threat or invasion. The *Dhimmah* status did not prevent voluntary conversion to Islam that would open higher levels of social mobility as far as assuming the office of the Muslim sovereign. There were ex-slaves, as in the case of Ali Golom, "who freed Gao from the domination of Mali."[42] The word Golom is very likely the corrupted version of the Arabic *Ghulam* which has historically denoted adult male slave. The fact that an ex-slave could have found the Sis or Sonnis line of the Songhay kingdom is indicative of the fact that among medieval Muslims, it was not the race or ethnicity but the very act of conversion to Islam that allowed for the rise to the highest position of power. As observed by Bosworth:

---

40   Bosworth, Clifford Edmund, (1996), *The New Islamic Dynasties: A chronological and genealogical manual*, (New York, Columbia University Press), p. 125.

41   Bosworth, Ibid., p. 125.

42   Bosworth, Ibid., p. 125.

At the end of the fourteenth century, Songhay became completely independent of Mali, and a powerful empire, with both military and naval forces, was built by Sonni 'Ali Great, penultimate ruler of the Si line and the real founder of the Songhay Empire. Shortly after Sonni 'Ali's death, his commander Muhammad Ture, of Sonkine origin, seized the throne and founded a new dynasty of his own, that of the Askiyas. Under him, Islam became the imperial cult, and Timbuktu developed as a centre of Islamic learning.[43]

This raises a question: how did the colonizers (be Christians or Muslim) resolve the inherent conflict between slavery and the confessional tenets of their faith that proclaimed do unto others, as you would have them do to you? Slavery was the antithesis of this idea, yet it comprised the base of a very lucrative international trade in human capital as slaves. The very act of enslavement inflicted all kinds of physical, mental, cultural and psychological violence and unwarranted injustice on people who had never committed any injustices on their captors, be it European or Muslim. Ironically, the Qur'an is adamant that no one is allowed to enslave themselves to mortal beings other than to Allah who is the one and only source of high morality and values. In fact, the term Muslim means one who has submitted to Allah thus he or she is not allowed to enslave themselves to mortal beings, neither is he or she allowed enslaving others. Thus, the very act of submission to Islam means a total denunciation of the evil act of enslavement of others, be it men, women or children. The same view can be found in the Bible. So how did the slave masters resolve this conundrum? They resolved it first by dehumanizing the would-be object of enslavement so as through proselytizing "rescue-humanize" the enslaved.

Legitimizing Slavery

One theory was premised on the notion that Black Africa was living in its "natural" state devoid of any discernible culture, religion, and those sublime values that separated man from beasts. How else could one explain those "bizarre" traditions of the African tribes be it in the Ivory Coast, Sierra Leon, Zanzibar, Cape of Hope and other ports from which African slaves were imported to the New World? How could skin color, the shape of the skull, the texture of hair of the African slave be explained other than biological "inferiority"? How could traditions such as cannibalism, worship of totems, strange music and dances and voodoo be anything but "primitivcness" pondered pseudo-scientific theories that mushroomed in the post-Great Exploration era in Europe and later found its niches in the New World.

Another legitimating theory developed by the Christian Missionaries was premised on the notion that Black Africa had not been exposed to Christianity. The temporal blackness of the African Continents was not as important as the presumed

---

43   Bosworth, Ibid., p. 125.

'blackness' of the soul theorized as being due to a lack of exposure to the majesty of the Holy Trinity: God the Father, the Son, and the Holy Spirit. If only the logic and inherent beauty of the Holy Trinity could be explained to these lost souls, thus, went the reasoning behind one of the most intense proselytizing efforts that took place in the annals of Christianity during the colonization of Africa. Whether inadvertently, or intentionally, slave masters and Christian missionaries followed the same logic, one was to "civilize", the other to "proselytize" for the salvation of the soul and body of the "Dark Continent" Africa.

Another legitimating theory was that although certain parts of Black Africa had experienced Islam giving some semblance of superficial civility to Africa, it was far from being civilized for the simple reason that *Mahomet* was a false prophet who had concocted a religion whose teachings, although borrowed from both Judaism as well as from Christianity, were nonetheless corrupted by this "devilish" Mahomet; missionaries were to save Africa's soul and body from Islam's "abhorrent" teachings.

The institution of Transatlantic Slavery created the text, the context, and the sub-text for the initial dehumanization of the African element to be subsequently "rescued" and "humanized" by its White, Anglo-Saxon overlords in North America. The Jewish and Arab slave merchants and ship-owners played an important role in this scheme and thus the seed of the historical animosity between the Jew and the Black was planted in this fashion.

The case of Latin America was different for there was a qualitative difference between the Latin American view of slavery and those of the Anglo American. As observed by Gunnar Myrdal, the Spanish Conquistadores did not differentiate between African and non-Africans when it came to the issue of racial supremacy. The Conquistador was the *sin qua non* master, and all other races were his inferior and deserved to be slaves, be it the natives, the Asian functionaries at his service, or his African slaves. Myrdal compares and contrasts this disposition of the Conquistador towards slavery with those of the US slave masters who had to legitimize slavery in a social setting that had a deep sense of Judeo-Christian values; a social medium that espoused to the Jeffersonian ideal that men were created equal in the image of God. If men were deemed created equal, how could men enslave other men? This is an American dilemma observes Myrdal, a dilemma that can only be resolved if it could be shown that this dictum does not apply to all races.[44]

Thus, the demonization of ex-slave Blacks became the only viable alternative to resolve this dilemma after slavery was abolished in the United States in the 1860s. In contrast to the re-demonization attempts in the post-bellum Southern States of the United States, the abolition of slavery in Latin America facilitated ex-slaves' incorporation into the main stream society and economy. The American experience was quite different. It is not ironic that during the struggle for social justice and equity, the African American community produced giants such

---

44   Myrdal, G., (1994), *An American Dilemma*, New York, NY, Harper & Row.

as Frederick Douglas, Booker T Washington, W. E. B. Du Bois, Malcolm X, Thurgood Marshall, and Martin Luther King, Jr. Neither is it ironic that Black churches, synagogues, and mosques were at the forefront of this struggle. The Black churches, synagogues and later, Black mosques, next to Black institutions of higher learning, and Black educators, have helped in the creation of an African American social and historical conscience; these institutions have produced formidable intellectuals and orators (e.g., Reverends Martin Luther King Jr., Jessie Jackson, Malcolm X, etc.) who have raised the Black consciousness about social, economic, political and legal justice in the twentieth century.

African American intellectuals, social critiques, academicians, and community leaders have been concerned with the plight of indigent and urban minority communities and their offending populations (both adult and youth categories) as well as with and their treatment in the American criminal justice system. Most seem to argue that the general test of the fairness of any system of justice and conflict resolution depends on the manner in which the socially disenfranchised members of society are treated. This premise has been defended both from the standpoints of common sense and of the logic of the etiology of crime. It is a matter of common sense that members of the disenfranchised social strata face more hurdles in Common, Civil, and Islamic Law systems. The power differential inherent in modern class societies puts this category in a more disadvantageous position in terms of posting bail to secure pre-trial release, and having the ability to mount a viable defense strategy.

In sum, because the thrust of the Western colonial proselytizing literature was saving, rather than enslaving Africans, this literature provided a powerful legitimating mechanism for slave masters as how to save those "lost souls" from eternal damnation by presenting them to Christianity. Was this an empty rhetoric? Some scholars have contrasted the British colonization procedures with those of the Spanish Conquistadors arguing that the former tried to adhere to true Christian doctrine whereas the latter followed an insatiable thirst for looting and pillaging, to the effect that the drafters of the British colonial charters found it imperative to remind all parties involved in the colonization processes of their duties—the moral mandates of the British imperia in colonial ventures.[45] Whereas slavery was being legitimated in the eyes of colonial penologists as a Judeo-Christian salvation mandate, human action that included, among others, a rational explanation as to why people committed anti-social acts.

---

45   See for example, Stanley Johnson, "John Donne and the Virginia Company," at web page http://links.jstor.org. The original article is published by the *ELH*, Vol. 14, No. 2. (Jun., 1974), pp. 127–138.

Post-Colonial American Penology

Post-colonial American penology, notwithstanding its relative humanization efforts, relied, by and large, on incarceration to both deter and incapacitate criminal culprits. In fact, compared to the British penal system which applied the death penalty to around 168 crimes until very recent times, the American colonial penal system gradually restricted the application of the death penalty to much fewer and only to capital crimes. Incarceration, on the other hand, has a different connotation and meaning for the American penologists. This state of affairs, it should be noted, did not come about easily. Hugo Adam Bedau states that:

> Almost every aspect of reduction in the use of penal execution is a result of efforts by those who would do away with it completely; every important change in its continual administration short of abolition represents a compromise between the two contending forces.[46]

Bedau argues that the American criminal justice system's reliance on death penalty gradually lessened as a number of important developments took place in penal and judicial philosophy. These were:

a.   inventing degrees of murder
b.   reducing the variety of capital offense
c.   ending public executions
d.   expanding the role of appellate courts
e.   experimenting with total abolition
f.   reducing the number of executions.[47]

These developments arguably humanized the American penal philosophy by extending both *de facto* and *de jure* the borders of the etiology of crime on the one hand. On the other hand, American criminology as an academic discipline started giving more attention to the contributory role of social, economic and political factors. For example, with the development of modern medicine, biology, germ theory, clinical psychiatry and genetics, no longer could a simple morality-based pathology explain the causes of crime. The rise of modern American criminology also made the etiology of crime more a concern of the state rather than the community. This, in turn, allowed racial and ethnic groups to raise questions about the propriety of disproportionate application of capital punishments as, for example, the death penalty to minority offenders. The humanization process of

---

46   Bedau, H.A., "Background and Development" p. 3, in Hugo Adam Bedau (ed.), *The Death Penalty in America*, third edn, New York, NY, Oxford University Press, 1982, pp. 3–28.
47   Bedau, Ibid., pp. 3–4.

the penal philosophy, however, was an arduous process that was not welcomed universally. For example, Bedau writes:

> The idea that murder can be distinguished into crimes of certain degrees has not always been hailed as an improvement over the common-law notion of murder. It is arguable whether the common-law concept of "malice" is really clarified by the equally shadowy notions of willfulness, deliberateness and premeditation. But, it was an effective compromise of the policy that murderers should be punished with death; the jury was left to decide in each case whether the accused, though guilty, had committed homicide with sufficient calculation to deserve the maximum punishment.[48]

There were those judges, the likes of Benjamin Cordozo, who a century after the adaptation of the doctrine of degrees of murder, still questioned even the intelligibility of the "concept of degrees of murder," points out Bedau. Even in Britain, as late as 1953, the Reporter of the Royal Commission on Capital Punishment maintained that:

> There are strong reasons for believing that it must inevitably be found impracticable to define a class of murderers in which alone the inflicting of the death penalty is appropriate. The crux of the matter is that any legal definition must be expressed in terms of objective characteristics of the offense, whereas the choice of the appropriate penalty must be based on a much wider range of considerations, which cannot be defined but are essentially a matter for the exercise of discretion.[49]

In Britain, incarceration, as a punitive measure, has developed through a long process of trial and error and in conjunction with the evolution of the British penal system, a system which originally was designed to serve the law and order interests of centuries-old British monarchy at the apex of the British aristocratic power structure. British penologists, social thinkers, judges, barristers and members of the parliament conceived of incarceration as a necessary evil whose historical roots extended as far as the medieval times perhaps when the theory of the King's Peace prevailed. The theory maintained that the king's rule was divinely ordained and legitimated by the king's ability to provide the realm with peace and security for its subjects. Sin and crime, because they corrupted the King's Peace, had to be excised through just and equitable punishments. For most ordinary sins and crimes, the form of the punishment was not as important as the desired end result of it. There were specific diabolical crimes such as sorcery, witchcraft and satanic rituals that necessitated ritualistic punishments that had to be performed by the priests. According to Stephen Pfohl, those accused of such

---

48   Bedau, Ibid., p. 5.
49   Bedau, Ibid.

diabolical crimes could be subjected to trial by ordeal which was in essence "trial by torture."[50] The "evidence," usually consisted of confessions that were extracted from the accused through torturous methods. As common law went through stages of elaboration and sophistication in the 16th, 17th and 18th centuries, such practices (e.g., torture or inquisitions by the ordained priests) were largely abandoned in England. Incarceration, however, remained a dominant form of punishment in both England and colonial America with the proviso that in the North American colonies, incarceration was much more humane as it was to replace the much harsher death penalty that was prevalent England.

Making a comparison between the two circa 1749–1758 and 1790–1799 (in terms of number of persons executed in Britain), Leon Radzinowicz has documented how British penal system gradually moved to a "divergence" between law and practice to the effect that between 1800–1810, out of a total of 939 capitally convicted cases, only 123 persons were executed. Making a comparison between these three periods, Radzinowicz writes:

> The importance of the conclusions which may be drawn from these figures cannot be over-emphasized. In the years 1749–1758, more than two-thirds of the offenders who were capitally convicted were executed; in the years 1790–1799, the proportion fell to less than one in three. But in the next eleven years (1800–1810) only about one offender out of every seven sentenced to death was executed.[51]

On the other hand, American colonies sought to inculcate, in the mantle of Protestantism, the "true" Judeo-Christian values such as charity, compassion, forgiveness towards every member of the colony that included the sinners, criminals and wrong-doers. Incarceration reflected these ideals at the same time that rehabilitation was sought.

Equity in American Penology

Equity in punishment has been a core value in American penology. The evolution of equity in punishment principle has its Judeo-Christian history as reflected in some of the documents that we cited above; however, from modern perspective, reference should be made to the United States Constitution upon which the Original Thirteen Colonies built America. It was within the parameters of the American

---

50   Pfohl, Steven., (1994), *Images of Deviance and Social Control: A Sociological History*, New York, McGraw-Hill, Inc., p. 25.

51   Radzinowicz, L., (1971), "The Purpose of Punishment Related to Enforcement: A Case History from Capital Punishment" pp. 105–113 in L. Radzinowicz and M. Wolfgang (eds), *Crime and Justice, Volume II, The Criminal in the Arms of the Law*, New York, NY, Basic Books, Inc., Publishers, p. 105.

Constitution that the Union derived its principles of equity applicable to both law and punishment. For example, all colonies believed in the Biblical notion that an eye for an eye, and a tooth for a tooth, reflected the criteria of justice in punishment. This retributive notion of punishment reflected a basic Judeo-Christian rationale that colonial penologists adhered to in their writings and public deliberations.

The puritanical view of punishment was harmonious with the colonists' view that man had made a contract with God to perpetuate God's ideals on earth which included among many others, the application of God's Law. Melvin I. Urofsky observes that it was because of this view that, "… Governor John Winthrop and his associates initially tried to run Massachusetts as a Calvinist oligarchy. In order to preserve the religious nature of the colony, they limited freeman status only to members of the church."[52] Although ideally speaking, proportionality applies in the Biblical *lex talionis*, but in practice, such punitive measures could not be adhered to because they ran the mood of the time that favored humane forms of punishment such as imprisonment instead of cruel punishments. As observed by James W. Marquart and Jonathan R. Sorensen, the idea of systematic imprisonment emerged in England as a reaction to cruelty in punishment inflicted on convicts. The eighteenth century, observe the authors, was also the time of general enlightenment, a time that produced such humanist social philosophers as Voltaire, Montesquieu, Beccaria and Bentham.[53] In fact, the emergence of the notion, as well as the institution, of a criminal justice system, argues Pieter C. Spierenburg, has to be located in the context of the rise of modern state whereby a rational, systemic and centralized penology replaced the vengeance based punitive system of pre-modern era. Tracing the origin of this replacement as far back as twelfth century Europe, Spierenburg, draws upon the work of P. W. A. Immink, to conclude that the "birth of punishment" or the "emergence of public penal law," ought to be placed "… in the context of changing relationship of freedom and dependence in feudal society."[54] In other words, the term punishment should be used in the context of a central authority that has a penal code as well as the requisite legitimacy to impose a regulated form of punishment.

Penance Ideal in American Penology

The rationale for punishment from an American penal perspective was religiously inspired by Quakers. This could be seen in the first correctional institutions in Colonial America. Following the rationale of the Quaker notion of penance as a

---

52 Urofsky, M.I., (1988), *A March of Liberty: Constitutional History of the United States*, New York, McGraw-Hill, Inc., p. 11.

53 Marquart, J.W., and Sorensen, J.R., (eds), (1997), "Introduction" pp. 1–2 *Correctional Context: Contemporary and Classical Readings*, Los Angeles, CA, Roxbury Publishing Company, p. 1.

54 Spierenburg, P.C., "The Specter of Suffering" pp. 3–15, in *Correctional Context*, p. 3.

legitimate form of punishment, criminal offenders have historically been segregated or placed in penitentiaries as places whereby the criminal offenders could reflect upon their anti-social acts as well as sharing their sin and crime experiences with their fellow convicts. The ideal of segregating or grouping and housing similarly situational offenders was for repentance. By learning from others experiences, the penitentiaries would engender an atmosphere of sorrow and yet dignified reflection of a multitude of men who have fallen victim to their own temptations and therefore have been involved in sinful-criminal acts, but now they want to redeem their souls next to redeeming their human worth and place in society. At the same time, through a regime of hard work, iron clad discipline, and Judeo-Christian morality-based education system in the penitentiaries, the punitive and yet rewarding rehabilitative process would steer the inmates towards penance. In short, the American ideal of penance has historically been structured so as not only to reflect the Judeo-Christian basic premise that punishing criminal offenders is indispensable, but that punishment ought to be corrective and redemptive rather than solely vengeful.

Market Economy and the American Penal Philosophy

The American criminal justice system is undoubtedly one of the most complex systems of justice and conflict resolutions ever known in the annals of human history. The system has evolved from its colonial background to its present format which reflects a modern notion of crime and penology reflecting the economic infrastructure upon which it has been structured, modern industrial (and now post-industrial) capitalism. Although American penology during its Quaker movement reflected an agrarian base of Colonial America, the criminal justice system has developed parallel with the overall prerequisites of modern capitalism from late nineteenth century to the present. For example, although the American Bill of Rights prohibits the infliction of cruel and unusual punishments such as public hanging, lynching, quartering, flogging (that were deemed appropriate punishments in Colonial America), this prohibition has yet to cover the issue of the length of incarceration. A lifelong sentence without possibilities of parole for capital crimes has yet to be researched adequately in terms of the cruel and unusual parameters of the Eighth Amendment to the US Constitution. Although there are cases such as *Weems v. United States* (1910) in which the Court deemed that, "... the Eighth Amendment had been violated by a law which allowed a person convicted of falsifying a public record to be assessed a heavy fine, sentenced to fifteen years at hard labor and subjected to several other sanctions."[55] The notion that the length of incarceration constitutes cruel and unusual punishment has yet

---

55   See *Weems v. United States*, 217 U.S. 349 (1910), cited in *Congressional Quarterly's Guide to the U.S. Supreme Court*, Washington, D.C., Congressional Quarterly Inc., 1979, p. 575.

to be tackled by the US Supreme Court. This is important because after the Court ruled in *Trop v. Dulles* (1958), it has become customary to consider the following statement of Chief Justice Earl Warren as the yard stick for what is cruel and unusual punishment:

> The basic concept underlying the Eighth Amendment is nothing less than dignity of man. While the State has the power to punish, the Amendment stands to assure that this power to be exercised within the limits of civilized standards. Fines, imprisonment and even execution may be imposed depending upon the enormity of the crime, but any technique outside the bounds of traditional penalties is constitutionally suspect .... The Court [has] ... recognized that the words of the Amendment are not precise, and that their scope is not static. The Amendment must draw its meaning from the evolving standards of decency that mark the progress of a maturing society.[56]

It is commonly known that the constituents of the American criminal justice system (courts, police, and corrections) are complex and of a multifaceted social nature employing large numbers of persons from all segments of society. This complexity is further compounded by the fact that each constituent is locally, rather than nationally, financed and managed. The communal differences impact the overall operational dynamics of the system in the distribution of justice. Some states are more progressive than others and therefore, differ in their manner and style of the administration of justice, but not necessarily in their incarceration of the indigent, urban African-American males who, by and large, disproportionately occupy the system. Incarceration is the end result of a long process known as the criminal case processing which involves investigation and arrest, pre-trial activities, adjudication and sentencing and correctional stages.[57] The entire process, despite all its federal and state based constitutional checks and balances, is nonetheless of an adversarial nature requiring the paid-services of competent legal counsel and representation from the very beginning (e.g. the arrest) through pre-trial (bail and pre-sentence release) and post-trial activities (e.g., appeal).

The profoundly financially-based process has made justice a product, like any other product, with complex market mechanism based on price and demand and supply structures. Those who can afford its price can obtain the legal services of the most competent criminal defense lawyers from the very beginning of the process to the end. Those who can't, are allowed to opt for a number of legal remedies that are financed by public funds so as not to leave indigent defenders vulnerable to the negative realities of the adversarial system. Most states have provided state-sponsored indigent defense funds, they also have required law firms to provide

---

56   See *Trop v. Dulles*, 356 U.S. 86 at 99 (1958), cited in *Congressional Quarterly's Guide to the U.S. Supreme Court*, p. 575.

57   Schmallerger, F., (1999), *Criminal Justice Today*, fifth edn, Upper Saddler, NJ, Simon & Schuster Company, p. 21.

pro bono defense services for indigent defendants as well as availing the services of the Public Defense Office and court appointed attorney services for indigent clienteles. Even at this level, a certain gender, race and social class based disparity and outright discriminatory practices hinder the just resolution of the conflicts. For example, due to historical legal paternalism towards female criminality, female indigent cases are, by and large, handled by overworked court appointed attorneys. Whereas the male indigent cases are usually handled by the Public Defense Office which is more competent with considerable resources at its disposal to enter into pre-trial plea bargaining. In other words, even at the indigence level, factors of power differentials enter the justice process.

It is commonly understood that in all four stages of the criminal case processing, the odds are against those racial and ethnic minorities who are economically indigent, socially disenfranchised, and politically dispersed and divided. Due to the class nature of the American criminal justice system, indigent African-American and Hispanic males are disadvantaged as they enter the justice process usually through the disproportionate arrest and booking mechanism which initiates the justice process. Thanks to the untiring efforts of both progressive white and minority (African-American, Hispanic and Asian) criminologist and community leaders, more attention, and policy-generated resources, are now being directed to the manner in which the justice process is initiated and applied to various social, ethnic and racial groups, including to the African-American communities. For example, it is widely known that the media, the entertainment industries, and the American popular culture have played a central role in depicting predatory street crime (both violent and property) as the equivalence of "Black" or "minority-based" crime. The media depicts that the young, indigent, and urban African-American and Hispanic males commit the bulk of predatory crimes throughout American metropolises from the East Coast to West Coast. This depiction is misleading not because I intend to argue that there is a conscious media conspiracy to depict these two categories of the American youth as the main culprit for the majority of predatory urban crimes, or that African-American and Hispanic males do not commit predatory and violent street crimes, but that this is a superficial representation. For example, as shown by Samuel Walker et al., it is the young, indigent, and underclass white, rather than the African-American or Hispanic-American, males who commit the bulk of the predatory urban crimes. However, due to the sensationalist nature of the news and print media, the typical offender is depicted as a young, indigent and urban African-American or Hispanic males who victimize whites.

Utilizing data on victims and offenders, Walker et al. reason that due to the role of the media's sensationalist style of news coverage, a false depiction perception is created about both crime and offender-victim pairs. Accordingly, a typical crime is portrayed in the media as a violent crime (assault, robbery, murder, rape) which is committed by either a young African-American or Hispanic male against a typical victim, a white male or female.[58] Walker et al. then caution the reader that one has to be informed about the myths and realities of crime commission in the US. Not only is the above picture misleading, but in fact victimization data " ... reveal that racial minorities are more likely than whites to be victimized by crime."[59] Walker et al., make a distinction between crime being intra- and inter-racial; the first being the victimization of the members of one race at the hand of their own race, the second as victimization of the members of one race at the hand of the members of another race. The authors also utilize data from various victimization surveys to dispel this sensationalist view of typical victim-offender nexus.

The 1992 data on victimization used by Walker et al. covers the following racial and age differences as they pertain to (1) homicide rates, (2) household victimization, and (3) victimization for crimes of violence. In each of these, African Americans are victimized by much higher rates.

Table 2.1 A comparison between White and African-American homicide rates in 1992

White	4.9 per 100,000 persons
Black	34.0 per 100,000 persons

Source: Adopted from data provided by Walker et al., *The Color of Justice: Race, Ethnicity and Crime in America*, p. 27.

Table 2.2 A comparison between White and African-American household victimization rate in 1992

White	146.0 per 100,000 households
Black	199.1 per 100,000 households

Source: Adopted from data provided by Walker et al., *The Color of Justice: Race, Ethnicity and Crime in America*, p. 27.

58   Walker et al., Ibid., p. 25.
59   Walker et al., Ibid., p. 25.

**Table 2.3 A comparison between White, African-American and Hispanic
American victimization rates for crimes of violence in 1992**

White	88.7 per 100,000 persons aged 12 or older
Hispanic	110.1 per 100,000 persons aged 12 or older
African-American	110.8 per 100,000 persons aged 12 or older

Source: Adopted from data provided by Walker et al., *The Color of Justice: Race, Ethnicity and Crime in America*, p. 27.

From the above and similar data Walker et al. have reached the conclusion that:

> For most of their history in this country … blacks were victims, not initiators, of violence. In the Old South, violence against blacks was omnipresent–sanctioned both by custom and by law. Whites were free to use any methods, up to and including murder, to control 'their Negroes' ….There was little blacks could do to protect themselves. To strike back at whites, or merely to display anger or insufficient deference, was not just to risk one's own neck, but to place the whole community in danger. It was equally dangerous, or at best pointless, to appeal to the law.[60]

The counter argument is not that once freed from the chains and shackles of slavery, the newly emancipated became violent criminals. In fact, with the abolishment of slavery in the 1860s, it took almost a century for ex-slaves to attain their full legal status in this country. However, from the decades of the 1960s to present, the disproportionate incarceration of African-American males has led to the rise of a powerful belief among Black leaders and political activists that incarceration is a powerful tool at the hands of the American criminal justice to not only deprive the ex-slaves of their well deserved share of the American dream, but also to marginalize and dehumanize a good segment of African-American communities.

Finally, one must also consider the impact of modern penal law on American penal philosophy. Writing on the subject of American penal law and its relationship to British common law, John Kaplan and Robert Weisberg, opined that:

> Taken together, the legislative provisions defining crimes and prescribing punishments are usually referred to as the penal law, although they are also called the criminal law. The penal law in virtually all states of the United States

---

60   Walker et al., Ibid., p. 29.

is legislative in origin. That is, the conduct is not criminally punishable unless it has been proscribed by statute.[61]

Kaplan and Weisberg argued that this has not always been the case. After, giving a synopsis of the development of the British common law from the time of Norman Conquest of England in 1066, to the colonization of the New World, they write:

> In the colonization of the British North America, the common law of crimes was received and applied. With the rupture of sovereignty in the colonies at the time of the American Revolution, however, a strong movement arose to establish all law, including the criminal law, on the foundation of legislative enactment. Initially, this took the form of legislative enactments that simply declared the common law, including the common law of crimes, to be in effect except as displaced by particular statutory provisions. However, the principle was established in many states that the definition of crimes was the province of the legislatures and not the courts.[62]

The legislative process codifying criminal behaviors had an inevitable impact on post-colonial American penal philosophy for the simple reason that a move in that direction opened the flood gates of a re-consideration of that which was the province of religion, and that which was the province of the state. At the same time, the legislative processes adopted by each colony, after they become States of the Union, forced a reconsideration of the doctrine of social harm and the principle of liability, according to Kaplan and Weisberg.[63] It was "... Jeremy Bentham whose utilitarianism," argue Kaplan and Weisberg, "afforded a coherent basis for ordering the law of crimes according to the principle of degrees of social harm."[64] Bentham's rationale found its way into post-colonial American jurisprudence and into the many reforms that have proceeded since then as, for example, in the "the Model Penal Code promulgated by the American Law Institute in 1962."[65] The Code, maintain Kaplan and Weisberg established the following:

---

61 "Appendix A: A Note on Criminal Justice System" p. 1131 in Kaplan, J., and Weisberg, R. (eds), *Criminal Law: Cases and Materials*, Boston, MA, Little, Brown and Company, 1991, second edn, pp. 1129–1164.

62 Ibid., Kaplan et al., pp. 1131–1132.

63 Ibid., p. 1132.

64 Ibid.

65 Ibid.

a. a hierarchy of substantive criminal proscriptions
b. a corresponding hierarchy of social values
c. principle of criminal liability
d. definition of various specific crimes.[66]

These were important developments that gradually took place in post-colonial American view of penal philosophy. This was not because the British common law was devoid of these concepts, but these were due to the social dynamics and realities of the New England. The American Constitution and the addendum to it represented these dynamic realities engendering a powerful humanization process in both penal philosophy and penal institutions in this country from 1789 to present. Naturally, this was not a monist development and as Dean J. Champion notes, there is a definite chronology of these developments that penal historians have identified. For example, citing Adamson, Dean J. Champion gives the following six periods relating to developments that have taken place in American penology from 1790 until the beginning of the Great War:

a. The post-revolutionary period, 1790–1812
b. The recession following the War, of 1812
c. The Jacksonian period, 1812–1837
d. The mid-century period, 1837–1860
e. The post-bellum south, 1865–1890
f. The industrial northeast, 1865–1914[67]

Other scholars such as Thomas P. Roth and Anthony P. Travisono have extended their analyses to World War II, and from post WWII, to present era, respectively. Thus, although the first prisons in Massachusetts and other colonies were relatively primitive, within a short period of time a specifically American penal institution i.e., "Penitentiary" developed with its philosophy of "Penance." The genesis of this development can perhaps be observed in the Great Law of Pennsylvania.

The Impacts of Sin-Crime Synergy on Colonial Penology

The colonial belief in a sin-crime synergy had both positive and negative consequences on the rising Anglo-American penology. On the positive side, the notion that sin was causally related to crime was consequential for a structure of social mannerism that did not promote acts and thoughts that were antithetical to the doctrine of Christianity. On the negative side, the notion that sin led to crime facilitated the imposition of cruel and unusual punishments that were meted out

---

66   Ibid.
67   Champion, D.J., *Corrections in the United States: A Contemporary Perspective*, Upper Saddle River, NJ, Prentice Hall, 1998, second edn, p. 12.

publicly. Thus, corporal punishments served various purposes such as inculcating the fear of authority in the minds of those potential trouble makers and serving as a mechanism of social control. Corporal punishments were deemed especially effective for deterring evil agents from the soul and body of the possessed. These punishments ranged in severity, in the manner of execution, and in their presumed deterrent impacts. A literary of this perspective is found in the *Comedia* of the medieval Italian poet, Dante Alighieri (1265–1321). The Inferno section of the *Comedia* depicts the medieval Italian view of the sin-crime synergy including its diabolical mechanism. As Dante allegorically descends through the spiraling cantos of the Inferno, guided by the soul of his inspirational muse, the poet Virgil, he notices the incremental rise in the severity of various forms of punishment applied to the sinner-criminal culprits dwelling in each canto. The symbolism implies that the lower one gets through the cantos in Hell, the heavier is the burden of the sin which gets the sinner closer to the very persona of Satan, who is depicted as having eternally been immersed "up to his waist" in a frozen ocean of ice that covers the lowest of the lowliest pits of the ninth canto of the Inferno. Each canto, therefore, depicts the classification of sinner-criminals housed in Hell's wards being subjected to a variety of cruel and unusual punishments that the Hell-dwelling ghouls and goblins and demons mete out eternally on the souls and bodies of sinners. Although *Comedia* is an allegory, it nonetheless depicts a typical medievalist Roman Catholic view of an ideal regime of just and equitable punishment, one that ought to be of a supra-class, supra-gender, supra-race and supra-ethnic in nature. Punishment ought to be swift, certain, but of an eternal duration. This Italian penal philosophy prevailed, *mutatis mutandis*, throughout Europe until the rise of the Enlightenment era of the eighteenth century. Under the impacts of the Enlightenment penal measures and systems experienced reform including those applied in post-colonial American penal system.

Chapter 3
American Penal Philosophy: An Overview

The thrust of this book is that modern American penal philosophy is facing a profound moral challenge when it comes to dispensing penal justice to a large segment of the offending population. This segment is by and large poorly educated, socially and economically underprivileged residing in large inner city ghettoes, barrios and slums. Its offending pattern is mostly of a non-violent nature centered on the commission of petty theft, gambling, prostitution, or illicit drug-possession/distribution. When involved in predatory crime, it is mostly of an intra- rather than inter-racial nature. This book is mostly concerned with the plight of inner-city African-American offenders. In particular, the book addresses what is known as the disproportionate incarceration paradigm which has been developed by critical criminologists. It maintains that the present rate of incarceration of minority offenders in general, and, that of the African-Americans in particular, is disproportionate to their total number in the general population. This chapter discusses the operational functions of the American penal philosophy as a prelude to a more systematic exploration of the disproportionate incarceration paradigm. It is within this frame work that Black Islam's challenge to modern American penology will be laid out.

Why Punish Offenders? Functions of Punishment

From its colonial era to present, American penal philosophy has experienced profound changes in both theory and practice. Incarceration, as explored later in this chapter, has played a significant role in crime control policies as well as in allowing the system to dispense justice. American penologists have explored various dimensions of this important question and have reached the conclusion that punishment achieves a number of important social functions. These major functions of punishment are: retribution, deterrence, incapacitation, rehabilitation, restitution and just deserts. A synopsis of the first four penal functions is provided below. However, the last two are not true correctional strategies comparable to the preceding four thus no discussion will be provided for restitution and just deserts.

Retribution

Historically, the question as to what constitutes retributive justice has played a significant role in the development of Western penal philosophy of which, the Anglo-American is the most complex constituent; the ideological thrust of this philosophy is expressed in the Code of Hammurabi, the Bible, the Qur'an and in the Greco-Roman legal treatises. These issues are addressed in some length in *Defendant Rights*.[1] The attainment of retributive justice comprises one of the oldest aims of punishment regimes in Western penal history. From biblical times to the rise of modern legal tradition in market economies, retribution was viewed as one of the most rational methods for restoring equity in justice between the victim and the perpetrator of crime. The rationale for retributive justice rested on the most innate aspect of the victimization process namely, because the criminal culprit inflicted harm on the individual victim, it was only just that he or she be subjected to retribution. The biblical form of it, known as *lex talionis*, (the law of retribution) has its Islamic equivalence as, *al-qisas* that even today applies in a number of Islamic countries and especially in the Islamic Republic of Iran (1979–present). With the rise of modern state and legal codes prohibiting the use of cruel and unusual punishments, the absolute majority of modern democratic societies no longer apply retribution as an acceptable form of punishment notwithstanding few failed states in the Middle East and North Africa that apply it.

Although ideally speaking, proportionality applies in the Biblical *lex talionis*, but with the arrival of modern legal traditions retribution-based penal measures are no longer applicable because the philosophy of retributive justice runs counter to humane penal measures as, for example, imprisonment instead of the many cruel punishments that were used in agricultural societies. For example, James W. Marquart and Jonathan R. Sorensen observed, the idea of systematic imprisonment emerged in England as a reaction to inordinate amounts of cruelty inflicted on convicts. The eighteenth century, observe the authors, was also the time of general enlightenment thanks to the works and thought of Voltaire, Montesquieu, Beccaria and Bentham.[2] In fact, the emergence of the notion, as well as the institution, of a criminal justice system, argues Pieter C. Spirenburg, has to be located in the context of the rise of modern state whereby a rational, systemic, and centralized penology replaced the haphazard and vengeance-based punishment system of pre-modern era. Tracing the origin of this replacement as far back as twelfth century Europe, Spirenburg draws upon the work of P. W. A. Immink, to conclude that the "birth of punishment" or the "emergence of public penal law," ought to be placed

1   Kusha, H.R., *Defendant Rights: A Reference Handbook*, ABC-CLIO, Inc., 2004.
2   Marquart, J.W., and Sorensen, J.R., (eds), (1997), "Introduction" pp. 1–2 *Correctional Context: Contemporary and Classical Readings*, Los Angeles, CA, Roxbury Publishing Company, p. 1.

"... in the context of changing relationship of freedom and dependence in feudal society."[3]

Deterrence

One central premise of Western penal philosophy is that deterrence is an important function of punishment, thus penal measures must be structured and applied so as to garner general deterrence against crime. The question is do modern penal institutions effectively deter people from committing offenses? It is a difficult question to answer with any degree of certainty, to be critiqued later in this chapter. Next to retribution, Western penal philosophers and justice practitioners have discussed different dimensions of deterrence as, for instance, Jeremy Bentham (1748–1832) whose *Principles of Penal Law* tackles these issues. In this treatise, Bentham presents his eight principles prefaced by the following observation:

> Punishment may be too small or too great; and there are reasons for not making
> them too small, as well as not making them too great. The terms *minimum* and
> *maximum* may serve to mark the two extremes of this question, which require
> equal attention.[4]

Bentham's eight rules putatively comprise the foundation of his principles of penal law.

Rule I establishes the proportionality between punishment and benefits that are driven from commission of a crime. He elaborates on what is meant by "profit of crime" and its criminogenic impacts.

Rule II is unspecified and the text jumps to Rule III which establishes the principle of deterrence through severity in punishment for crimes with different degrees of social harms. It reads: "When two offences come into competition, the punishment for the greater offences must be sufficient to induce a man to prefer the less."[5]

Rules IV and V are complementary to rules I and III to the effect that Bentham considers the first four rules as rules of proportion whose primary purpose is "... to mark out the limits of minimum side— the limits below which a punishment ought not to be diminished; the fifth will mark out the limits on the maximum side— the limits above which it ought not to be increased."[6]

---

3 Spirenburg, P.C., "The Specter of Suffering" pp. 3–15, in *Correctional Context*, p. 3.

4 Bentham J., *Principles of Penal Law*, p. 328, cited in Sanford H. Kadish and Stephen J. Schulhofer (eds), *Criminal Law and Its Processes: Cases and Materials*, Boston, MA, Little Brown and Company, 1989, fifth edition, pp. 328–330. Italics are in the text.

5 Ibid. Italics are in the text.

6 Ibid., p. 329.

Bentham also establishes the boundaries (minimum/maximum) levels or degrees of punishment. The rationale for this boundary definition is given as follows:

> The greatest danger lies in an error on the minimum side, because in this case the punishment is inefficacious; but this error is least likely to occur, a slight degree of attention sufficing for its escape; and it does exist, it is at the same time clear and manifest, and easy to be remedied. An error on the maximum side, on the contrary, is that to which legislators and men in general are naturally inclined: antipathy, or a want for compassion for individuals who are represented as dangerous and vile, pushes them onward to an undue severity. It is on this side, therefore, that we should take the most precautions, as on this side there has been the greatest disposition to err.[7]

Besides Bentham, other European social thinkers (e.g., Thomas Hobbes, Immanuel Kant, Cessare Beccaria, and John Howard) as well as American penologists (e.g., William Penn, Benjamin Rush, and Elam Lynds) have addressed some of these issues to which reference will be made as occasion arises. Although modern legal doctrines (e.g., the American Bill of Rights), are against, and prohibit, the infliction of cruel and unusual punishments such as public hanging, lynching, quartering, flogging, this prohibition has yet to cover the issue of the length of incarceration. In the American penal philosophy, the issue as to whether a life-sentence without the possibility of parole for capital crimes comprises cruel and unusual punishment has yet to be researched adequately in terms of the parameters of the Eighth Amendment of the Bill of Rights.

However, we also have to organize social and economic factors in such a way as to provide a more equitable opportunity for success in modern class societies. Put it differently, deterrence is not achievable through the application of a hierarchy of punitive measures for had it been possible to excise crime and deviance through such measures, many third-world police states who utilize cruel and unusual punishments would have long since achieved this objective. The complexity of modern and democratic class societies does not allow simple solutions to complex problems, at least not in the case of crime and deviance. This being said, there are correctional scholars who have argued that the American penal system has two sets of 'truisms' that some of these scholars have characterized them as rehabilitation versus deterrence. One consistent theme of this book, repeated throughout the pages, is that regardless of such truism arguments, the length of imprisonment is a very important factor in relation to deterrence: a penal philosophy that utilizes lengthy incarceration schemes is capable of engendering a deep sense of frustration and animosity in the inmate population; it is also capable of undermining the legitimacy of the

---

7   Ibid.

whole penal institutions especially if long sentences are applied indiscriminately and consistently against the indigent segment of the populace for non-violent drug-possession related offenses. As we shall explore shortly, the bulk of such offenders are African American and/or Hispanic minorities who end up in both State and Federal penitentiaries without drug-related rehabilitative accommodations and programs.

Based on the above, let us consider some modern penal measures that do not justly punish the culprits, but subject them to a lingering dehumanization process such as long-term incarceration for non-violent crimes as, for example, possession of illicit drugs for personal consumption. Covered under the title of the Possession Laws, these penal measures are applied in the United States against mostly socially and economically impoverished people with a vengeance since the passage of the Harrison Act in 1914. The Harrison Act of 1914 was originally designed to stamp out the use of narcotics by the immigrant Chinese laborers on the West Coast. It gradually led to a "War on Drugs" mentality that has led to the rise of what is known as narcotic-based terrorism under the control of an international crime cartel with a trillion dollar base to its worldwide operations aimed at supplying illicit drugs for a wide range of clientele in Asia, Europe and North America. The application of long-term incarceration to narcotic use for personal consumption has gradually led, among other social and health-related problems, to prison overcrowding in both state and federal penitentiaries. The question is this: is it just to subject those who possess narcotics for personal consumption to long-term incarceration? Does the length of incarceration have anything to do with the efficacy of deterrence through incarceration? There are other social ailments that long-term incarceration is capable of inducing on convicts whose drug-dependency is the main cause of their criminality in the first place. These are some of the more important questions and considerations that American penologists have tried to articulate in the context of the logic of incarceration to which reference shall be made later in this chapter.

Incapacitation

From colonial times to present, it has been taken for granted by American penologists that there exists an inverse relationship between social order and crime. Social order is a *sui generis* web of folkways, norms, values and mores that keeps society together and makes its orderly functioning possible. Therefore, those who violate the safety and well-being of the social order have to be neutralized and/or incapacitated; these penal measures can take various forms such as imprisonment, banishment, house arrest, blinding, or the ultimate form of incapacitation, death. With the rise of modern nation states and humane laws, incapacitation has gone through profound modification and humanization both in form and in content. For example in agrarian and/or tribal societies that preceded modern capitalist social relations, the well-being of the social order was the main concern of the governing elite and elders of the social institutions (e.g., the family and religious). The Mosaic Code, the Code Hammurabi, the Declarations of Cyrus the Great, the Achaemenid Emperor, the Islamic Shari'a, and the Roman Twelve Tablets are examples of this concern in pre-capitalistic social formations. The main commonality among these pre-capitalism laws was the notion that one who violated the prevailing social order, or presented a threat to social order had to be neutralized through harsh penal measures.

The reason these codes reverted to penal measures considered cruel and unusual by today's standards had a lot to do with the social and demographic realities of pre-capitalist social formations whereby each individual was of significance for the reproduction bases of society. In such limited population, violent crimes such as murder and mayhem had to be controlled through harsh measures to prevent society from falling into vengeance-based anarchy and crises; lenient and unjust punishments could enrage the victim's family into taking the law into their own hand which in turn could engulf other families and kinship groups. The delicate power-balance between various social groups necessitated the use of harsh measures to ensure the inviolability of individual life and to preserve social order. Thus, punishment was a balancing act between justice and order. With the rise of modern capitalism, capable of feeding millions leading to huge population-dynamics, we no longer face a limited demographic-based rationale for incapacitation *per se*, but one that has its dynamism in social and political disenfranchisement; the lower one is on the social and economic ladder, the greater the chances of one receiving an incapacitation-type of punishment at the apex of which stands long-term incarceration next to death penalty. That is why in the United States those states which have the highest incarceration rates (to be discussed in Chapter 4), have also the highest rate of death penalty that is disproportionately applied to ethnic and racial minorities.

Pre-Enlightenment Incapacitation Philosophy

The British colonists who gradually settled along the Atlantic shores of North America during the seventeenth and eighteenth centuries brought with them the British common law tradition as they tried to create a "New England" along these shores. The American colonial notion of deterrence through incapacitation emerged through an evolutionary process of trial and error. The colonists, however, were trying to create their New England free of the social malaise that had engulfed Continental Europe's penology, thus they could neither re-establish the old British penal system in its entirety, nor could abandon that heritage altogether. British penal philosophy of the sixteenth and the seventeenth centuries did not shy away from punishments that were extremely cruel and of a humiliating nature meted out in public. Such punishments and their procedural applications were deemed harmonious with the larger objectives of the European penal philosophy as articulated in the writings of the social contract theorists as, for example, Thomas

Hobbes (1588–1679). Hobbes, in his treatises such as *The Elements of Law* (1640), *De Cive* (*The Citizen*, 1642), and *Leviathan* (1651), elaborated on the notion that "man," prior to the rise of the civilization, existed in the state of nature, a kind of lawless and anarchic state of existence that, Hobbes theorized, preceded the so-called civil society.

Hobbes proposed that "civil society" was made possible through an invisible pact, or "social contract," that man, having left the "state of nature," had made with his fellow man in order to enter into the arms of civility, one in which the harmonious functioning of the society and economy was strategically related to the manner in which the application of law and justice was harmonized. This harmony necessitated the forceful subjugation of elements that endangered the supremacy of the provinces of law and order. What were these elements? These were sin, crime, deviance and anti-social acts—all manifestations of man's lowly inclinations. Left alone, these elements, argued social contract theorists, were capable of dragging the civil society and, in fact, the whole human civilization, into perpetual disorder and war of men against other men. However, punishment could not apply arbitrarily because any arbitrariness in the application of punishment would violate the integrity of the province of justice, which was conceived as a part of the province of law and civility.

Following Hobbes' logic, the British penologists of the eighteenth and nineteenth centuries were also convinced that penal measures, if they were based on the principles of swift justice, were profoundly functional in safeguarding the integrity of the society thus of the social contract. However, penal measures could no longer be applied in the exact manner of the past centuries. Nonetheless, the poor, the illiterate, the homeless, the mentally deranged as well as members of the working class were deemed more vulnerable to the lure of sin and crime in comparison to those who belonged to the so-called respectful members of higher social strata. Thus, in the British penal philosophy of the Enlightenment era, the form of the penal measures was as important as the manner in which they were meted out. This was due to centuries old, entrenched belief among British penologists that there was a causal relationship between the severity of punishment and general deterrence. This relationship seemed especially relevant in relation to the plight of the following groups: (1) repeat offenders; (2) political dissidents especially those reputed of harboring anti-Anglican Church sentiments; (3) those convicted of grave political or diabolical crimes; and (4) those who engaged in activities that not only threatened the stability of the entrenched order, but also the security of the church and state. These categories of offenders had to be neutralized in the most severe manner and form possible in various dungeons that were created and maintained for this purpose. A dungeon-based incapacitation was the most cruel and yet the most negatively efficacious form of neutralization because unlike modern incarceration whose main objective is correction *per se*, dungeons were places for the most gruesome form of death that would come through torture, malnutrition, and the sheer weight of total isolation.

The Thirteen Colonies that comprised the United States of America adhered, by and large, to Hobbes's theory of the social contract and therefore followed the logic that the severity of penal measures played a significant role in obtaining deterrence. The colonies also retained the British corporal and capital punishments, as for example, flogging, ducking stool, pillory, hanging convicts from their necks until death occurred. Ruth Masters and Cliff Roberson cite a partial list from "The Capital Laws of Massachusetts in the years 1641–1643," to give the reader an idea about colonial notion of punishment:

1. If any man after legal conviction, shall have or worship any other God, but the Lord God, he shall be put to death.
2. If any man or woman be a Witch, that is, hath or consulteth with a familiar spirit, they shall be put to death.
3. If any person shall blaspheme the Name of God the Father, Son, or Holy Ghost with direct, express, presumptuous, or high-handed blasphemy, or shall curse God in like manner, he shall be put to death.
4. If any person shall commit any willful murder, which is manslaughter, committed upon premeditate malice, hatred, or cruelty, not in a man's necessary and just defense, nor by near casualty, against his will; he shall be put to death.
5. If any person slayeth another through guile, either by poisoning, or other such devilish practice; he shall be put to death.
6. If any person shall slayeth another suddenly in his anger, or cruelty of passion, he shall be put to death.
7. If a man or woman shall lie with any animal, by carnal copulation, they shall surely be put to death and the animal shall be slain and buried.
8. If any person committeth adultery with a married, or espoused wife, the Adulterer and Adulteress, shall surely be put to death.
9. If any man shall unlawfully have carnal copulation with any woman-child under ten years old, either with or without her consent, he shall be put to death.
10. If any man steals, he shall be put to death.
11. If any man rises up by false witness, he shall be put to death.[8]

American colonial penologists, like their European counterparts, were concerned with the moral and structural safety of their colonies per above crime and punishments list. Colonial penologists took it for granted that the safety of each member of the colony was contingent upon the general safety and well-being of the colony, a complex patriarchal web of folkways, norms, values and mores that kept the integrity and functionality of the colony. Therefore, those who violated this order had to be neutralized/ incapacitated in the most appropriate

---

8   Masters, R., and Roberson, C., *Inside Criminology*, Englewood Cliffs, NJ, Prentice Hall, 1990, p. 56.

manner. This balancing act was regularly achieved through penal measures that grew in harshness from public frowning to the ultimate form of incapacitation, death, or banishment from the colony. In between, the culprit could be subjected to house arrest, or imprisonment.

Banishment was another popular punishment. American colonies banished their convicts to the hostile and untamed Western territories of the continental USA. However, with the passage of time, the colonies relied less on this type of punishment in the face of the social and political realties of an emerging American spirit of the land of opportunity. On the contrary, Britain, could afford to resort to banishment as an effective form of deterrence/incapacitation until very late. This was due to the fact that Britain, starting from the mid-seventeenth century, gradually rose to the pinnacle of an imperial maritime power in possession of various territories under her control. Britain not only utilized these territories for banishment, but this measure was also cost effective in terms of its ability to deflect the actual cost of incarceration. As noted by Dean J. Champion, "Between 1600 and 1776, England exported thieves, vagrants, political undesirables, and religious dissidents to the American colonies through transportation, a form of banishment .... Although estimates vary, 2000 or more convicts were transported to the American colonies during this period ..."[9]

Neither could American colonists remain indifferent to the social, economic, and political realties of colonial life—a set of realities that necessitated the construction and application of a somewhat different regime of punishment than the ones that prevailed in England or in Continental Europe. The end result was the specific North American penal philosophy of deterrence through swift penal measures and especially incapacitation whose colonial frame, though based on the British common law, had to gradually conform to the American Constitution with its Bill of Rights. This new frame contained, among other crime and justice related amendments, Amendment number 8 that prohibits the use of cruel and unusual punishments that other prevailing systems had no compunction in utilizing against convicts. With the passage of the American Constitution by Congress, it was no longer feasible to apply such measures to convicts, at least in theory. In a sense, banishment was one of the cruelest forms of punishments because it deprived the culprit of the love of mother land, a love which is almost intrinsic to all regardless of offending patterns. As will be discussed later, the American Constitution and the Bill of Rights also facilitated the gradual humanization of the colonial penology by repealing cruel and unusual punishments throughout the state and federal penal codes.

---

9 Champion, D.J., *Corrections in the United States: A Contemporary Perspective*, Upper Saddle River, NJ, Prentice Hall, 1998, second edn, p. 8.

Rehabilitation

Like their British counterparts, the American colonial penologists promoted the idea that a just regime of punishment could efficaciously correct and therefore, rehabilitate, those who had fallen victim to the clutches of crime. To achieve this goal, colonial penologists argued that a convict ought to be subjected to hard labor in order to restitute/compensate the individual victim(s) and/or the colonies for their losses incurred due to the culprits' criminal or law infracting conduct. This idea was made operational by a number of colonial penal systems as, for example, the Auburn and Pennsylvania, later discussed in this section. Both penal institutions adhered to the notion that in order to rehabilitate prisoners, they had to be removed from those negative attributes which facilitated crime commission. Prisoners were thought to lack strong moral foundation permeating in them a capacity for idleness, dishonest disposition towards work and malevolence and deception towards their fellow men. Therefore, it was incumbent upon the penal institutions to "correct" the convicts within the very iron-clad disciplinarian embrace of the penal institution thus the notion of systemic approach to corrective rehabilitation. Both institutions also adhered to the religious notion of penance which implied repentance in its Judeo-Christian context. They also focused the strategic importance of hard and disciplined prison-bound work on the grounds that the corrective processes could only be initiated and sustained through hard and disciplined work. The two penal institutions, however, differed in their "separate" versus "congregate" methods of punishing convicts during their incarceration periods.

The Pennsylvania System

In the Pennsylvanian "separate" system, introduced first at the Walnut Street Jail in Philadelphia, the corrective process was believed of effectuating through complete isolation of the individual convict from his/her fellow inmates in the penal institution as well as from the outside world.[10] In other words, penance was achieved through isolation and thus, the term "separate." The main intellectual force behind the Pennsylvania system, it is commonly agreed, was Dr. Benjamin Rush in conjunction with the Philadelphia Society for Alleviating the Miseries of Public Prisons. Dr. Rush's penal philosophy centered on the notion that imprisonment would serve its desired functions if it were multifaceted in its treatment of the convicts by providing personal discipline next to a set of prison-based meaningful vocational training for the inmates. Robert Johnson cites from the work of Beaumont and de Tocqueville, two French social critiques and travelers who have provided us eyewitness accounts of early American penal institutions, including of the Pennsylvania system. Accordingly, Beaumont and de Tocqueville were

---

10 Johnson, R., "Race, Gender and the American Prison: Historical Observations," p. 30 in Joycelyn M. Pollock (ed.), *Prisons: Today and Tomorrow*, Gaithersburg, MD, Aspen Publishers, Inc., 1997, pp. 26–47.

advocates of the Pennsylvania system because [the managers of the Pennsylvania system]:

> have thought that absolute separation of the criminals can alone protect them from mutual pollution, and they have adopted the principle of separation in all its rigor. According to this system, the convict once thrown into his cell, remains there without interruption, until the expiration of his punishment. He is separated from the whole world; and the penitentiaries, full of malefactors like himself, but every one of them entirely isolated, do not present to him even a society in prison ....[11]

With all its good intentions, the Walnut Street Jail was closed in 1835 because the system experienced a number of problems such as overcrowding, riots due to idleness of the prisoners, ineffective control of the prison staff over the inmates, observes Thomas P. Roth.[12] However, the idea of rehabilitation through penance did not end and has continued since then in other forms until present.

The Auburn System

The Auburn system was first introduced at the Auburn Prison in New York. In this system, following the ideal of rehabilitation through penance, the convicts were allowed to eat their meals and to perform prison hard labor together, but had to spend the night in solitary confinement. Beaumont and de Tocqueville observed the following about the Auburn system:

> ... in the most profound silence, and nothing is heard in the whole prison but the steps of those who march, or sounds proceeding from the workshops. But when the day is finished, and the prisoners have retired to their cells, the silence within these vast walls, which contain so many prisoners, is like that of death. We have often trod during night those monotonous and dumb galleries, where a lamp is always burning: we felt as if we traversed catacombs; there were thousand living beings, and yet it was a desert solitude ...[13]

The founder of the Auburn system, Captain Elam Lynds was "disciplinarian," writes Thomas P. Roth, adding that Lynds:

---

11   *Ibid.*, p. 50. Johnson cites the paragraph from a 1964 reprint of the 1833 book of Beaumont G. D., and A. de Toqueville, *On the Penitentiary System in the United States and its Application to France*, Carbondale, IL, Southern Illinois University, 1964, p. 57.

12   Roth, *Prison and Jail Administration*, p. 9.

13   Johnson citing Beaumont and de Tocquiville in *Prisons: Today and Tomorrow*, p. 31.

... believed that all inmates should be treated equally, and he used a highly regimented schedule of inmate activities, including lockstep marching and extremely strict prison discipline. Inmates were dressed alike in black and white striped uniforms, worked and prayed during the day, received no visitors, could not send or receive mail, and, for those who could read, read only the Bible. Advocates of the Auburn system believed that the strict routine would transform violators into law-abiding citizens.[14]

The Auburn system, like its counterpart, the Pennsylvania system, was plagued by overcrowding and similar malaise that, Roth notes were typical of the mid 1850s corrections preceding the Civil War; it was these systemic problems that led to the development of the "Reformatories" during 1870–1910. Roth notes that these developments, next to prison disturbances, made rehabilitation secondary to the emerging need of discipline and control of prison population throughout the country.[15] It was in the Reformatory stage that both education and vocational needs of young offenders were undertaken by a new prison management philosophy in the aftermath of the foundation of the National Prison Association, the precursor of the American Correctional Association. The main concerns of the new philosophy were the following according to Roth:

- prison overcrowding
- corporal punishment
- the physical conditions of prisons
- how to replace prisons with reformatories.[16]

These concerns found their practical solutions with the construction of the first modern reformatory in Elmira, New York, in 1877.

The Elmira Reformatory

Following the reformatory ideas of Sir Walter Crofton, Captain Alexander Maconochie, and Zebulon R. Brockway, Elmira Reformatory was built as a pioneering penal institution to reform offenders. Herbert A. Johnson and Nancy Travis Wolfe write that:

> The new era in penology was ushered in by the National Prison Congress held in Cincinnati in 1870. A gathering of wardens, prison officials and interested academics working in the area of penology, the Cincinnati Congress promulgated a *Declaration of Principles* which stressed the need for a professional prison civil service under centralized control of a state board. It asked for the institution

---

14   Roth, *Prison and Jail Administration*, p. 9.
15   Roth, Ibid., pp. 10–11.
16   Roth, Ibid., p. 11.

of a progressive form of prison discipline, echoing the Dwight-Wines *Report* of 1867, with its reliance upon the Crofton, or Irish system. The *Declaration* was based upon a paper by Zebulon Borckway titled "The Ideal of True Prison System for a State," which caught the attention of the Congress. The young prison warden from Detroit advocated a reformatory program that would prepare inmates for release and reduce the crime rate. Stressing that the central aim of a true prison system should be the protection of society against crime, and not the punishment of criminals, Borckway argued for intermediate sentencing, and the creation of an impartial board that would decide when it was safe to return inmates to society. A library and public hall would permit reading and other forms of entertainment, as well as a room for religious services. Industrial and agricultural departments would be established, as appropriate to the location of the prison, and these would be run as efficient business organizations, returning profits to the institutions and providing training in craft skills to the inmates.[17]

The revolutionary ideas of Borckway, argue Johnson and Wolfe, were tried out at the Elmira Reformatory which made the American penology the forerunner of an emerging international penology movement. Later (after 1908), the movement splinted into two wings: the Anglo-American, and the Continental European. The former's aim was rehabilitation. The latter, under the influence of Cesare Lombroso, an Italian medical doctor, moved in the direction of the positivist school of criminology whose aim was to scientifically cure criminals from their biologically and genetically based ailments. Thus, treatment became the main goal of the positivist view of crime and penology.[18]

The Positivist Rehabilitation

In the first half of the 20th century, American penology under the general influence of positive sciences moved in the direction of positivism. Positivism, as a philosophy of modern science, is built on the notion that modern science's main function is to explain the causality of events through modern scientific methods. Scientific method is positive because it is objective at the same time that it is also neutral; the scientist, ideally speaking, is an 'impartial' observer who collects, analyzes, and interprets data in order to explain cause and affect parameters, be it within the nature or within social settings. The ultimate aim of modern science is to observe in order to explain, in order to predict, in order to replicate and/or control events in the nature or in society. The positivist philosophy in science has deeply influenced various disciplines in social sciences, as for example, criminology and its sub-discipline of penology. Positivist criminology depicts crime as something that can be studied objectively and independently in its natural setting. The development

---

17   Johnson, H. A., and Wolfe, N. T., *History of Criminal Justice*, (Cincinnati, OH, Anderson Publishing Co., 1996), second edn, pp. 195–196.

18   Ibid., pp. 196–197.

of this perspective was partially due to the fact that American criminology has been thoroughly influenced by the European view of crime a synopsis of which was presented above. Of significance to positivist penology is the pathological perspective of crime and deviance that we discuss below.

The Pathological Rehabilitative Perspective

The pathological rehabilitative perspective relates to pathological view of crime and deviance that thrived in the early twentieth century American criminology. It was based on a simplistic and naive view as to what constituted the etiology of crime. On the side of no-crime naiveté, stood a set of "positive" values that made America great as against those which caused crime and deviance. By and large, positivist criminologists believed that the positive values belonged to the main culture and its core social groups, the Western European and/or Anglo-Saxons immigrants, the original founders of the New England on the North American Atlantic shores. It was these core groups whose values provided the yard stick of the social, political and economic positivism in the late nineteenth and early twentieth century America. Accordingly, whereas these groups were endowed with such positive values as hard work, honesty, intelligence and rugged individualism, the pathogens of crime and deviance lurked among those who did not belong to this group, nor were such groups deemed capable of getting rid of these pathogens. Thus, the farther new immigrants were from the positivist core's values, the higher their pseudo-scientifically presumed vulnerability to the pathological malaises of crime and deviance. It was with this intellectual naiveté that American positivist criminologists devised the Chicago School of Criminology whose theoretical prominence continued until the 1950s and then declined. A synopsis of the Chicago School's impacts on positivist rehabilitation is given below.

The Chicago School and pathology   The Chicago School of criminal pathology concentrated on the negative impacts of rapid change as the main pathological cause of urban crime; the theoretical thrust of the school was that urban crime is a result of deterioration of basic values and social structures, a multifaceted process that Chicago School criminologists theorized of taking place with observable regularity in the large inner city slums. Crime was not the result of individual, but of social groups' pathology. Prevalent until 1950s, and having produced powerful theories in almost every conceivable sub-field of criminology (e.g. juvenile delinquency, the process of ghetto formation, alcoholism, prostitution, illicit street drug sub-culture, professionalization of crime, urbanization to name a few), the Chicago School lost its theoretical edge when it was assailed by those who argued that the school suffered from its middle class bias. Pathological theories nonetheless influenced American penal philosophy and institutions. Anthony P. Travisono, after giving a synopsis of the post WWII social developments, argues that American corrections have gone through similar changes from the middle of the 20th century to present. In principal, Travisono concentrating on the "medical model," that rose to prominence during 1950s and continued until early 1980s,[19] argues that this model's purpose was threefold:

- diagnosis
- evaluation
- treatment.[20]

The thrust of the medical model is that it is incumbent upon the professional experts to "diagnose" the pathology of crime and/or deviance that afflicts the offending population so as to enable society to cure the offender from his or her crime commission or derivational anomalies and/ or ailments. This requires systemic observation of the offending population by those who have gained their expertise in appropriate diagnostic-evaluative institutions created for this purpose, institutions such as prisons, or psychiatric wards, or mental sanatoriums. The relationship between the offending population and their handlers in these institutions was presumed of one based on a therapeutic modulation: in the same manner that medical doctors attend their patients, so should the correctional staff and officers in penal institution attend the offending population. This philosophy has led to the classification of offenders not only in terms of the offense and security levels, but also the medical nature of it.

The New Penology and Rehabilitation

After World War II, the United States entered into a period of unprecedented social and economic prosperity, allowing the so-called American way of life to gradually dominate not only Europe—that was recovering from the ravages of the WWII—but also many developing societies be it in Africa, Latin America, or Asia. This hegemonic dominance of the American way of life, naturally influenced American criminological thinking in its approach to crime and punishment. In the post WWII period of American economic, social and cultural efflorescence, the predominantly white, Anglo-American upper and middle-class strata adhered to a masculine etiology of crime centered around the idea that good, decent, and hard working people do not commit crime, nor do they get entangled in the clutches of various forms of deviant behaviors one of which was, and remains, sin. This anti-criminogenic view, promoted by the American news and entertainment media, education system and various Christian denominations was well received by middle class America thanks to a thriving free-market economy. Subsequently, American society and economy went through a tumultuous differentiation process that is known as the post-industrialization period that took effect in mid 1960s as computer technology was applied to American service industries. Within two

---

19   Travisono, A. P., "American Corrections Since World War II" in *Prison and Jail Administration*, pp. 15–21.

20   Travisono, Ibid., p. 16.

decades, American manufacturing hegemony in steel, textile, automobile and home appliance industries was lost to the emerging powers in Western Europe, Japan and South East Asia (Taiwan, Malaysia, Singapore, Hon Kong and South Korea). This was devastating for all strata of the American lower middle and working class as well as large inner cities where a large segment of the lower working class strata resided. The economic disenfranchisement in conjunction with inner-city infestation with illicit drugs and drug-pushing gangs led to waves of crime which in turn prompted tougher law enforcement strategies and tactics. Tougher possession laws passed by Congress led to waves of arrests and long-term incarceration of petty offenders who mostly reside in large inner city slums. Ironically, it is in these areas that conversion to Islam is being sought and promoted as a remedial alternative to criminological pulls and pushes of the inner cities, a subject to be explored in more detail in subsequent chapters of this book.

Chapter 4
Black Incarceration:
A Historical Analysis, 1960–2007

This chapter explores prevalent factors that have played a role in the disproportionate incarceration of African-American males (both adults and juveniles) from the 1960s to the present. The thrust of this chapter is that historically speaking, it is only after the 1960s that the American crime scene has come across the specter of the so-called black crime problem. Although members of the African-American community, like other ethnic and racial groups, have committed crimes and misdemeanors in the past, it was only in the aftermath of the Civil Rights era that the black crime problem seems to have taken a new urgency to its etiological, epidemiological configuration prompting criminologists and criminal justicians to study it as a separate crime entity; it is in the context of this "rediscovery" that the pre-1960s "docile" black male has been transmuted into the epitome of the full-fledged predatory urban criminal capable of inflicting unimaginable levels of harm and violence on the American society. In this transmutation of the black male into the epitome of the *victimizer* of the whites, two macro social/institutional forces have played significant roles: First, the news media has consistently depicted the black crime problem as predatory and violent. Second, from the 1960s to the present, a large number of inner-city communities have experienced cycles of illicit-drug related violence propagating the popular notion that the bulk of black crime is of a predatory nature perpetrated by black males. This has occurred despite the fact research-based studies have shown that with the exception of rape and robbery, the rest of predatory crime is committed by poorly educated and economically challenged white males. We start with the general profile of American prisoners as a prelude to a more detailed exploration for the reasons of disproportional incarceration of the African-American males during the 1960–2007.

Who Goes to Prison and Why? American Prisoners Profile

One of the most distinguishing features of profiling inmates in jail and prison in the United States is that the bulk of the prison population consists of the socioeconomically impoverished urban poor. Writing on the profile of prisoners in 1999, Allen J. Beck observes that, "The total number of prisoners under the jurisdiction of Federal and State adult correctional authorities was 1,366,721 at

year end 1999."[1] Giving the number of 2,026,596 as representing the total number
of persons incarcerated in the US at the year end of 1999, Beck divides the
distribution of this number into the following categories that are quoted below:

- federal and state prisons (1,284,894, which excludes state prisoners in
  local jails)
- territorial prisons (18,394)
- local jails (605,943)
- facilities operated by or exclusively for the U.S. Immigration and Naturalization
  Service (7,675)
- military facilities (2,279)
- jails in Indian country (1,621)
- juvenile facilities (105,790, as of October 29, 1997).[2]

In so far as disparities in incarceration is concerned, Beck argues that factors
such as race and ethnicity play significant roles. Table 4.1 depicts this disparity:

Table 4.1 Race and ethnic origins of prisoners, 1990–1999

	Percent of prisoners under state or federal jurisdiction*	
	1990	**1999**
Total	100.0%	100.0%
White	35.6	33.0
Black	44.5	45.7
Hispanic	17.4	17.9
Other	2.5	3.4

Based on inmates with sentences of more than 1 year.

Source: Adopted from data provided by Allen J. Beck, Prisoners in 1999, U.S. Department
of Justice, Bureau of Justice Statistics Bulletin, NCJ 183476, p. 9.

The accuracy of the Justice Department's data on incarceration disparity, based
on socioeconomic status as well as race and ethnic origin, has been confirmed by
other studies. For example, Samuel Walker, Cassia Spohn and Miriam DeLone
present the following prison profile quoted below:

---

1   Beck, A.J., (August, 2000), "Prisoners in 1999," U.S. Department of Justice, Bureau
of Justice Statistics, NCJ 183476, p. 1.
2   Beck, Ibid., p. 1.

Half of all the prisoners in the United States (49.4 percent by January 1996) are African American, despite the fact that blacks represent only 12 percent of the U.S. population. Even more alarming, the incarceration *rate* for African American men is seven times the rate for white men (3,250 per 100,000 compared with 461 per 100,000).

Hispanics were 17.5 percent of all prisoners in 1996, up from only 10.9 percent in 1985.[3]

The inordinately high incarceration rates of African-American males—next to that of Hispanics—has continued (with some variations) unabated since the 1960s to present; this constitutes one of the most profound challenges that the American penal system is now facing in the new millennia. The epistemological foundations of this challenge, one of the purposes of this book, centers around a common perception among a large segment of the black community (regardless of the class strata as determined by their prospective socioeconomic indicators) that the American criminal justice system does not provide equity as it dispenses penal justice. There are black leaders and religious personalities (be it in the church, the synagogues and the mosques) as well as community activists who are adamant that the American criminal justice system practices uneven-handed justice against minority offenders in general but to African-American offenders in particular. The systematic disproportionate incarceration is seen as the outcome of a racist justice system. This view shall be critiqued shortly. What is the driving force behind the disproportionate incarceration of African-Americans? There are a number of factors to consider.

The Contributory Role of General Incarceration

Scholars posit that reasons vary for the high incarceration rates of the African-American males within the context of general incarceration which is much higher for the US in comparison to other advanced democratic societies around the world. For example, Hugh D. Barlow writes that "Since 1980, the number of prison inmates has grown every year, increasing by an average of 8.7 percent."[4] This same trend also applies to the jail population for the reason that any aggregate rise in the general rate of incarceration does adversely affect the jail population. In midyear, 1997, Barlow writes, "the nation's 3,304 local jails were operating at 97 percent of capacity, with 567,079 inmates (including over 9,000 juveniles). This

3   Walker, S., Spohn, C., DeLone, M., (2001), *The Color of Justice: Race, Ethnicity, and Crime in America*, third ed., Belmont, CA, Wadsworth Publishing Company, pp. 1–2. See also the fourth edition of the same source for similar data.
4   Barlow, H.D., (2000), *Criminal Justice in America*, Prentice Hall, Upper Saddle River, New Jersey, p. 578.

total was the largest number ever recorded."[5] Making a comparison with fourteen other nations, the United States, observes Barlow, occupies the second highest rank next to Russian incarcerated population.

Allen J. Beck observes that as of midyear 1999, "... the Nation's prisons and jails incarcerated 1,860,520 persons. Federal and State prison authorities held in their custody 682 persons per 100,000 U.S. residents."[6] This means that from year-end 1990 to midyear 1999, the following developments had taken place in the American incarceration process:

- The rate of incarceration increased from 1 in every 218 US residents to 1 in every 147.
- State, Federal, and local governments had to accommodate an additional 83,743 inmates per year (or the equivalent of 1,610 new inmates per week).[7]

Where factors such as race, ethnicity, and gender are concerned, Beck observes that as of June 30, 1999:

- An estimated 11% of black males, 4% of Hispanic males, and 1.5% of white males in their twenties and early thirties were in prison or jail.
- Men were nearly 12 times more likely than women to be incarcerated. There were 106 female inmates per 100,000 women in the United States, composed to 1,261 males inmates per 100,000 men.[8]

Table 4.2 is a partial representation of the prison population as of June, 1999.

Another set of historical data is presented in Table 4.3 below showing a historical incarceration trend that has been recorded in the United States from 1850s to present.

From Tables 4.2 and 4.3, the following observations can be made concerning the rate of incarceration in the United States. First, from 1850 to 1870, a steep incarceration rate followed a relatively stable rate until 1940s. Following WWII, until 1960, another rising trend was recorded followed by yet another steep rise in the general incarceration rate reaching to the unprecedented rate of 461 per 100,000 population in 1998. Second, this trend can be summarized as: high incarceration rates in the Southern and industrial Northeast States, followed by comparatively low incarceration rates in sparsely populated Western and North Western States. The one notable exception is the State of California. The high incarceration rate in California can be explained by the combined size, population and cultural diversity.

---

5   Barlow, Ibid., p. 580.

6   Beck, A.J., (April 2000) "Prison and Jail Inmates at Midyear 1999," US Department of Justice, Bureau of Justice Statistics, NCJ 181643, p. 1.

7   Beck, Ibid., p. 1.

8   Beck, Ibid., p. 1.

Table 4.2 State-based differences in incarceration rate

The prison situation in the United States, June 30, 1999			
Sentenced prisoners per prison population*	Number of inmates	Incarceration rate, 6/30/99	100,000 State residents**
10 highest			
California	164,523	Louisiana	763
Texas	146,180	Texas	704
Federal	130,378	Oklahoma	653
New York	73,960	Mississippi	613
Florida	68,599	South Carolina	550
Ohio	47,084	Alabama	538
Michigan	46,253	Georgia	524
Illinois	44,355	Nevada	518
Georgia	41,655	Arizona	500
Pennsylvania	36,511	California	489
10 lowest			
North Dakota	909	Minnesota	121
Vermont	1,507	Maine	128
Wyoming	1,634	North Dakota	130
Maine	1,724	New Hampshire	188
New Hampshire	2,257	Vermont	193
South Dakota	2,517	West Virginia	203
Montana	2,799	Utah	207
Rhode Island	3.246	Nebraska	216
Nebraska	3,663	Washington	252
West Virginia	3,699	Massachusetts	252

*All inmates under legal authority of the prison system, regardless of sentence.

**The number of prisoners with a sentence of more than 1 year per 100,000 in the resident population. The Federal Bureau of Prisons and the District of Columbia are excluded.

Source: U.S. Department of Justice, Bureau of Justice Statistics, "Prison and jail inmates at midyear 1999", April, 2000, NCJ 181643, p. 4.

Table 4.3 Incarceration rates in the United States, 1850–1998

Year	Incarceration rates per 100,000
1850	29
1860	60.7
1870	85.3
1880	61
1890	72
1904	69
1910	75
1925	79
1930	104
1935	113
1940	131
1945	98
1950	109
1955	112
1960	117
1965	108
1970	96
1975	111
1980	138
1985	200
1990	292
1995	403
1998	461

Source: Adopted from Margaret Werner Cahalan's constructed data from *Historical Corrections Statistics in the United States, 1850-1984*, Rockville, MD: Westat, Inc., 1986 Bureau of Justice Statistics, source Book of Criminal Justice Statistics, 1994, Washington, D.C.: U.S. Department of Justice, 1995 and Bureau of Justice Statistics, State and Federal Prisoners, June 30, 1995, Washington, D.C.: U.S. Department of Justice, 1995.

Third, interestingly enough, there seems to be a close correspondence between the States that have the highest incarceration rates and those with high rates of capital punishment. "From January 1, 1977, to December 31, 1998," writes Tracy L. Snell. "500 executions took place in 29 States." The bulk of these executions took place in 5 States. These were Texas (164), Virginia (59), Florida (43), Missouri (32), and Louisiana (24).[9] In so far as the race and ethnic composition of state executed inmates, the following has been observed per Table 4.4:

---

9   Snell, T.L. (December 1999), "Capital Punishment 1998," US Department of Justice, Bureau of Justice Statistics, NCJ 179012, p. 1.

Table 4.4 Race and ethnic composition of convicts on death penalty, 1990–1998

Race of the Convict	1990	1998
White	1,381	1,906
Black	942	1,488
American Indian	25	29
Asian	14	18
Other	1	13
Total	2,363	3,441

Source: U.S. Department of Justice, Bureau of Justice Statistics, "Capital Punishment" 1998 December 1999, NCJ 179012.

The highest percentage of change in the application of the death penalty were given to black convicts (from 39.86 percent of all executions in 1990 to 43.24 percent of all executions in 1998), followed by the white executions (from 58.44 percent in 1990 to 55.39 in 1998). Whereas the net rate of the execution of black convicts increased by 3.38 percent, the net rate of the execution of the white convict dropped by 5.05 percent.

The Contributory Role of Crime-Control Policies 1960–2007

What drives this high incarceration rate in the US? Barlow argues that the inordinately high rates of incarceration in the US are highly influenced by crime policies rather than the actual commission of crime. Accordingly, "… the United States sends more people to prison for lesser crimes, and keeps them there longer …"[10] The end result of longer incarceration for less serious crimes has prompted James Austin and John Irwin to reach the conclusion that American penology has entered its "imprisonment binge," a phrase that harks back to the insidious warehousing of the prisoner philosophy.

When explaining the reasons for this binge, Austin and Irwin argue that this strategic return to incarceration, as a cure for all social malaise of this country's potential offending population, is based on a conservative political agenda whose foundation is built on a set of fallacies that the authors summarize as follows:

- The War on poverty, which sought to fight crime through education, job training, and rehabilitation in the 1960s and 1970s, was a total failure.
- Dangerous criminals repeatedly go free because of liberal judges or decisions made by the liberal Supreme court that help the criminals but not the victim.

---

10   Barlow, Ibid., p. 581.

- Swift and certain punishment in the form of more and longer prison terms will reduce crime by incapacitating the hardened criminals and making potential law breakers think twice before they commit crimes.
- Most inmates are dangerous and cannot be safely placed in the community.
- It will be cheaper to society in the long run to increase the use of imprisonment.
- Greater use of imprisonment since the 1980s has in fact reduced crime.[11]

Austin and Irwin, then, present the imprisonment binge data reproduced in Table 4.5.

Table 4.5 Percentile change in adult correctional population, 1980–1998

	1980	1998	% Change
Probation	1,118,097	3,417,613	206%
Jails	163,994	592,462	261%
Prisons	329,821	1,302,019	295%
Parole	220,438	704,964	20%
Totals	1,832,350	6 ,017,058	184%
Adult population	162.8 million	192.6 million	18%
Percentage of adults under supervision	1.1%	3.0%	173%
Adult arrests	6.1 million	8.6 million	46%
Reported index crimes	13.4 million	12.3 million	-8%

Source: U.S. Department of Justice, Federal Bureau of Investigation, *Uniform Crime Reports: Crime in the United States, 1980 and 1997*; U.S. Department of Justice, Bureau of Justice Statistics, *Prisoners in 1998; U.S* Department of Justice, Bureau of Justice Statistics, *Probation and Parole Populations in the United States, 1998.*

Table 4.5 shows that during 1980–1998, the adult correctional population increased dramatically in each correctional category. This increase continuing today, is manifestly disproportionate to percentage increases in both reported indexed crimes as well as in the adult population. Whereas in the 1980–1998 period, the number of reported indexed crimes showed a -8 percent decline, a 46 percent increase was recorded in the category of adult arrests during the same period. More importantly is the discrepancy between the rise in the adult population (18%), and adult arrests (46%). This discrepancy can either be explained by the

---

11   Irwin, J., Austin, J., (2001). *Its About Time: America's Imprisonment Binge*, third ed., Wadsworth, Belmont, CA, pp. xiii-xiv.

arbitrary arrest mechanisms utilized by police throughout the country, or that certain adult populations get arrested with a higher frequency than others, or both. With the mounting costs of defending civil liability suits pertaining to false arrests and other police misconduct that accompany false arrests, it is quite unlikely that American police can afford the discriminatory arrest policies of the past decades (e.g., the 1980s and 1990s). The only viable explanation is the second one. As observed by Austin and Irwin, "Those under the control of correctional authority do not represent a cross-section of the nation's population. They tend to be young African-American and Hispanic males who are uneducated, without jobs, or, at least, marginally employed in low-paying jobs."[12] This fact has been established in prior research, it will be revisited shortly. Irwin and Austin summarize their findings quoted below:

- Almost 1 of 3 (32.2 percent) African-American men in the age group 20–29 is either in prison, jail, probation, or parole on any given day.
- More than 1 of every 10 Hispanic men (12.3 percent) in the same age group is either in prison, jail, probation, or parole on any given day.
- For white men, the ratio is considerably lower: 1 in 15 (or 6.7 percent).
- Sixty years ago, less than one-fourth of prison admissions were nonwhite. Today, nearly three-fourths are nonwhite.
- African-Americans and Hispanics constitute almost 90 percent of offenders sentenced for drug possession.
- African-American women have experienced the greatest increase in correctional supervision, rising by 7.8 percent from 1989 through 1994.[13]

The above is self explanatory. However, the long-term criminogenic effects of the systematic and disproportionate incarceration of adult African-American males is yet to be fully appreciated, a secondary purpose of this book.

The Contributory Role of the News Media

Some studies on the relationship between the American news media and general crime have deciphered a complex process through which crime-related news are selected, put in the context of crime-as-a-news-item, and presented for public consumption during prime time television viewing in this country. This process may have a deleterious effect on the general public's perception as to whether the American penal philosophy and/or criminal justice components are soft on those who victimize others thus legitimizing the need for harsher treatment of offenders through longer and harsher sentences. For example, Ray Surette maintains that the news media plays a significant role in the "social construction of reality" including

---

12   Irwin and Austin, Ibid., p. 4.
13   Irwin and Austin, Ibid., pp. 4–5.

that of crime.[14] Where the criminal justice system and news media is concerned, Surette notes that whereas the former seeks to establish "legal guilt", the latter is involved in the construction of a social reality of crime whose parameters are much wider than that of the legal ones.[15] The criminal justice system, at the same time that is theoretically geared to control crime, operates, ideally, on a case-by-case basis whereby a person's constitutional rights have to be safeguarded against any systemic abuse that might be inflicted against such rights in the justice process. The news media is not encumbered by the strict legal code of the conduct, but by other constraints of the profession such as time and rating.

Another characteristic of the news media is in its ability to transcend the fear of crime across time and culture. For example, thanks to the transcendentalist nature of the news media, the construct known as the fear of crime is no longer a local or even a national one as a social phenomenon. This impacts the image of the criminal. Surette observes:

> The image of the criminal that news media propagate is similar to that found in the entertainment media. Criminals tend to be of two types in the news media: violent predators, or professional businessmen or bureaucrats .... Furthermore, as in entertainment programming, they tend to be slightly older (twenty to thirty years old) than reflected in the official arrest statistics .... In general news media underplay criminals' youth and to some degree their poverty, while overplaying their violence .... Additionally, many times crimes are reported without any description of the perpetrator and the public is left to fill in the image .... It follows that since most crime news is about violent interpersonal crime, the image that is filled in it is that of a faceless predator. Thus, Graber (1980), found that the public's image of criminals reflected the stereotypical street criminal— A young, unemployed male.[16]

Critical criminologists have followed the same rationale in relation to the role of the news media. Walter S. DeKeseredy and Martin D. Schwartz observe that although serious questions have been raised regarding the causal relationship between news media and crime (e.g., does the media exposure of the crime causes the fear of crime among general populace), nonetheless the bulk of research supports the notion that "media can influence people's concern about crime as a social issue."[17] Like Surette, DeKeseredy and Schwartz have noted that media can "cause" crime because the media can present or construct the how and when associated with the commission of crime ranging from sexual violence to

---

14   Surette, R. (1992), *Media, Crime, and Criminal Justice: Images and Reality*, Belmont, CA, Wadsworth, Inc, p. 3.

15   Surette, Ibid., p. 6.

16   Surette, Ibid., pp. 63–64.

17   DeKeseredy, W.S., Shwartz, M.D., (1996) *Contemporary Criminology*, Belmont, CA, Wadsworth, Inc., p. 11.

domestic terrorism. These scholars also concentrate on the "strength" of the news media's abilities to present crime stories and news to lay audience. According to DeKaseredy and Schwartz, factors giving the strength to news media's crime presentation are as follows:

- The media provide more extensive information than most people ever directly experience.
- The media offer different types of knowledge than a person would likely encounter directly, such as information on gang violence and racketeering.
- As a public institution, the media facilitate the exchange and sharing of personal knowledge. Consequently, the media could transform various individual's beliefs and opinions into a "general will" of consensual public opinion, based on which collective action might be taken.
- Media knowledge holds out the promise of allowing us to move beyond our limited experiences by applying our knowledge to a wide base.
- Media knowledge is so central in policy debates that it becomes important in its own rights, whether or not it accurately reflects people's experiences...[18]

The news media, through its multifaceted strength in covering and disseminating crime news, assists components of the American criminal justice system in legitimating policies, procedures and concerns in the application of the justice process. The news media, for example, is capable of providing pseudo-scientific reasons for the disproportionate high arrest rates that research has shown to be responsible for massive incarceration. The news media is a double-edged sword that if used properly, can inform the public on the plight of minorities be it in the justice process, or in other social, political and legal realms.

The Contributory Role of the Criminal Justice System

The contributory role of the criminal justice system to the disproportionate incarceration of minorities in general, and, that of the African-American males in particular, is a controversial issue. It is the hub of much passionate debate some of which has been quite rancorous and emotional. The gist of the debate centers around the degree to which the system's operational functions is permeated on racism. There are several schools of thought of this matter. First, some argue that the criminal justice system is a manifest form of institutionalized racism. Thus, the system arrests, prosecutes and imprisons minorities at inordinately high rates achieved through legal racism. For these scholars, the disproportionate incarceration of African-American males is due to the systemic rather than the occasional malevolence of the system. By and large, instrumentalist Marxist

---

18   DeKeseredy and Schwartz, Ibid., p. 20.

criminologists and activists adhere to this view, reasoning that the justice system is a mechanism used to control certain segments of the US population.

Second, other scholars argue the criminal justice system dispenses justice by being neutral to extralegal factors of race, gender and ethnic origin of the offenders. Accordingly, the system treats everyone, *mutatis mutandis*, on the basis of legal equity principles by following the Anglo-American ideal of justice namely, that everyone is equal in the proverbial eye of law. For those who adhere to this view, it is the crime that leads to incarceration; these criminologists and practitioners contend that the American justice system is the best of its kind in the industrialized world notwithstanding problems that emerge every now and then. By and large, conservative criminologists adhere to this view, reasoning crime seriousness determines appropriate punishment.

The truth, as usual, lies somewhere in-between: as suggested by realist (both White and African-American) criminologists and justice practitioners, the system is neither institutionalized racist nor flawless. Both legal and extralegal factors play roles in the manner in which the system operates and dispenses justice. Thus, it can be argued that: First, the American criminal justice system is dynamic despite the fact that American penal philosophy has a long gestation period from colonial times to present. Gradually, and through the putative efforts of enlightened reformers, functional checks and balances have been inculcated in the system as well as in its sub-components. From the above, we can extrapolate the following: it is first the premise of this book, that the American criminal justice system dispenses justice as a *social product* whose quality depends on the offender's social and economic status (abbreviated as the SES in the pertinent literature). The SES is of a multivariate nature determined by the offender's class affiliations comprised of one's level of wealth, prestige and power. The higher an offender's SES in American society, the greater the person's likelihood to garner justice in comparison to one whose SES is at a lower level. This does not mean that high SES offenders do not get punishment; the emphasis is on the quality of justice.

Second, the American criminal justice system is vast, complex and highly structured despite the fact that there are jurisdictional differences that permeate the operational dynamics of the system, be it at the state, or at the federal levels. Thus, it is the second premise of this book that next to SES, there is also the contributory role of the race, ethnicity and gender. These factors have historically played significant roles in determining who receives justice in both traditional and modern legal systems. These are innate factors thus we do not have much control over them. Ideally, one would desire to be processed in a legal system that does not take into consideration extralegal factors in dispensing justice. In reality, all legal traditions do, including the Anglo-American.

It is the third premise of this book that because the American justice system is of an adversarial nature, it allows justice to be served through the dynamics of a much larger force, a force which can be considered as the Justice Market which is a subsection of the larger American Market Economy. Those who are more successful in the larger market get a better deal in the justice market than those who are less successful. Thus, to reduce the chances of consistently getting a raw deal in the justice market, efforts should be made to systemically reform all aspects of the justice process while struggles occur for a more just and equitable economic market capable of providing opportunities for economic success. This important issue will be explored along with its implications within the framework of Islam's challenge to American penology in subsequent chapters. Suffice it to state at this juncture that no matter how hard efforts are made to reform American penal institutions and/or other components of the justice system, it is through success in the economic market that improvements can be made in the justice market. This is the battle cry of Black Islam's challenge to American penology.

It is the final premise of this book that the disproportionate incarceration of black males deprives the African-American community of its male adults, one of the most important Human Capital factors that has historically enabled other communities to succeed in American patriarchal society and economy. It is the adult male who, in his dual capacity as the father-husband, has historically functioned as the provider of the legitimate economic goods for the family, thus acting as the legitimate authority figure for the offspring, especially the male. In both traditional and modern democratic societies, the economic role of the female figure is undeniable, so is the crucial role that females provide as mother-wife. However, the absolute majority of societies around the world are of a patriarchal nature whereby the authority of the female has been socially, economically, and politically entrenched as only secondary to that of the male figure. It is the male figure who sets, identifies, and normalizes the social, legal, economic and political parameters of authority on the one hand. On the other hand, it is, again, the male figure who promulgates law and penal philosophy. Finally, it has always been the male figure who has defined and committed the bulk of crime, be it violent or property.

The world of crime and justice has been and remains a male dominated universe whereby the adult male has a central role in defining the boundaries of acceptable social behavior, language, conduct, thought structure, ideology and manner of expression. Naturally, deviation from these realms takes place, at home or society at large. However, it is in the absence of the male authority figure that these deviations, trivial at the outset, could or may turn into serious experimentation with the boundaries of social values that separates simple infractions from serious ones that ultimately leads to criminality. Again, it is the male figure who guards the offspring as he or she roams in this terrain; this is not intended to devalue the role of the female figure. However, the stark realities of the patriarchal structures in capitalist societies such as the United States have overwhelmingly put the burden of authority on the shoulders of the male figure in relation to crime and justice in almost all major cultures and sub-cultures throughout the world. Once deprived of its share of legitimate male authority figures, the alternative role model is the female figure who shoulders the burden of both motherhood and fatherhood in patriarchal social settings.

This does not mean that each category is incapable of carrying out these burdens simultaneously. They can, and the legendary role of Black woman as the authority figure in Black families is undeniable. However, the thrust of the literature on juvenile delinquency and crime is one of rude awakening to the undeniable reality that depriving any community of its legitimate male role models would have a manifestly deleterious and criminogenic impact, especially on the juveniles. Having these points in mind, the next section discusses the incarceration of African-American juveniles.

The Profile of the African-American Youth Offenders

On February 2000, the US Department of Justice's Bureau of Justice Statistics released a "Special Report" authored by Kevin J. Strom titled "Profile of State Prisoners under Age 18, 1985–1997." The highlights of the Special Report, directly quoted below, give us a general idea about the extent of the incarceration of African-American juvenile males in American correctional institutions:

> On December 31, 1997, less than 1% of inmates in State prison were under age 18, a proportion that has remained stable since the mid-1980's.
>
> The number of offenders under age 18 admitted to State prison has more than doubled from 3,400 in 1985 to 7,400 in 1997, consistently representing about 2% of new admissions in each of the 13 years.
>
> In 1997, 61% of persons admitted to State prisons under age 18 had been convicted of a violent offense compared to 52% in 1985.
>
> The violent arrest rate for persons under age 18 did not change dramatically between 1980 and 1988, but increased over 60% from 1994, then fell to 23% from 1994 to 1997.
>
> Relative to the number of arrests, the likelihood of incarceration in State prison has increased for offenders under age 18. In 1997, 33 persons were sentenced to prison for violent offenses for every 1,000 arrests for violent offenses, up from 18 per 1,000 violent arrests in 1985.
>
> Among persons under age 18 sentenced to State prison in 1997, the average maximum sentence for violent offenses was about 8 years, and the minimum time expected to be served was nearly 5 years.[19]

---

19   Strom, J.K., (February, 2000), "Profile of State Prisoners under Age 18, 1985–97," p. 1, Special Report, the US Department of Justice, Bureau of Justice Statistics, NCJ 176989.

The Special Report further identifies the race and gender characteristics of these juvenile offenders. They are reproduced per Table 4.6 below.[20]

Table 4.6 Characteristics of State prisoners under age 18 in 1997

	Admitted to prison	Held in prison
Gender		
Male	97%	92%
Female	3	8
Race/Hispanic origin		
White non-Hispanic	25%	19%
Black non-Hispanic	58	60
Hispanic	15	13
Other	2	8
Most serious offense		
Violent	61%	69%
Property	22	15
Drugs	11	11
Public order	5	5

Source: U.S. Department of Justice Bureau of Justice Statistics Special Report, February 2000, NCJ 176989.

The significance of the Special Report stems from the fact that in the United States, juvenile felonies and misdemeanors, characterized as delinquency, are processed in the juvenile, rather than in the adult, criminal justice system, the purpose of the next section.

The Contributory Role of the Juvenile Justice System

The American juvenile justice system has its separate terminology, court structure and correctional authorities that operate in every state. Although states in their respective jurisdictions differ in their approach to juvenile offenders, they follow a common philosophy when it comes to addressing juvenile crime. The juvenile justice system, from its inception in the late 19th century to the present, has operated on the premise that juveniles ought to be given as many rehabilitative chances as

---

20   Strom, Ibid., p. 1.

possible in non-penal yet corrective institutions separated from adult offenders. The adult system, on the other hand, stressed the importance of deterrence that the system has theorized as achievable through a variety of penance-rehabilitative as well as treatment strategies, a point to be explored in more details in subsequent chapters of this book.

The "get tough" policy of the juvenile justice system—to which reference shall be made shortly, reflected a higher rate of juvenile cases to the adult system resulting in a higher number of juveniles in adult prisons. This is important because the American society is one of the richest, most dynamic and youth-oriented cultures that has sprung in the New World. As such, American society is endowed with much potential for reforming its social structures and of the complex web of social relations in the context of which juvenile law-infracting behavior takes place. Naturally, intervention and prevention programs have their roots in the social, political and ideological parameters that surround crime as a social product, a topic that will be addressed shortly.

Based on the aforementioned Special Report's data, 75 percent of all persons under age 18, who have been incarcerated in state prison, have committed serious offenses. The Report classified these acts as violent, property and drug-related offenses whose commissions have resulted in the incarceration of juveniles in state prison in the past last two decades (1980 and 1990s). A disproportionate 58 percent of this juvenile population is African-American youths who live in large urban slum areas. Of this percentage, 60 percent were held in prison, a percentage that is 3, 5, and 8.5 times respectively as high as White, Hispanic, and Other youth categories in prison. In other words, African-American juveniles are admitted to prison at a disproportionate rate to the number of African-Americans in the general population (12 percent of the American population), but the percentage held in prison (rather than released early for good behavior, or paroled) is also quite disproportionate to other racial and ethnic youth groups that commit serious crimes. Are young African-American offenders victims of a racist juvenile justice system? Or, is this the result of disproportionate confinement strategies applied to minority and especially, to the African-American youth offenders? We have already documented the disproportionate incarceration of African-American adults.

The Contributory Role of Disproportionate Confinement

In a 1998 study commissioned by the Office of Juvenile Justice and Delinquency Prevention (OJJDP from now on), Patricia Devine, Kathleen Coolbaugh, and Susan Jenkins observe that:

> The 1988 amendment to the Juvenile Justice and Delinquency Prevention (JJDP) Act of 1974 (Pub. L. 93-415, 42 U.S.C. 5601 *et seq.*) Required that States participating in the JJDP's Act's Part B Formula Grants program address the disproportionate confinement of minority juveniles in secure facilities.

Specifically, this provision required State plans to assess the level of such confinement and implement strategies to reduce disproportionate minority representation where it is found to exist.[21]

Having recognized the disproportionate aspects in the minority youth's confinement as early as 1991, the OJJDP chose Arizona, Florida, Iowa, North Carolina and Oregon as pilot states to analyze factors that lead to "Disproportionate Minority Confinement (DMC)." The DMC is defined as "the proportion of juveniles detained or confined in secure detention facilities, secure correctional facilities, jails, and lockups who are members of minority groups … exceeds the proportion of such groups represented in the general population."[22] The authors of the study also note that a large number of studies have pointed out that when it comes to "processing decisions," many state juvenile justice systems "are not racially or culturally neutral."[23] Table 4.7 presents four variables that Devine et al., have identified as contributors to DMC.

Table 4.7 is self-explanatory. By and large, juveniles from the lower social and economic strata of American society are in a disadvantageous position with regard to risk factors that may lead to DMC. Each risk factor is important and should be carefully studied so as to assess its contributory role to DMC. However, there is no doubt that the four underlying factors that contribute to DMC are not of the same magnitude in terms of their criminogenic impacts. Therefore, it is logical to presume that the relationship between the four factors, dynamic, structured, and contributory as it is, lends itself to a hierarchy of importance. For example, it is logical to assume that juveniles who do not commit serious delinquent acts do not come before the juvenile justice system of their jurisdictions and therefore do not face DMC risk perpetrated by the system. Simply put, a family that adequately manages its juvenile(s) renders DMC risk factors perpetrated by the juvenile justice, education and communal systems ineffective.

21   Devine, P., Coolbaugh, K., and Jenkins, S., (December, 1998), "Disproportionate Minority Confinement: Lessons Learned From Five States", The U.S. Department of Justices, Juvenile Justice Bulletin, p. 1.

22   Devine et al., Ibid., p. 2.

23   Devine et al., Ibid., p. 2.

Table 4.7 Variables affecting disproportionate minority confinement

Underlying Factors That Contribute to Minority Over-representation			
Juvenile Justice System	**Socioeconomic Conditions**	**Educational System**	**The Family**
Racial/ethnic bias	Low-income jobs	Inadequate early childhood education	Single-parent homes
Insufficient diversion options	Few job opportunities	Inadequate preventions programs (early dropouts)	Economic stress
System labeling	Urban density/high crime rates	Inadequate quality education overall	Limited time for supervision
Barriers to parental advocacy	Few community support services	Lack of cultural education, cultural role models	------
Poor juvenile justice system/ community integration	------	------	------

Source: Adopted from U.S. Department of Justice, Juvenile Justice Bulletin, December, 1998, Figure 1, p. 8.

The Contributory Role of the Risk Factors

Ideally speaking, the preventive measures ought to effectuate in the family, enhanced by similar measures in the community, school, and peer group socialization processes. One could even argue that juvenile delinquency can be prevented at the individual level. This proposal focuses on the role of moral values that the family ideally inculcates in children. The problem is that crime and delinquency are social products committed by various segments of the population and for various reasons. Therefore, even the most individualistically-centered criminological theory put forward to explain the etiology of juvenile (or adult) crime cannot escape the fact that individuals are not islands of morality in themselves, being immune to pulls and pushes of law-infracting behavior, delinquency and crime. Nonetheless, family is the logical place for inculcating anti-crime values and norms of propriety in conduct in children. The role of the father in this complex undertaking is indispensable. This premise does not mean that only fathers can play this role, but it is the premise of this book that fathers have a unique and irreplaceable role in the modern American family which by and large is of a patriarchal structure whereby it is the male who is personified as the legitimate authority figure for children. One of the most complex social problems facing the African-American family is the fact that it is losing its legitimate male authority figure much faster than any other racial and ethnic groups in this country, a point that is overwhelmingly supported by research and acknowledged by African-American community leaders and activists in this country.

Returning to our analysis of the aforementioned pilot states' racial and ethnic composition, presented in Table 4.8 below shows that juveniles of minority status are disproportionately arrested, processed, and confined.

Table 4.8 Pilot states' ethnic and racial composition based on 1990 census

State	White American	Hispanic American	African American	Indian American	Asian American
Arizona	72 %	19 %	3 %	5 %	1 %
Florida	73 %	12 %	13 %	0.3 %	1 %
Iowa	96 %	1 %	2%	1 %*	1 %*
North Carolina	75 %	1 %	22 %	1 %	1 %
Oregon	91 %	4 %	2 %	1 %	2 %

Source: Adapted from data provided by Patricia Devine, Kathleen Coolbaugh and Susan Jenkins' Study, Disproportionate Minority Confinement: Lessons Learned From Five States U.S. Department of Justice, Juvenile Justice Bulletin, December, 1998.

Devine et al., found that in all pilot states except Arizona, a discernible degree of DMC applied to minority and especially the African-American youth offenders. In Arizona, "The extent and nature of differential justice treatment varied between white and minority juveniles, among minority juveniles, and from point to point in the system."[24] In contrast to Arizona, in Florida, "African-American juveniles were over-represented at every stage of the juvenile justice process."[25] In Iowa, with its overwhelming white population (96%), minority youth not only were over-represented in comparison to white youths, but also were subjected to longer stays at the correctional facilities.

In North Carolina, a similar pattern existed. Minority youths, observe Devine et al., were over-represented in ten pilot counties of North Carolina. This over-representation applied to arrest, intake, referral to juvenile court as well as referral to secure confinement facilities.[26] Finally, in the pilot state of Oregon with its 2% of African-American juvenile population, a similar pattern of this segment of the

24   Devine et al., Ibid., p. 3.
25   Devine et al., Ibid., p. 5.
26   Devine et al., Ibid., p. 8.

youth population has been observed, maintain Devine et al. However, this trend has been of a less pronounced nature for other minority youth groups.[27]

Devine et al., observe that, "To fully understand the effects of race/ethnicity on juvenile justice system decision making, an analytical model developed by Feyerherm and colleagues was refined during OJJDP DMC initiative."[28] The following "major decision points common to virtually all juvenile justice systems," include:

- Decision to arrest a juvenile, who then appears in juvenile court for intake processing.
- Decision at intake either to dispense or to process further.
- Decisions to remove the juvenile from the current living arrangements during processing (e.g., detention or shelter home care).
- Decision to file a formal petition of delinquency, engage in other formal action such as a citation or fine, or seek informal resolution such as a warning or a remand of a juvenile to his or her parents without going to court.
- Decision to resolve the case by informal probation, formal probation, or custody transfer. Informal probation includes diversion programs and other mandated activities for nonadjudicated youth. Formal probation is for adjudicated youth who are not assigned to detention or confinement, but have a court-appointed probation officer and court-defined responsibilities (e.g., frequency and type of contact, frequency of urine analysis, etc.).[29]

This is the tip of the iceberg where the age of onset of juvenile criminality is concerned.

The Contributory Role of the Age of Onset of Youth Crime

The conventional wisdom is that there is an inverse relationship between the onset of the age of delinquency and criminality: the earlier the onset, the greater the likelihood of full-blown criminality. Jeffery A. Butts, and Howard N. Snyder, having studied the crime data from the Federal Bureau of Investigation (FBI) and the National Crime Juvenile Court Data Archive about young delinquents (under age 15) found the following alarming statistics about the lowering of the age of the onset of youth criminality pertaining to 1980–1995:

27　Devine et al., Ibid., p. 9.
28　Devine et al., Ibid., p. 5.
29　Devine et al., Ibid., p. 5.

- Offenders under age 15 represent the leading edge of the juvenile crime problem, and their numbers have been growing.
- Violent crime arrests, for example, grew 94% between 1990 and 1995 for youth under age 15, compared with 47% for older youth.
- Consequently, the age profile for juvenile offenders has changed somewhat since 1980. Offenders under age 15 accounted for an increased proportion of all juvenile arrests for violent crime in 1995 (30%) compared with 1990 (28%), 1985 (29%) and 1980 (25%), the most significant increase occurring between 1980 and 1985.
- However, recent trends are encouraging. Between 1994 and 1995, decreases in the number of juvenile arrests for violent crime were greater for offenders ages 13 and 14 (down 6%) than for those age 15 or older (down 2%).
- Because offenders under age 15 have a high risk of continued criminal involvement, yet are often more amenable to services and sanctions, juvenile crime policy should continue to focus on early and effective interventions with these youngest delinquents.[30]

Butts and Snyder provide estimated data on serious crime committed by three juvenile age categories that are reproduced in Table 4.9.

Table 4.9 shows that as of 1996, three age categories of juveniles have been involved in the commission of both index and non-index crimes. Index crimes cover both property and violent crimes, whereas non-index is a category that covers crimes to the exclusion of property and violent crimes.

30　Butts, J.A., Snyder, H.N., (September 1997) "The Youngest Delinquents: Offenders Under age 15," U.S. Department of Justice, Juvenile Justice Bulletin, p. 1.

Table 4.9 Arrest (%) for three juvenile age category offenders in 1995

	Juveniles Age 12 or under	Juveniles Ages 13 and 14	Juveniles Ages 15 or older
Offense			
Total	9%	25%	66%
Crime index total	12	27	60
Violent crime index	8	23	70
Murder and non-negligent manslaughter	3	10	6
Forcible rape	11	26	63
Robbery	6	22	72
Aggravated assault	9	23	68
Property crime index	13	28	58
Burglary	12	27	61
Larceny-theft	15	29	56
Motor vehicle theft	4	25	72
Arson	35	33	33
Nonindex			
Simple assault	3	28	59
Forgery and counterfeiting	3	10	87
Fraud	4	22	74
Embezzlement	3	7	90
Stolen property (buying receiving, possessing)	6	22	72
Vandalism	19	29	53
Weapons (carrying, possessing, etc.)	8	22	70
Prostitution and commercialized vice	5	12	83
Sex offense (except forcible rape and prostitution)	18	33	49
Drug abuse violations	2	15	83
Gambling	3	13	83
Offenses against the family and children	8	22	70
Driving under the influence	2	1	97
Liquor law violations	1	9	90
Drunkenness	2	12	85
Disorderly conduct	9	26	65
Vagrancy	4	17	79
All other offenses (Except traffic)	7	21	72
Suspicion	6	21	73
Curfew and loitering	5	24	71
Running away	8	35	56

Note: Percentages may not add to 100% because of rounding.

Source: Authors' analysis of data from the Federal Bureau of Investigation, Crime in the United States 1995 (Washington, DC: U.S. Government Printing Office, 1996).

Table 4.10 Estimated juvenile crimes, arrests and percentile change for three juvenile age categories between 1980–1995

	Juveniles Age 12 or Younger	Estimated Percent Change Arrests 1980–1995	Juveniles Age 13 and 14	Estimated Percent Change 1980–1995	Juveniles Age 15 or Older	Estimated Percent Change Arrests 1980–1995
Total*	256,300	24%	680,400	54 %	1,808,300	18%
Crime index total	109,300	5	243,000	23	532,800	-2
Violent crime index	11,500	102	33,300	92	103,000	47
Murder and nonnegligent manslaughter	100	209	300	88	2,800	72
Forcible rape	600	190	1,400	62	3,500	-3
Robbery	3,200	41	12,400	45	39,900	16
Aggravated Assault	7,600	139	19,100	147	56,800	85
Property crime index	97,800	-1	209,800	16	429,800	-9
Burglary	16,600	-35	36,500	-32	82,700	-46
Larceny-theft						
Motor vehicle theft	2,900	31	19,900	53	57,00	23
Arson	3,600	29	3,400	54	3,400	-8
Nonindex*						
Simple assault	28,700	170	60,600	196	126,500	115
Stolen property (buying, receiving, possessing)	2,500	7	9,300	20	31,000	14
Vandalism	26,000	-7	39,900	28	73,700	13
Weapons (carrying, possessing, etc.)	4,500	206	12,600	167	39,200	93
Sex offenses (except forcible rape and prostitution)	2,900	125	5,300	68	7,800	4
Drug abuse violations	4,100	129	28,000	101	157,700	67
Liquor law violations	1,200	31	11,300	19	107,500	24
Disorderly conduct	16,000	63	45,600	102	112,300	17
Curfew and loitering	7,100	136	35,900	170	106,700	96
Running away	21,100	47	88,100	80	140,300	56

Notes and Source for Table 4.10

Note: Between 1980 and 1995, arrests for Violent Crime Index offenders doubled for juveniles age 12 or younger, although these youth accounted for just 8% of juvenile arrests for Violent Crime Index offenses in 1995.

Increases in the number of arrests between 1980 and 1995 were relatively greater for juveniles ages 13 and 14.

Detail may not add to totals because of rounding.

* Not all offenses included in the nonindex category are represented.

Source: Author's analysis of data from the Federal Bureau of Investigation, Crime in the United States 1980 and Crime in the United States 1995 (Washington, DC: U.S. Government Printing Office, 1981 and 1996, respectively).

The Contributory Role of the Juvenile Crime

Table 4.10 gives the estimated numbers in each crime category accompanied with the percentage change in the juvenile commission of crimes between 1980–1995. The two tables, when taken together, give an idea of the extent of juvenile involvement in various crimes between 1980 and 1997. At the same time, these tables inform the reader of the early age of onset of juvenile crime, a factor that is very important in gauging the effectiveness of preventive measures that the American juvenile justice system has undertaken during the past several decades in order to prevent juvenile delinquents' transformation into adult criminals.

In Table 4.10, Butts and Snyder caution the reader about their data. It is common knowledge that the Federal Bureau of Investigation (FBI), collects data on arrests made by law enforcement agencies throughout the United States and publishes its results in the Uniform Crime Reports (UCR) and now as National Incident Based Report System (NIBRS) on an annual basis. The above data reflect the number of juveniles who have been arrested by law enforcement agencies. "The FBI does not calculate national estimates for arrests involving persons under the age 18," caution Butts and Snyder. The national estimates are for the "total number of arrests for various offenses." Butts and Snyder have utilized the national estimates in order to estimate the proportion of youth arrests in each offense category writing:

> The juvenile arrest estimates presented in this study were developed by deriving the proportion of youth arrests in each offense category from the data reported by UCR-participating jurisdiction and then applying that proportion to the UCR national estimate of total arrests for the offense.[31]

It goes without saying that these estimates of youth crime and violence, based on Butts and Snyder's methodology, are lower than the actual crime and violence

---

31   Butts and Snyder, Ibid., p. 3.

perpetrated by the youths in this country. After analyzing various statistical data pertaining to the three age category juveniles, Butts and Snyder conclude that:

> The findings of this study confirm that the number of offenders age 14 or younger in the Nation's juvenile justice system has increased disproportionately in recent years. Relative to the 1980s, arrests and juvenile court cases involving youth under the age 15 increased more than those juveniles age 15 or older. However, the actual number of offenders age 14 or younger remained relatively small as compared with the caseload of older juvenile offenders seen by law enforcement agencies and the courts. Thus, juvenile offenders as a group have not become markedly younger in the past decade. Offenders age 12 or younger represent the same proportion of juvenile arrests (9%) and juvenile court cases (11%) they did more than a decade ago, and the percentage of offenders age 13 and 14 increased slightly.[32]

Despite this finding, the authors caution that there is a public perception that offenders are becoming younger. Butts and Snyder provide five reasons for this false perception:

1. The overall growth in the number of violent juveniles.
2. Change in the nature of offenses.
3. Doubling of delinquency case loads since 1970.
4. The everlasting negative image that young offenders imprint in the minds of prosecutors, judges and jury members.
5. The role of the news and print media in disseminating the shocking news of young offenders' crimes in the public mind and conscience.[33]

The question as to why juveniles as young as 12 years of age—and in some cases as young as 10—commit the kind of serious crimes that Table 4.9 depicts above, is a serious question. Many studies conducted by researchers have addressed this simple yet intriguing question. These studies have covered almost all aspects of social life through child socialization in the family, school, peer group and community. In addition, various negative and crime causing aspects as well as positive aspects of American social life and their impacts on child socialization have been studied. What is the current rate of juvenile crime in United States?

An Institutional Remedy: Juvenile Monitoring

The Office of Juvenile Justice and Delinquency Prevention (OJJDP) in its report titled, "Juvenile Monitoring Program: 1998 Report to Congress," informs Congress about the recent decline in juvenile arrests (Snyder, 1997), then gives

---

32   Butts and Snyder, Ibid., pp. 9–10.
33   Butts and Snyder, Ibid., p. 11.

the following as the factors responsible for the decline: "a 9% decrease in the juvenile violent arrest rate; a 14% reduction in the number of juveniles arrested for murder; a 9% and 10% reduction respectively in weapons related arrests and motor vehicle theft; an 8% reduction in the number of juveniles arrested for robbery."[34] The Report, however cautions Congress observing that, "Juvenile crime remains exceptionally high. Youth involvement with gangs and associated gang related criminal activities continue to be a problem for many of our communities."[35] Referring to risk-focused prevention strategies, the Report identifies the following as factors that contribute to the ongoing high rate of juvenile delinquency and serious. According to the Report:

- family members no longer routinely remain in the communities in which they grew up—families often are isolated;
- fathers, mothers and older children frequently work outside of the home creating an increased need for alternative child care for younger children, and a higher incidence of unsupervised youth in the absence of such alternative care;
- the increases in both rates of divorce and rates of single teens during the early 1990s resulted in more families being headed by one rather than two parents–further exacerbating parental isolation;
- increases in gang crime and domestic violence and other violent behaviors have diverted scarce community resources from family support services to criminal investigations and prosecutions;
- prevalence of alcohol and drug abuse led to both family and community upheaval, and to physically, mentally, and emotionally damaged youth who must struggle to function effectively and productively; and
- ready availability of guns increases the likelihood that crimes will be increasingly lethal.[36]

In short, the 1998 Report to Congress concentrates on both risk and protective factors pertaining to family, school, personal and peer group, and community, to propose that juvenile delinquency and serious crime can be prevented more effectively if these social institutions were to function in their preventive capacities. Table 4.11 provides risk and protective factors that the 1998 Report to Congress has identified their relationship to juveniles' commission of crime.

34   Bilchik, Shay, "Juvenile Monitoring Program: 1998 Report to Congress," U.S. Department of Justice, Office of Juvenile Justice and Delinquency Prevention, p. 3.
35   Bilchick, Ibid., p. 3.
36   Bilchick, Ibid., p. 6.

Table 4.11 Risk and protective factors pertaining to community, family, personal/peer, and school

Community	Family	Personal/Peers	School
Risk factors	*Risk factors*	*Risk factors*	*Risk factors*
Easy availability of drugs and guns	Parental alcohol or drug abuse	Friends who use drugs, engage in delinquent behaviors	Poor grades
Extreme economic deprivation	Lack of adequate supervision	Working more than 20 hours per week	Being behind grade level
High mobility and transitions	Family conflict or violence	Low impulse control, or sensation seeking behavior	Sense of isolation from/prejudice by peers
Community	**Family**	**Personal/Peers**	**School**
Protective Factors	*Protective Factors*	*Protective Factors*	*Protective Factors*
High neighborhood attachment	Parental disapproval of delinquency and ATOD use	Perceived importance of religion or prayer	Realistically high parental expectations for achievement
Protective community organization	Feeling of warmth, love and caring from parents	Sense of social belonging	Connectedness and positive engagement with school
Community norms unfavorable toward crime and drug use	Clear standards and consistent discipline	Meaningful, challenging opportunities to contribute to family/community	Perceived caring from teachers

Source: Adopted from Bilchik, Shay, Juvenile Monitoring Program: 1998 Report to Congress, The U.S. Department of Justice, Office of Juvenile Justice and Delinquency Prevention, Exhibit 1:1, p. 8.

The 1998 Report to Congress details various monitoring strategies, support programs, and various agencies involved in reducing the risk factors that push juveniles into crime and delinquency. These findings, supported by similar research, indicate that juvenile crime while as complex as it may look, is, nonetheless, a symptom of an alarming trend in the rise of the risk factors that surround inner city youths, irrespective of race or ethnicity. One remedy is to fight the risk factors with enhanced protective factors, a strategy that the 1998 Report to Congress has identified as JUMP which stands for the Juvenile Monitoring Program. It originated as "Part G of the Juvenile Justice and Delinquency Prevention (JJDP) Act of 1974, as amended in 1992 (Pub. L. 93-415:42 U.S.C. 5667 et seq.) ...."[37] This program is designed to prevent juveniles from drifting into delinquency, experimenting with alcohol and drugs, and involvement with criminal gangs through juveniles' engagement with monitors who would steer the youth energies into proper and productive social channels—something that the family, school, and peer and community processes of socialization do in the United States and other parts of the world.

Monitoring juveniles by concerned adults is not a new concept, neither is it a new practice. Citing Freedman, Bilchik observes that "Examples can be found as far back as the late 19th century when the Friendly Visiting campaign, supported by charitable societies, recruited hundreds of middle-class women to work with poor and immigrant comminutes ...."[38] The Big Brothers/Big Sisters of 1904 is another example of monitoring efforts that followed the "Friendly Visiting" program according to Bilchik.[39]

There are other juvenile centered programs funded by federal and state governments in the United States to help youths who become known as "youth at risk" to the effect that we now possess a compendium of such programs according to Eileen M. Gary.[40] Out of 150 programs designed to help youth at risk, the editors of this compendium, reports Gary, chose 46 programs characterizing them as those which provide tangible results. The principles that separate effective programs from non-effective ones have been identified as the following:

- quality of implementation
- caring, knowledgeable adults
- high standards and expectations
- parent/guardian participation
- community involvement
- youth as resources/community service and service-learning
- work-based learning
- long-term services, support, and follow up.[41]

In short, it is safe to argue that juvenile crime is a reflection of the manner in which America treats its children through its social, economic and political processes.

---

37   Bilchik, Ibid., p. 1.
38   Bilchik, Ibid., p. 4.
39   Bilchik, Ibid., p. 4.
40   Gary, M. E., (November, 1999) "A Compendium of Programs That Work for Youth," Fact Sheet, The U.S. Department of Justice, Office of Justice and Delinquency Prevention.
41   Gary, Ibid.

The Contributory Role of Crime Pathology and Treatment

There is a lot of lip service given by the liberal academicians, juvenile justice practitioners and policy makers to the notion that crime (both adult and juvenile) is a social product. In reality, however, predatory and violent crimes are by and large treated as pathological, rather than as social, products. Thus, more adults as well as juveniles are incarcerated in prisons, despite the fact that serious crime has declined in this country in the past decade. More juvenile cases are being transferred from juvenile to adult courts. For example, the "Special Report" cited above, notes that:

> Defendants under age 18 are prosecuted in either adult courts or juvenile courts, with State statutes defining the maximum age of juvenile court jurisdiction. In three States (Connecticut, New York, and North Carolina) all offenders age 16 or older are excluded from the juvenile system and handled in adult court. In 10 States (Georgia, Illinois, Louisiana, Massachusetts, Michigan, Missouri, New Hampshire, South Carolina, Texas, and Wisconsin) all offenders age 17 or older are automatically proceeded against in adult court. In the remaining 37 States and the District of Columbia, all defendants age 18 or older are processed as adults in criminal court.[42]

The fact that in thirteen states juveniles as young as sixteen are involved in the commission of serious crime requiring certification from juvenile to adult courts is indicative of the American juvenile justice system's inability to rehabilitate a segment of the youth offending population characterized in the literature as Serious and Violent Juvenile Offenders (SVJ) according to Gail A. Wasserman, Laurie S. Miller, and Lynn Cothren, to be dealt with shortly. Strom also notes in the special Report that:

> Defendants whose age are below these State-specified ranges can be statutorily excluded from juvenile court because of age and offense seriousness or can be transferred to adult court. As of 1997, all States had at least one mechanism that allowed persons under age 18 to be handled in the adult criminal system.[43]

Other mechanisms for the transfer of juvenile cases, maintains Strom, include: (1) statutory exclusion laws, (2) prosecutorial direct-file provision, and (3) judicial wavier. The last category is the most frequently used form, and it is divided into three categories: discretionary waiver that in 1997 was utilized in 46 states and the District of Columbia, mandatory waiver statutes utilized in 14 states, and presumptive waiver utilized in 14 states and the District of Columbia. In addition, many states have adopted "blended sentencing options" allowing a state to utilize

---

42 Strom, "Profile of State Prisoners under Age 18, 1985-97" Ibid., p. 1.

43 Strom, Ibid., p. 1.

both juvenile and adult courts in dealing with juvenile crimes.[44] When utilized, this system allows a juvenile court to impose sanctions suspending adult court's sanctions provided that the juvenile refrains from future law violations. Despite these efforts, the number of juvenile offenders, incarcerated in prisons due to commission of serious crime, has increased as shown in Table 4.12.

Table 4.12 Juveniles incarcerated in State prisons for serious offenses, 1985–1997

	1985		1990		1997	
Most serious offenses	**Number**	**%**	**Number**	**%**	**Number**	**%**
All offenses	3,400	100	5,100	100	7,400	100
Violent offenses	1,730	52	2,270	45	4,510	61
Murder*	230	7	310	6	500	7
Sexual assault	230	7	180	4	300	4
Robbery	930	28	1,020	20	2,360	32
Aggravated assault	230	7	570	11	1,060	14
Property offenses	1,410	42	1,780	35	1,590	22
Burglary	930	28	940	19	950	13
Larceny/theft	230	7	300	6	230	3
Motor vehicle theft	110	3	320	6	160	2
Drug offenses	70	2	820	16	840	11
Public-order offenses	140	4	200	4	360	5

Note: All data are estimated. Includes only those with a sentence of more than 1 year.

In 1997, 1% of offenders under 18 were admitted for "other" offense types. Other offense types are not shown in detail. See *Methodology* for procedures used for calculating national estimates.
* Murder: includes nonnegligent manslaughter.
Aggravated assault: Includes forcible rape and other sexual assaults.

Source: U.S. Department of Justice, Special Repot, "Profile of State Prisoners under Age 18, 1985-97, February 2000, NCJ 176989, Table 2, p. 4.

Table 4.12 records that the number of juveniles incarcerated in prison for serious offenses more than doubled (2.17 time), rising from 3,400 in 1985 to 7,400 in 1997. The actual number of those juveniles incarcerated in prisons for property offenses rose steadily from 1,410 in 1985 to 1,780 in 1990 to 1,590 in

---

44   Strom, Ibid., pp. 1–2.

1997. The most dramatic increase occurred in the number of juveniles arrested for drug offense that rose from 70 in 1985 to 820 in 1990 and 840 in 1997.

This picture, as disturbing as it is, is incomplete insofar as the extent of the juvenile involvement in crime and misdemeanors is concerned. Table 4.13, reproduced from the Special Report, sheds light on the extent of juvenile criminality.

Table 4.13 Serious juvenile offenses and felony convictions

	Uniform Crime Report (UCR)	National Judicial Reporting Program (NJRP)		National Correctional Reporting Program	
Most serious offenses	**Number of persons arrested age 13–17**	**Number of felony convictions**	**Number of felony convictions per 1,000 prison**	**Number of admissions to State prisons**	**Number of admissions to State prisons per 1,000 convictions**
Violent offenses	138,470	9,161	66	4.180	456
Murder	2,820	998	354	500	501
Sexual assault	18,970	793	42	310	391
Robbery	47,340	4,375	92	2.280	521
Aggravated assault	69,340	2,995	43	1,090	196
Property offenses	622,720	8,750	14	1,420	162
Burglary	119,040	5,256	44	1,030	196
Larceny /theft	433,390	2,877	7	240	83
Motor vehicle theft	70,290	617	9	150	243
Drug offenses	207,120	6,019	29	860	143

Note: All data are estimated. See Methodology for estimation of arrests (UCR), felony convictions in State courts (NJRP), and State prisons admissions (NCRP) by offense. NRJP estimates a total of 29,000 State felony convictions of persons under age 18 at time of arrest.

As shown in Table 4.13, as of 1996, 138,470 persons aged between 13–17, were arrested for violent offenses. Of this number, 9,161 juveniles were convicted with almost half of them (4,180) sentenced to state prison giving the number 66 representing "number of felony convictions per 1,000 arrests," and number 456 representing "number of admissions to State prison per 1,000 felony convictions" as specified by Strom. In comparison to violent offense, property offenses perpetrated by juveniles had a much lower number of felony convictions resulting in a much lower admission of juveniles to state prisons. For example, from the estimated total of 622,720 property offenses committed by juveniles aged 13–17 in 1996, only 8,750 juveniles are estimated of having been convicted resulting in 1,420 juveniles admitted to state prison. Among property offenses, burglary had the highest number of felony convictions (5,256) of juveniles resulting in the largest number of admission to state prison next to drug offenses. Among the violent offenses committed by juveniles, the crime of murder had the highest number of felony convictions (354) resulting in the estimated admission of 500 juveniles to state prison followed by the crime of robbery and aggravated assault resulting in 2,280 and 1,090 juveniles admitted to state prison in 1996. What is the implication of this and similar data? Are we witnessing the rise of a new type of juvenile offender who engages in the most violent crimes? Has the American juvenile justice system strategically failed to rehabilitate juvenile offenders in general and minority youths in particular?

A New Type of Young Offenders

After a two-year study and collaborating with others, Wasserman et al., argue that in the 1990s, they discovered a new type of juvenile offender characterized as Seriously Violent Juvenile Offenders (SVJ).[45] It represents juvenile offenders that are different from regular juvenile delinquents. As a group, it possesses a set of early discernible behavioral and antisocial characteristics. These are defined as "risk factors." The researchers argue, "Identifying the risk factors for these behaviors is important in developing strategies to prevent violent offending."[46] The authors also stress the importance of identifying the risk factors for prevention purposes and categorize them into two distinct sets: (1) Distal or community risk factors that include factors such as poverty, accessibility of guns or drugs, or both, and (2) Proximal risk factors which include factors such as parental and/or peer group relationships, or low IQ. The purpose of the research is multi-dimensional. The authors write:

> This Bulletin explores these proximal risk factors, reviews the early developmental
> precursors to violent offending, and summarizes approaches to prevention. It
> also discusses components of intervention programs; limitations of single-focus

45   Wasserman, G.A., Miller L.S., and Cothern L., (April, 2000) "Prevention of Serious and Violent Juvenile Offending," *Juvenile Justice Bulletin*, p. 1.
46   Wasserman, et al., Ibid., p. 1.

preventions; examples of well-designed, multi-systemic intervention programs that target proximal risk factors; and limitations of prevention strategies.[47]

Based on this approach, Wasserman et al., focus on the contributory roles of ADHD (Attention Deficit Hyperactivity Disorder) as well as on ODD (Disruptive Behavior Disorders). Wasserman et al., argue that early detection of these two categories of risk factors is important for implementing measures that would prevent the adolescent child from progressing into SVJ status. The preventive measures include:

1. Family- and Parent-Focused Components
2. Child-Focused Components
3. Classroom-Focused Components
4. Peer-Group Focused Components

After describing these components and their applicability in the preventive measures, the authors conclude:

> Antisocial behavior is rarely the result of a single risk factor. Youth live in layered and complex environments that contain multiple risk factors at different levels. As a result, successful approaches to prevention must incorporate components directed at more than one type of risk factor. As a result, successful approaches to prevention must incorporate components directed at more than one type of risk factor.[48]

In sum, American criminologists and justice practitioners have postulated various explanations for the disproportionate incarceration rate of African-American males. These explanations (including those of the African-American criminologists to be dealt with in the next chapter), vary along the consensus-conflict paradigmatic approaches to the etiology of crime and delinquency. Consensus criminologists posit African-Americans have higher rates of incarceration because of their involvement in crime.

Conflict criminologists posit the reasons for the disproportionate incarceration of minorities lie within the operational dynamics of the larger social, economic and political forces within American society and economy. However, the author of this book uses a realist-conflict perspective and argues the importance of crime commission as a factor, but also considers the contributory role and importance of social, economic, and political forces. The thrust of my argument is that although it is true that "it takes a village to raise a child," but for that child not to fall victim to the influences of criminality, society must socially and economically structure and maintain all of its villages upon the ideal of social justice. On a macro level,

---

47   Wasserman, et al., Ibid., p. 1.
48   Wasserman, et al., Ibid., p. 9.

the disproportionate incarceration of African-American males as discussed in some details in this chapter, has deprived the American criminal justice system from one universal ingredient that gives legitimacy to any system of conflict resolution, equity in the process of dispensing justice. By the term equity, I aim at both the tangible process of delivering justice, as well as the historical legacy that permeates a certain racial, or ethnic, group's view of the process.

Chapter 5
Adverse Impacts of Incarceration

This chapter briefly discusses some of the more prevalent negative impacts of incarceration on African-American community and family life. Incarceration, especially if of a disproportionate and continuous nature not only exacts a heavy toll on inmates' physical and mental health, but also deprives African-American community from one of its most important human capital elements, adult males thus negatively impacting youths socialization within both family and community structures.

Life in American Penal Institutions

The established wisdom is that daily life in American prisons is by and large a negative and dehumanizing experience despite important legal, custodial as well as structural changes that American penal institutions have gone through within the past half century. Prison life has been studied by modern scholars in different branches of social sciences. The paradigmatic approach to the study of life in American penal institutions has evolved from one of conceptualizing prison as a "primitive institution" to one of "total institution" of the modern era as spearheaded by the Chicago School of Criminology that emerged with the establishment of the Department of Sociology at the University of Chicago, IL in 1894. It dominated American modern criminology as well as penal philosophy up until 1960s and then gradually declined. Chicago School criminologists were process-oriented in their approach to the root causes of social problems that they regularly studied, be it the inner-city crime or poverty, juvenile delinquency, or the use and spread of illicit drugs and/or alcoholism, including the social realities of daily life in penal settings.

Chicago School criminologists also studied different dimensions of life in American penal institutions as for example, Hans Reimer, a prominent sociologist who in 1935 volunteered a three-month lock up in a minimum security prison so as to observe as many social processes that unfolded within the penal setting.[1] The inmate population was apparently not aware of who he was, nor did most of the staff. Upon release, Reimer reported his observational findings to the American

---

1   Schmalleger, F., *Criminal Justice Today: An Introductory Text for the 21st Century*, Pearson Prentice Hall, 2009, p. 501.

Prison Association.[2] The report portrayed daily life in penal settings as one marred with criminogenic and debilitating processes. In 1939, another prominent sociologist, Edwin H. Sutherland, who had already studied the lifestyle and *modus operandi* of a class of criminals that he characterized as "professional thieves," published an article in the American Journal of Sociology theorizing that, "criminal behavior is learned in interaction with persons in a matter of communication."[3] This simple yet coherent argument provided the foundational base of Differential Association theory in relation to deviance and crime. In contrast to biological theories of crime developed by the twentieth century European criminologists, as for example, Cessare Lombroso, Sutherland concentrated on the learned aspect of criminal behavior. Sutherland's principles of differential association went through modification and refinement until it reached its present format in 1947. Sutherland's nine principles, developed with the help of his student and co-author, Donald R. Cressey, when applied to prisons settings added depth and explanatory power as to why prison life negatively impacted inmates especially the young, the inexperienced and socioeconomically disenfranchised.

In the 1960s, Erving Goffman published one of the most influential studies on the social environment of American mental institutions, *The Asylum*. Goffman characterized the mental hospitals and psychiatric wards as total institutions. He argued that the psychiatric wards controlled every aspect of social life of the mental patients subjecting them to abuse and dehumanizing processes whose aim was to control rather than mental or psychiatric rehabilitation. Applying Goffman's rationale to penal settings, there were, then and now, scholars who argue that American prisons manifest total institution characteristics. Accordingly, prison social environments are thoroughly criminogenic subjecting convicts to a wide range of exploitations and dehumanization practices that are structured within the prison subculture. Prisons function as total institutions similar to other total institutions such as mental hospitals, the army, concentration camps, or religious convents and monasteries. An example is the work of Gresham M. Sykes and Sheldon L. Messinger who studied the formation of inmate norms and values within prison subculture.[4] Sykes et al., also identified elements of prison

---

2   See Reimer, H. "Socialization in the Prison Community," pp. 152–153 in *The Proceedings of the American Prison Association 1937*.

3   See Miles, A.R., (1965) "The Relationship of Social Theory to Practical Utilization in Criminology" pp. 7–16, *The Prison Journal*; 45; 7, pp. 7–8. Miles cites this information from Donald R. Cressey, "The Theory of Differential Association: An Introduction," *Social Problems*, Vol. 8, No.1 (Summer 1960), p. 1.

4   Gresham M. Sykes and Sheldon I, Messinger, pp. 5–19 "The Inmate Social System," in Richard A, Cloward et al., (eds), *Theoretical Studies in Social Organization of Prison*, New York: Social Science Research Council, 1960, pp. 5–19.

subculture that included, among others, prison typology, prison argot language and convict relationship within and without the prison walls.[5]

In the first half of the twentieth century America, penal institutions were considered as places that by and large turned young and inexperienced petty criminals into full fledged career criminals. Penal institutions were also conceptualized as places for the second victimization of convicts especially those who could not stand up to the harsh, masculine pecking order at the apex of which stood the prison warden followed by the prison guards and correctional officers all the way down to various inmate typologies. Todd R. Clear et al. quote a former inmate by the name of Chuck Terry, to the effect that, " … male prisoners must project an image of 'fearlessness' in the way they walk, talk, and socially interact."[6] Those inmates, who show sign of weakness, become easy targets for physical or mental abuse or both. For example, prison-bound forced-homosexuality is one of the most abusive yet prevalent realities of prison life to which reference shall be made in this chapter. In fact, there is a physical strength-based prison subculture with its resultant inmate typology that researchers have identified in both state and federal prisons. John Irwin, in his classic *The Felon* argued that the rise of inmate typology was due to convicts' pre-conviction lifestyle and practices.[7] Once in prison they adopt those patterns of prison subculture that best fit their pre-conviction patterns of life notwithstanding the imposed restrictions that imprisonment entails. Thus the rise of inmate typologies is an adaptive reaction to prison environment predicated by their pre-incarceration life style and personality patterns. Irwin identified the following inmate typology: (1) Hustler; (2) Dope Friend; (3) Disorganized Criminal; (4) State Raised Youth; (5) Square John; (6) Head; (7) Thief; and (8) Lower Class Man.[8] Other researchers have come up with similar inmate typologies as, for example, Frank Schmalleger, who by utilizing these studies has identified nine inmate typologies as follows: (1) Mean dude; (2) Hedonist; (3) Opportunist; (4) Retreatist; (5) Legalist; (6) Radical; (7) Colonist; (8) Religious; and (9) Realist.[9]

Of special importance for the subject matter of this book is the profile of inmates who are religious in their perspective, or become religious in prisons. Concerning inmate religious typology, Schmalleger states that, "Some prisoners profess a strong religious faith. They may be 'born-again' Christians, committed Muslims

---

5   See for example, Erving Goffman, *Asylum: Essays on the Social Situation of Mental Patients and Other Inmates*, Garden City, NY: Anchor, 1961.

6   Tood, E.C., George F. Cole and Michael d. Reising, *American Corrections*, eight edn, Thomson Wadsworth, 2009, p. 268.

7   See Irwin, J. *The Felon*, Prentice Hall Publishers, 1970.

8   See *The Felon* by John Irwin, Englewood Cliffs, N.J: Prentice-Hall Inc. 1970, reviews by Albert Elias, *The Journal of Criminal Law and Criminology* (1973), Vol. 64, No. 1, (Mar., 1973), pp. 132–133.

9   Schmalleger, *Criminal Justice Today*, pp. 504–506.

of even satanists (*sic*) or witches."[10] As to their motives, he opines that, "While it is certainly true that some inmates have a strong religious faith, staff members are apt to be suspicious of the overtly religious prisoners."[11] Whatever the motives of the religious typology, one thing is certain: the rehabilitative potentials of religious faith have comprised a place in American penal philosophy from colonial times to present. In post 9/11 concerns with terrorism, the role of faith-based organizations and especially of Islam is seriously being reconsidered, a subject to be dealt with in some detail in Chapters 5 and 6 of this book.

Defining Characteristics of Total Institutions

There are several defining characteristics that are common to total institutions such as the army, psychiatric wards, concentration camps and penal institutions. One common characteristic is the fact that every aspect of daily life is structured by the institution so as to enable those in charge to perform their social and legal responsibilities successfully and in the most efficient manner possible. Another common characteristic of total institutions relates to the nature of their services, clientele and purpose for which they have been institutionalized. Barring exceptions, entrance into, or exit from, total institutions is not of a voluntary nature. For example, prior to the creation of a voluntary-based military corps in the US, young men who reached a certain age were legally obligated to report for conscription into military for a specified amount of time, a practice that was followed then and now in many countries around the world. Mandatory conscription into military has historically been deemed as an important step in young men's passage from adolescence into adulthood. One reason for this has a lot to do with iron-clad military discipline that the conscripts have to face and cope with its detailed regulative requirements. The rationale for military discipline is the fact that the purpose of the military is to face external threat to national sovereignty that nations face and to be prepared to repel it. It is generally believed that military discipline prepares young men for such eventualities thus it creates its norms, values and ethos of bravery and dedication to cause, next to a subculture that utilizes these parameters in creating military spirit de corpse. Within the military settings, those who can't march to the tunes of military discipline face the prospect of dishonorable discharge.

What is the rationale of incarceration? Unlike other total institutions whose rationale is to significantly reshape and improve the world view, the behavioral, and normative as well as personality traits of their constituents, be it the clientele or those in charge of the institution, the rationale of incarceration has historically been one of incapacitation of those who violate the criminal law. However, thanks to the Judeo-Christian thrust of the Anglo-American penal philosophy, this incapacitation must also be fair. The thrust of modern prisons from the time of the Chicago School of Criminology to present has been the establishment of an ideal,

---

10   Schmalleger, Ibid., p. 505.
11   Schmalleger, Ibid.

yet functional balance between the two. We want convicts to do their time, give their dues to society, get rehabilitated in penal institutions, and once released get positively re-integrated in society and economy. In short, we want the convicts to not recidivate once they have experienced life in prisons. This is a noble tall order that we all admire, but is quite hard to deliver for various reasons that we shall discuss in the rest of this chapter.

Why Prisons Don't Rehabilitate?

From the time of arrival until the time of exit from any state or federal custodial jurisdiction, inmates are subjected to the regulatory requirements of a wide range of rules that apply to every aspect of life within the penal settings. This structured restriction is necessary because the main functional goal of modern penal institution, be it state or federal, centers around four intertwined outcomes: (1) public safety; (2) offender rehabilitation; (3) reintegration of convicts once released from prison; and (4) victim assistance and restitution. Modern penitentiaries adhere, *mutates mutandis*, to these principles. An example is Texas Department of Corrections (from now on TDC) that manages one of the largest state prison systems in the USA. Its jurisdiction covers six regions with around 105 state and private prisons scattered throughout different counties of the State of Texas. The mission of TDC is, "... to provide public safety, promote positive change in offender behavior, reintegrate offenders into society and assist victims of crime."[12] The Offender Orientation Handbook of Texas Department of Corrections details offender's rights and responsibilities that are covered within four chapters. A synopsis of the contents of each is given below to familiarize the reader with the complex and structured nature of daily life of inmates in American penitentiaries.

Chapter One of the TDC Offender Orientation Handbook is about "Offender Access to Services for Behavior Reception and Diagnostic Process". It is comprehensive, covering issues related to intake custodial operations, offender custodial classification levels (from 1 to 5), administrative committees as well as considerations for good conduct time. An important part of Chapter One is about offenders "Standards of Behavior" while in custody. These include standards of hygiene, grooming and clothing next to those which apply to living areas, showers, toilets, recreation yards, commissary, safety and general rules of conduct. Under the caption of "Safe Prison Programs" subjects such as offender protection, sexual assault and what to do in case such assaults were to take place against an inmate are covered. Next to disciplinary rules and procedures, Chapter One also covers subjects such as educational, heath, recreational issues as well as inmate grievance procedures, parole information, sex offender treatment programs and crime stoppers behind the wall.

---

12   See Texas Department of Criminal Justice Mission Statement in Texas Department of Criminal Justice: Offender Orientation Handbook, November, 2004.

Chapter Two of the TDC Offender Orientation Handbook covers a wide range of rules pertaining to inmate visitation rights and responsibilities as well as under what circumstance suspension of visitation rights may occur. Included in this chapter are subjects such as visiting special offender categories (e.g., mentally retarded, psychiatric out-patient, transient offenders). A segment relates to lockdown status, administrative segregation, death row inmates and the so-called special visits that include visits by spiritual advisors, prospective employers, visits by attorneys etc.

Chapter Three of the TDC Offender Orientation Handbook covers rules regarding offender correspondence with the outside world that, among others, include both permissible and restricted correspondence as, for example, with the media, publishers as well as legal correspondence. There is a list of rules pertaining to custodial handling of offender correspondence.

Chapter Four of the TDC Offender Orientation Handbook is of special significance as it covers offender rights to access the courts, counsel and public officials. Because of these rights, allowance has been made for offender access to law books and legal compendiums in both state and federal penitentiaries. The quality of the so-called prison law libraries differs among correctional institutions. What is certain is that there are the so-called Jail-House lawyers who use this service regularly petitioning courts to hear a wide range of prison-bound grievances. Statistics compiled and published by The Bureau of Justice Statistics indicate that these grievances range from frivolous to those that have raised important constitutional violations related to conditions of quality of life in prisons and jails. Incarceration does not negate inmate rights to a set of minimums that the Section 1983 Litigation of the U.S. Code has identified and upheld by the United States Supreme Court to which reference shall be made shortly.

Other states of the Union have come up with similar offender manuals as, for example, Florida Department of Corrections (from now on FDC) that houses a large number of offenders throughout four custodial jurisdictions. As of 2006, Florida's correctional population put the State of Florida among "the big four in corrections" as observed by Todd Clear et al., who gave the following numbers respectively pertaining to prison (62,743), probation (278,606), and parole (4,484) in Florida.[13] Florida Department of Corrections has one of the most comprehensive faith-based programs that operate throughout the system. An example is The Wakulla Correctional Institution that based on FDC publications, as of November 2005 comprised "Florida's third, and nation's largest Faith-and character-based Institution."[14] The rationale for this initiative was based on the notion that, "Faith based programs promote the reintegration of offenders into society and address life

---

13   Clear, Todd R., George Cole and Michael D. Reising, *American Correction*, eight edn, Thomson/Wadsworth 2007, p. 14.

14   Wakulla Correctional Institution: Dedication as Faith-and Character-Based Institution Ceremony, November 23, 2005 at http://www.dc.state.fl.us/secretary/press/2005/FaithBasedWakulla.html.

skills from a spiritual perspective."[15] The Fact Sheet of the Wakulla Correctional Institution gives a number of reasons for the apparent potential success of the program. Accordingly, admittance to the Faith-and Character-Based initiative is voluntary, inmates don't have to make a choice in which faith program to attend, and attendance is complementary to regular work assignments of the inmates and not a substitute for it. The administrators are hopeful that the program will be effective stating that, "While [it is] too soon to calculate recidivism rates, inmates in Faith-and Character-based programs have proven to have fewer fights, get fewer disciplinary reports, and may even have fewer crisis mental health events (seasonal depressions, anxiety attacks, explosive anger, etc.)."[16]

California Department of Corrections and Rehabilitations (from now on CDCR) has custodial jurisdiction over the largest number of inmates housed in 33 adult institutions and 6 juvenile facilities in California. There are also 13 community correctional facilities that house the following numbers respectively pertaining to prison (170,676), probation (384,852), and parole (110,262) in California.[17] The CDCR has enunciated seven strategic goals that it is trying to implement during 2007–2012. These goals are (1) Workforce Excellence; (2) Technology; (3) Organizational Effectiveness; (4) Risk Management; (5) Crime Prevention, Rehabilitation Programming, and Safety; (6) Rehabilitation and Reentry; and (7) Health Care Delivery. To achieve these goals a set of strategies have been envisioned for implementation by the CDCR staff and management to which reference shall be made as occasion arises in this chapter.

Of special significance for our subject is the fact that in states with large inmate population (e.g. California, Texas, Florida, Ohio, New York, North Carolina, Michigan), much attention has been directed towards issues such as crime prevention, rehabilitation and safety within the penal settings that is indicative of the criminogenic nature of life in state penitentiaries in the USA. For example, the aforementioned Goals 5 and 6 of the California Department of Corrections and Rehabilitation are the most comprehensive among its seven goals. Goal 5 combines crime prevention, inmate rehabilitation and a safety measure in order to achieve this goal's stated objectives. It is stated that, "The Department must provide for the safety and security of our employees as well as offenders and the public including disaster and emergency preparedness."[18] The document emphasizes that next to the need of research for identifying the most appropriate approach to crime reduction and prevention within the penal institutions in California, "We must establish a systematic approach to correctional services from the time of

---

15   Spirit Life Inside at http://www.dc.state.fl.us/pub/compass/02spring/10.html.

16   Wakulla Correctional Institution: Dedication as Faith-and Character-Based Institution Ceremony, November 23, 2005 at http://www.dc.state.fl.us/secretary/press/2005/FaithBasedWakulla.html.

17   Clear, Todd R. et al., Ibid.

18   See California Department of Corrections and Rehabilitation Strategic Plan 2007-2012, p. 11. The document was accessed at http://www.cdcr.ca.gov/.

arrest to reintegration into the community. Implementation of strategies to reduce overcrowding in adult institutions is paramount to the success of rehabilitation efforts."[19] To achieve these, the document has envisioned five strategies for Goal 5. These are: strategy 5.1 that aims at reduction of prison overcrowding; strategy 5.2 that aims for safety as well as safe structures for both staff and inmates; strategy 5.3 that aims at gender issues within the penal institutions of the State of California; strategy 5.4 which aims for safety and rehabilitation of juvenile offenders; and strategy 5.5 that aims at victim service programs as well as offender rehabilitation and accountability.

Goal 6 of the CDRC Strategic Plan combines rehabilitation and reintegration strategies. It is stated that, "Departmental success in rehabilitation and reentry requires a network of support at the time of reception and while on parole."[20] Studies of the prison inmate profile, to which reference has been made in previous chapters of this book, show that an absolute majority of both State and Federal prisoners come from the lower social and economic strata of American society. Once under penal custody, inmates have to cope with the many prison-bound rules and regulations that apply to every aspect of daily life behind bars. It goes without saying that the effective implementation and success of these reform programs and initiatives depends, among others, on public expenditure for constructing and managing penal institutions, be it federal, state or local. One could systematically analyze different State Correctional Departments' custodial regulations, but it is very likely that similar results would be garnered.

The core problem for prison administration is the custodial management of a large segment of the inmate population that has already been victimized by all kinds of socioeconomic depravities and now has been put within the embrace of a total institution whose main purpose is to correct them. This endeavor entails cost, administrative and managerial talent and know-how. Based on the latest statistics, "The United States incarcerates more people than any country in the world, including the far more populous nation of China. At the start of the new year, the American penal system held more than 2.3 million adults."[21] As to the actual number of correctional populations, the following applied according to the latest Bureau of Justice Statistics: "At the year end 2006, over 5 million adult men and women were under Federal, state or local probation or parole jurisdiction: approximately 4,237,000 on probation and 798,200 on parole."[22] The Public Safety Performance report of the Pew Charitable Trust, in its latest report titled,

---

19   CDRC Ibid., p. 11.

20   CDRC Ibid., p. 14.

21   The Pew Center on the States: One in 100: Behind Bars in America 2008, published by The Pew Charitable Trust, Washington, D.C., February, 2008. p. 5.

22   See Probation and Parole Statistics of the Bureau of Justice Statistics of the U.S. Department of Justice & Office of Justice Programs. Accessed through http://www.ojp. usdoj.gov/bjs/panp.htm.

"Public Safety, Public Spending" predicts the following trends in relation to public spending on prisons during 2007–2011 that are bulleted below:

- By 2011, without changes in sentencing or release policies, Alaska, Arizona, Idaho, Montana, and Vermont can expect to see one new prisoner for every three currently in the system.
- Similarly, barring reforms, there will be one new prisoner for every four now in prison in Colorado, Washington, Wyoming, Nevada, Utah and South Dakota.
- Incarceration rates are expected to spike in Arizona and Nevada, from 590 and 540 prisoners per 100,000 residents, respectively, to 703 and 599. Particularly worrisome is the growth in the population of young males, the group at highest risk of criminal activity ….
- Louisiana, which has the highest incarceration rate among states, with 835 prisoners per 100,000 residents, expects that figure to hit 852 by 2011.
- Florida is anticipated to cross the 100,000-prisoners threshold within the next five years, the only state other than Texas and California to do so.
- None of the states is projecting an actual decrease in its number of prisoners between 2006 and 2011. The report projects no growth in Connecticut, Delaware and New York.
- The Midwest's prison population continues to rise primarily because of increases in new prison admissions and parole violations. Iowa's prison population is expected to increase at a slower rate than other Midwest states.
- Though the Northeast boasts the lowest incarceration rates, it has the highest cost per prisoner, led by Rhode Island ($44,860), Massachusetts ($43,026) and New York ($42,202). The lowest costs are generally in the South, led by Louisiana ($13,009), Alabama ($13,019) and South Carolina ($13,170).[23]

It is an established fact that a large number of state and federal law enforcement operations center on enforcing Possession Laws that date back to Harrison Act of 1914 as previously mentioned. It is Possession Law based-incarceration that has led to prison overcrowding from 1960s to present; most penologists would agree that prison overcrowding is the main cause of collapse of many penal reforms during the past half century in America. There are critical criminologists who have argued that by decriminalizing illicit drugs we can strategically alter prison overcrowding, one of the most enduring problems that prison administrators face in many prisons. This is much easier said than actually done for one obvious reason: prison life is marred with practices that enhance inmate's sense of helplessness against victimization. On the one hand, prison life is highly structured and regulated; on the other hand there is a concrete prison subculture and its resultant inmate typology. Putatively these structures create, enhance, and perpetuate a social environment that rewards those inmates who are the most apt in surviving in the hostile penal

---

23   See "Public Safety, Public Spending: Forecasting America's Population 2007-2011," The Pew Charitable Trusts, Washington, D.C., pp. iii-iv.

social settings and environments. The Chicago School criminologists studied this impact of the penitentiaries, as for example, Donald Clemmer in the 1940s. He called this impact as "prisonization," a term that denoted different debilitating impacts of long-term imprisonment on convicts. Clemmer in his research showed that prisonization gradually deprived many convicts from ability to cope with the non-criminal interpersonal demands of the society once released from prison. What are some of these negative impacts?

Mental Health Problems

The Bureau of Justice Statistics (BJS) in one of its "Special Reports," presents the following picture with respect to the need for mental health facilities in American penitentiaries:

> On June 30, 2000, 1,394 of the Nation's 1,558 State public and private adult correctional facilities reported that they provide mental health services to their inmates. Nearly 70% of facilities housing State prison inmates reported that as a matter of policy, they screen inmates at intake; 65% conduct psychiatric assessment; 51% provide 24-hour mental health care; 71% provide therapy/counseling by trained mental health professionals; 73% distribute psychiatric medications to their inmates; and 68% help released inmates obtain community mental health services.[24]

The Special Report gives an indication of the depth of the mental health problem which is especially acute in facilities which house offenders convicted of serious and capital crimes:

> Mental health screening and treatment policies were more frequently reported by maximum/high-security facilities than by minimum/low-security facilities ... Almost all maximum-security confinement facilities (99%) reported conducting screening and providing some form of treatment. The most common (95%) was the distribution of psychiatric medications and providing mental health therapy/counseling.[25]

The Special Report also provides an educated estimate of the number of mentally ill inmates who are currently housed in various penal institutions throughout the country:

---

24   Beck, Allen, J., (July 2001), Health Treatment in State Prisons, 2000, Bureau of Justice Statistics, NCJ 188215.
25   Beck, Ibid.

In the Special Report, Mental health Treatment of Inmates and Probationers (NCJ 174463), BJS estimated that 16.2% of State prisoners were mentally ill. Drawing from inmate surveys conducted in 1997, BJS found that 10.1% of State inmates reported a mental or emotional condition and 10.7% said they had stayed overnight in a mental hospital or program. Though these estimates depend on inmate self-reports, they provide an overall measure of the need for mental health treatment in State prisons. Assuming these percentages have not changed since the surveys were conducted, an estimated 191,000 inmates in State prisons were mentally ill as of midyear 2000.[26]

Prison-Bound Violence and Addiction

Prison life is also marred with physical violence perpetrated by inmates on one another. This type of violence is partially due to the subculture of aggression, and a pecking order of exploitation of the weak by the stronger that has traditionally prevailed in modern prisons; it is partially also due to the widespread use of alcohol and illicit drugs among inmate population in both state and federal correctional facilities. Another Special Report of the Bureau of Justice Statistics on this subject maintains that:

> In the 1997 Survey of Inmates in State and Federal Correctional Facilities, over 570,000 of the Nation's prisoners (51%) reported the use of alcohol or drugs while committing their offense. While only a fifth of State prisoners were drug offenders, 83% reported past drug use and 57% were using drugs in the months before their offense, compared to 79% and 50% respectively, in 1991. Also 37% of State prisoners were drinking at the time of their offense, up from 32% in 1991.[27]

The highlights of the above cited Special Report on substance abuse among inmate population is of special significance for our argument in this chapter. Accordingly:

- In 1997 over 80% of state and over 70% of federal prisoners reported past drug use; about 1 in 6 of both reported committing their current offenses to obtain money for drugs.
- About 40% of state and 30% of federal prisoners reported a prior binge drinking experience; over 40% of both had driven drunk in the past.
- Overall, 3 and 4 in 5 federal prisoners may be characterized as alcohol- or drug-involved offenders.

---

26 Beck, Ibid., p. 3.

27 Mamula, Christopher, J., (January, 1999), "Substance Abuse and Treatment, State and Federal Prisoners, 1997" Bureau of Justice Statistics, NCJ 172871.

- Over 50% of state and over 40% of federal prisoners had ever (sic) participated in treatment or other programs for substance abuse; a third of state and a quarter of federal prisoners had participated since their admission.
- Among both state and federal prisoners who had used drugs in the month before the offense, about 1 in 7 had been treated for drug abuse since admission; nearly a third had enrolled in other drug abuse programs.
- Since admission 14% of both state and federal prisoners drinking at the time of offense had been treated for alcohol abuse; a third had enrolled in other alcohol abuse programs.[28]

The types of illicit drugs used in prisons give an indication of the oppressive nature of incarceration. Inmates consume alcohol and illicit drugs for various reasons one of which is to psychologically detach the incarcerated-self from the oppressive realities of the larger and collective prison life as well as from its multifaceted dehumanizing subculture of violence. This said, there is no doubt that the consumption of alcohol and illicit drugs is one of the main causes of physical violence (see Tables 5.1 and 5.2) perpetrated within the prison confines by inmates on one another.

As Table 5.1 clearly shows, during 1991–1997, general illicit drug use in state correctional facilities went up by 3.6%. When categorized into types of illicit drugs used, the highest percentage of change (3.2%) applied to Marijuana/hashish, a category which is considered as recreational whose main impact is to alter the mind and therefore the mood of the user. Next, is the hallucinogenic category whose consumption went up by (1.8%). Other categories include drugs such as crack cocaine, heroin as well as both depressants and stimulants whose consumption went down by 0.2%, 0.7%, 0.3% and 1.4% respectively. It is plausible to suggest that the use and pushing of illicit drugs in both the state and the federal penitentiaries is perhaps tolerated to some extent to placate inmates. Access to illicit drugs is allowed perhaps with the idea that such allowance would make the drab realties of incarceration more palatable. This is problematic considering the fact that both the illicit drugs and alcohol differ in their comportment. Some users become more amenable to the social surroundings, others become more obtuse, violent and unmanageable. What is certain is that alcohol and illicit drugs are responsible for a wide range of crime and deviance that take place as documented in Table 5.2.

---

28   Mamula, *Ibid.*

Table 5.1 Illicit drugs used in State correctional facilities between 1991–1997

Type of drug	1997	1991
Any drug	83.0%	79.4%
Marijuana/hashish	77.0	73.8
Cocaine/crack	49.2	49.4
Heroin/opiates	24.5	25.2
Depressants	23.7	24.0
Stimulants	28.3	29.7
Hallucinogens	28.7	26.9
Inhalants	14.4	–

Source: Adapted from Table 2 of the Special Report, Substance Abuse and Treatment, State and Federal Prisoners, 1997, NCJ 172871.

The prison setting also breeds an exploitative web of relationships at the apex of which is the Prison Industries exploiting inmate population as an almost unlimited source of cheap labor. Next is a kind of tacitly approved prison-bound, and, yet, underground market whose primary products include: illicit drugs, cigarettes and chewing tobacco, alcoholic beverages, pornographic material, prostitution and gambling. This underground market is controlled and regulated by a range of criminal enterprises that may include gang affiliated prison inmates, and even correctional staff. Writing about Los Angeles County Jail, Noah Lhotsky depicts the following picture of this underground market in one of the largest jail facilities in the USA:

When you get processed into this place, you are packed like sardines into holding cells where it's literally standing room only. You'll be there for about six hours or so, until you and a large group of people are finally taken into a room where you strip out of your clothes, never to see them again. At least I never did.

Then you take a fast cold shower and put on your County blues, take a photo, eat a sandwich, watch a video welcoming you to the jungle, and are asked if you have any medical problems. Then you are put in another crowded holding area dirtier than Tijuana, for another six hours, people pulling tobacco and crack pipes out of their assess, junkies getting sick. The Homies kickin' it talking neighborhood ped, fools getting beat up for their shoes or tobacco, and you might breathe a sigh of relief when some steroided-out deputies come and call names. And if you are one of those names, you go to the infamous 9500 dorm to search for a bunk to kick it on, because you ain't getting no sleep here: lights on continuously, fights, beatings, the Homies looking for victims.[29]

29   Lhtosky, Noah, (2000), "The L.A. County Jail" p. 211, in Robert Johnson and Hans Toch (eds), *Crime and Punishment: Inside Views*, (Los Angeles, CA, Roxbury Publishing

Table 5.2 Alcohol or illicit drug induced offenses during the time of commission in USA

Type of offense	ENSP	ENFP	SPUDI%	FPUDI%	SPUAI%	FPUAI%
Total	**1,046,705**	**88,018**	**52.5**	**34.0**	**37.2**	**20.4**
Violent offenses	494,349	13,021	51.9	39.8	41.7	24.5
Murder	122,435	1,288	52.4	52.4	44.6	38.7
Negligent manslaughter	16,592	53	56.0	----	52.0	----
Sexual assault	89,328	713	45.2	32.3	40.0	32.3
Robbery	148,001	8,770	55.6	37.6	37.4	18.0
Assault	97,897	1,151	51.8	50.5	45.1	46.0
Other violent	20,096	1,046	48.2	37.2	39.6	32.2
Property offenses	230,177	5,964	53.2	22.6	34.5	15.6
Burglary	111,884	294	55.7	----	37.2	----
Larceny/theft	43,936	414	54.2	----	33.7	----
Motor vehicle theft	19,279	216	51.2	----	32.2	----
Fraud	28,102	4,283	42.8	14.5	25.2	10.4
Other property	26,976	757	53.2	34.6	36.0	22.8
Drug offenses	216,254	55,069	52.4	34.6	27.4	19.8
Possession	92,373	10,094	53.9	36.0	29.6	21.3
Trafficking	117,926	40,053	50.9	35.0	25.5	19.4
Other drug	5,955	4,922	59.2	29.0	29.9	19.7
Public-order offenses	103,344	13,026	56.2	30.2	43.2	20.6
Weapons	25,642	6,025	41.8	37.1	28.3	23.0
Other public order	77,702	7,001	60.9	24.1	48.1	18.5

Source: Adapted from Table 1, Special Report, "Substance Abuse and Treatment, State and Federal Prisoners, 1997, p. 3. ENSP: Estimated Number of State Prisoners ENFP: Estimated Number of Federal Prisoners SPUDI: State Prisoners Under Drug Influence (during commission of crime) SFUDI: Federal Prisoners Under Drug Influence (during commission of crime) SPUAI: State Prisoners Under Alcohol Influence (during commission of crime) FUPAI: Federal Prisoners Under Alcohol Influence (during commission of crime).

Co.), pp. 211–213.

However, the jails provide the first and yet a temporary step in the incarceration process. Therefore, it could be argued that the above picture is misleading insofar as the nature of prison life is concerned. In fact, one could argue that unlike jails, prison inmates have constitutionally protected rights enumerated in various statues some of which we discuss below.

Prison Reform

American penal institutions are no longer conceived as "primitive" due to many reforms that both state and federal prisons have gone through; in the post 9/11 terrorism events, prisons are conceived as potential recruiting grounds for Islamic terrorism. In the past, convicts upon release sought the helping hand of the community and the Judeo-Christian spirit of forgiveness for positive reintegration into society. The Civil Rights era ushered in state and federally sponsored programs that attempted to reform the penal institutions as well as helping post-release reintegration. Examples include accreditation criteria against which the efficacy of penal measures and programs administered in federal, state and local penal institutions must be measured for further operation allowance. These criteria were created by the American Correctional Association in 1954. The American Correctional Association, among other stated objectives, aimed to professionalize American Corrections, one of the colossal components of the American Criminal Justice System that administers correctional population composed of jail, prison, parole and probation population.

Another reform came through the auspices of the President's Commission on Law Enforcement and Administration of Justice (1967) that, among other reform measures, provided much needed research funds and wherewithal for improving the conditions of correctional institutions. Similar attempts were exerted as the American Friends Service Committee (1971) tried to articulate a more comprehensive justice-based correctional reform measures. The National Advisory Commission on Criminal Justice Standards (1974) also tried to strategically overhaul American criminal justice system. Other developments, more of legal reform nature, included efforts to inculcate equity into the sentencing schemes as, for example, Determinate Sentencing in California (1977), or the United States Sentencing Guidelines (1987) whose objective was to overcome some of the more egregious disparities in sentencing practices. Correctional literature has dealt with both the rate of success and failure of such post-release reintegration programs.

Civil Rights in American Prisons

Inmates in both state and federal prisons enjoy a number of constitutionally protected civil rights as previously mentioned. These rights, observes Jon R. Ferrar, relate to the First, Sixth, Eighth, and Fourteenth Amendments to the Constitution of the US.[30] Accordingly, these amendments provide the following protective rights:

1. freedom of speech;
2. freedom of religion;
3. freedom of press;
4. the right to be informed of the nature and causes of the accusation;
5. the right to have assistance of counsel to his defense;
6. the right to be free from cruel and unusual punishment;
7. the right to due process and equal protection of the law.[31]

Theoretically speaking, the violation of these rights of the inmates may constitute a cause of action for filing a suite at both state and federal courts by any inmate; in doing so, the inmates may allege that one or several of their constitutionally protected rights have been violated. It is through the provisions of 42 U.S.C. Section 1983 that inmates file civil rights violation suites in federal courts.[32] To prevail in such suits observes Farrar, the inmate has to show that (1) the prison staff and administrators violated a certain protected right under the so-called collar of the state, and (2) that such was a clear violation of a statute, or of constitutionally protected rights of the inmate by the officials in charge of the penitentiaries.[33] Giving various examples, Farrar writes that:

> The major cases of the 1970s and 1980s have been class action lawsuits involving prison conditions. In Texas, for example, the entire prison system was examined. The United States District Court for the Eastern District of Texas issued remedial orders concerning almost every facet of the operation of the prison system (see *Ruitz v. Estelle*, 1982).[34]

The US Supreme Court has confirmed that prisoners do indeed have rights albeit stressing that these are fewer in number compared to those of the free citizens, subject to both the security and safety considerations of the penitentiaries and of their staff. The case in point is *Wolff v. McDonell*, 1974.[35] Writing about the case, Louis Fisher maintains that:

---

30   Farrar, Jon R. (1996), "IV. Civil Rights" p. 287, in Marilyn D. McShane and Frank P. Williams III (eds), *Encyclopedia of American Prisons*, New York, NY, Garland Publishing, Inc., pp. 287–289.
31   Farrar, Ibid.
32   Ibid.
33   Ibid.
34   Ibid.
35   Ibid., p. 289.

The *Wolff* standard divided the Court 5 to 4 in 1995 when it held that Due Process Clause did not afford a prisoner a protected liberty interest to prevent prison officials from denying him the right to present witnesses during a disciplinary hearing that led to segregated confinement.[36]

In 1967, The President's Commission on Law Enforcement and the Administration of Justice was instituted by an Act of Congress. One purpose of the act was to inform the public of the plight of crime and justice in this country at a time that urban America seemed almost under the choking hold of crime. In addition, the Report shed light on how American penitentiaries handled prison-bound turmoil (e.g., illicit drug pushing petty criminals, prisons riots). It was this Commission, writes Rick Steinman that " ... recommended grievance procedures for prisoners."[37] The federal prison system followed suit and in 1974 initiated its inmate grievance procedure.[38] Ironically, the federal government had passed The Civil Rights Act of 1871 under whose 1983 Section state prisoners are allowed to file suits alleging the violation of their civil rights due to inadequate conditions of confinement.[39] Following the case of *Patsey v. Florida Board of Regents*, Congress reconsidered the conditions under which a section 1983 suit could be filed with the end result being the adoption of "exhaustion requirement of section 1997e" observes Steinman.[40]

Another safeguard is The Civil Rights of Institutionalized Persons Act of 1997. The Act has three main components which Steinman has reproduced in his article as follows:

* The United States attorney general may institute a civil action in a US District Court against a party he has reasonable cause to believe is violating the act, in order to ensure that corrective measures are taken (42 USC 1197a).
* Inmates must first "exhaust the internal prison grievance" process prior to personally filing a lawsuit under the act. This permits a federal court to continue an inmate action filed under 42 USC 1983 (commonly referred to as a 1983 federal civil rights action), for a period not exceed ninety days, so that an opportunity is available for the matter informally through a prison grievance system (42 USC 1997e(a)(1)).
* It must be certified that state inmate "grievance systems" follow specified minimum standards. The U.S. attorney general or the applicable U.S. district court must determine that state administrative remedies (prison grievance

---

36   Fischer, Louis (1999), *American Constitutional Law, volume 2, Constitutional Rights*, Durham, NC, Carolina Academic Press, third edn, p. 1010.

37   Steinman, Rick, (1996), "Civil Rights of Institutionalized Persons Act," p. 83, in *Encyclopedia of American Prisons,* pp. 83–86.

38   Steinman, Ibid.

39   Steinman, Ibid., pp. 83–84.

40   Steinman, Ibid., p. 84.

systems) are in "substantial compliance" with the minimum acceptable standards. If not, a court will not permit a ninety-day continuance to resolve a 42 USC 1983 action (42 USC 1997e(b)(2)).[41]

The Act provides an internal administrative venue next to an external one for prison inmate grievances to be redressed. This said, there is no doubt that a prison is theoretically designed for both penance and rehabilitative purposes. Thus prisons, as penal institutions, must be secure enough to safeguard the general public from convicts housed in them. Correctional scholars have addressed the relationship between the security concerns of the penitentiaries and their impacts on the nature of the prison life. For example, Norval Morris writes that, "Prisons range in security from double-barred steel cages within high-walled, electronically monitored perimeters to rooms in unlocked buildings in unfenced fields."[42] After giving a number of examples in regard to this diverse nature of the prisons, Morris observes further that:

> It would be an error to assume that most of these late-twentieth-century mutations of the prison tend toward leniency and comfort. The most common prisons are the overcrowded prisons proximate to the big cities of America; they have become places of deadening routine punctured by bursts of fear and violence. Nor is there a clear trend in either direction: traditional, massive prisons and modern, smaller prisons both proliferate.[43]

To those readers who may raise objection to making life easy for convicted criminals, my response is that a thoughtfully constructed penitentiary is capable of being turned into a place for both penance and rehabilitation provided that American penal philosophy were to remain loyal to its original intent: the centrality of penance in the rehabilitation of the convict next to its punitive aspects. American penitentiaries, however, have egregiously digressed from their original rehabilitative agenda that the humanitarian penologists, the likes of Benjamin Rush, had proposed. Gradually being transformed into oppressive and dehumanizing institutions, the American penitentiaries of the twentieth century, by and large, have basically functioned to warehousing the urban indigents be it white, black, or Hispanic. This is despite the fact that the history of American prison reform extends as far as 1790 whence the Walnut Street Jail was opened in Philadelphia.

---

41   Steinman, Ibid.

42   Morris, Norvall, "The Contemporary Prison" p. 202, in Norval Morris and David J. Rothman (eds), *The Oxford History of the Prison: The Practice of Punishment in Western Society*, New York, NY, Oxford University Press, pp. 202–231.

43   Norvall, Ibid.

Forced-Homosexuality and HIV Infections in Prisons

American state and federal penitentiaries have inadvertently been transformed into semi-shooting galleys in which inmates have access to all kind of illicit drugs and alcoholic beverages for daily consumption, being exposed to a subculture of violence and forced homosexuality marred with predatory crime which if were to occur in public, the perpetrator would be charged with the crime of aggravated rape in most cases. Next to mental health, there are other health problems such as HIV infection among both prison and jail populations. The Bureau of Justice Statistics gives the following picture pertaining to the prevalence of HIV in state penal institutions quoted below:

> Between 1995 and 1999 the number of HIV-positive prisoners grew at a slower rate than the overall prison population (19%).
>
> At year-end 1999, 3.4% of all female State prison inmates were HIV positive compared to 2.1% of males.
>
> New York held more than a quarter of all prison inmates (7,000) known to be HIV positive at year- end 1999.
>
> In State prisons 27% of HIV-positive inmates were confirmed AIDS cases; in Federal prisons, 37% had AIDS.
>
> The overall rate of confirmed AIDS among the Nation's prison population (0.60%) was 5 times the rate in the U.S. general population (0.12%).
>
> The number of AIDS-related deaths has been dramatically decreasing since 1995. In 1999 there were fewer than a quarter of AIDS related deaths (242) than in 1995 (1,010).
>
> Among jail inmates, the HIV infection rate was highest in the largest jail jurisdiction. In 43 of the 50 largest jurisdictions that reported data, 2.3% were HIV positive compared to 1.1% in jurisdictions with fewer than 100 inmates.
>
> New York City, the second largest jail jurisdiction, held 1,165 jail inmates known to be HIV positive (7.1% of its inmates).
>
> Between July 1, 1998, and June 30, 1999, 1 in 12 deaths among jail inmates were due to AIDS-related causes.[44]

44   Maruschack, Laura, M., (July 2001), "HIV in Prisons and Jails, 1999" Bureau of Justice Statistics Bulletin, NCJ 187456.

The data is self-explanatory. The spread of HIV infection in prison settings is due to the forced nature of homosexual relationships and the wide-spread use of intravenous use of narcotic drugs. This subculture of illicit drugs and predatory crime and violence could and should be stopped.

Adverse Impacts of Incarceration on African-American Community

One central premise of this book is that in modern open-ended class societies built on the dynamics of the free-market and its patriarchal culture, adult males play an irreplaceable role in the proper socialization of children within the family structure; it is the patriarchal family that in conjunction with the patriarchal educational system prepares the youngsters for success within the complex and multifaceted web of socioeconomic parameters. As discussed in previous chapters, from 1960s onwards, the inner-city African-American community is gradually being deprived of its adult males either lost to the intra-racial violence or to the correctional institutions. This disappearance is now manifesting its deeply adverse social, economic and behavioral impacts on inner-city African-American community in general, and on the institution of black family and youths in particular. This disappearance is of a multifactor rather than a monist nature thus the rationale for characterizing it as the Black Male Disappearance Syndrome in this book. The rest of this chapter briefly discusses the consequences of the disappearance syndrome as a prelude to positing prison-bound Islam's challenge to American penology.

Black Male Disappearance Syndrome

Disproportionate incarceration of the African-American males is not solely due to crime commission, but one that is also being engendered by the operational functions of a complex legal process though which American criminal justice system dispenses penal justice. Historically speaking, American criminal justice system has been structured to dispense penal justice through the establishment of legal guilt which is different than actual guilt. Legal guilt is established through an adversarial process governed by the constitutional checks and balances and case law on the one hand. On the other hand this adversarial process is being impacted every step of the way (from arrest to resolution of the criminal case) by what is known as the SES (Social and Economic Status). The established wisdom is that criminal defendants who can better maneuver within the federal or state criminal trial systems fare better than those who are less able to do so.

   The core problem of American inner-cities where large number of ghettoes, barrios and slums are located is that they are no longer viable for raising functional families, properly educating youngsters and preparing them for success within the periphery, let alone mainstream, American socioeconomic structures. The inner-cities are the areas that have historically housed a large segment of the African-American community from the 1930s to present. There was a time that inner-city was viable as, for example, during post World War I. Examples include the Harlem in New York, Oakland in San Francisco, and various inner city neighborhoods in Chicago, Boston, Baltimore, Saint Louis, Houston and Raleigh to name but a few. One main reason for the viability of these inner-city neighborhoods during industrialization of America in late nineteenth and early twentieth centuries had something to do with the strength of the Black family and church and synagogues next to black pride in hard and honest work. Of especial significance was the fact that inner-city communities were being served by a chain of what has historically become known as "the mamas and papas" shops and business ventures that gave both meaning and strength to the socioeconomic viability of inner-city communal life. A look at the cadre of Black leaders (in politics or religious and civic circles next to musicians, artists, writers, poets and civil servants) that the post WWI era produced is a tale that tells of this era's viability and strength. In fact, a number of important Black movements (e.g., the Harlem Renaissance, 1916–1939) and organizations such as the NAACP, and the NOI were founded on this very inner-city strength to which reference shall be made later in this and subsequent chapters.

In contrast to the first half of the twentieth century, in the second half of the twentieth century and especially from mid 1960s to present inner-city life in America has gradually become subjugated to the retrogressively adverse impacts of what is known as Post-Industrialization. During its ascendency, American industrialization priorities centered around world supremacy in steel and manufacturing industries that occurred during late nineteenth and early twentieth centuries. This supremacy enabled American manufactured products (e.g., automobile, textile and home appliances) to saturate internal as well as external markets. Post-Industrialization, spearheaded by the application of modern computers to American Service Industry, led to the gradual demise of American steel and manufacturing industries which in turn drastically restructured American economy, work, education and employment practices. As a result of further stages of post-industrialization, inner-city life and economy suffered tremendously due to chronic unemployment that in conjunction with the migration of the various strata of the middle class to the suburbs, left the inner-city to its own devices. Thus the once socioeconomically viable inner-cities were transformed into dysfunctional, socially disorganized and criminogenic ghettoes, barrios and slums, populated with a large segment of the low-skilled and poorly educated strata of the working-class next to outright socioeconomically disenfranchised. Organized criminal gangs found inner city barrios, ghettoes and slums suitable grounds for pushing of highly addictive illicit drugs; as these criminal gangs were mushrooming around the lucrative illicit drug niches and markets, they also structured a wide range of petty-criminal networks who proliferated inner-city neighborhoods with illegally obtained and or smuggled hand guns and ammunition that resulted in much of the inner city drive-by shootings and other type of intra-racial animosity. The so-called black on black violence was the natural outcome of these factors.

Among some radical circles the disappearance syndrome is due to a deliberate and multifaceted genocidal policy that white America is allegedly pursuing against black America for two intertwined long-term purposes: (1) to either wipe out adult black males from American society altogether, or (2) to further reduce inner-city African-American neighborhoods to a life of perpetual poverty, infested with drug-induced violence and crime.[45] The academic approach to the causes of the black male disappearance syndrome is more sophisticated than the monist approach of radical circles because academic approach tries to articulate the contributory role of social, economic, political and legal factors that have historically worked against a more comprehensive integration of the African-American community in main stream American social and political life.

African-American Criminology on Disappearance Syndrome

One academic paradigm on black male disappearance syndrome has been articulated by the African-American criminologist and justice practitioners. The disproportionate incarceration of the African-American males in conjunction with other correctional strategies—some of which we mentioned in previous chapters—has given a powerful voice to a new cadre of African-American criminologists and justice practitioners to critique the issue of the fairness of the American penal philosophy. By and large, this cadre argues that American penal strategies, applied regularly against economically-challenged black males, are unjust representing legalistic racism. To remedy this state of affairs, a number of African-American criminologists and justice practitioners have proposed that American criminological thinking is desperately in need of an "insider-based" explanatory paradigm to explore various dimensions of the disappearance syndrome. The insider-based paradigm is intellectually generated by those scholars who have established a generic relationship with inner-city African-American neighborhoods and thus are capable of providing both unbiased data and analytical strategies for a more thorough explanation of the causes of the black male disappearance syndrome.

The Etiology of Black Crime: The Insider-Based Perspective

Writing on the importance of an "insider-based" view of causes and consequences of the Black crime problem, Vernetta D. Young and Ann T. Sulton acknowledge the fact that crime is one of the most urgent issues that African-American community faces. The authors caution that for almost a century, there existed an "insider-based" explanation of the etiology of Black crime problem thanks to the untiring

---

45   Miller, Jerome G., *Search and Destroy: African-American Males in the Criminal Justice System*, Cambridge University Press, 1997; see also Jawanza Kunjufu, (2004), *Countering the Conspiracy to Destroy Black Boys*, (African American Images).

efforts of African-American criminologists who have vigorously studied it.[46] Thus, the problem of the American criminology is not that it lacks an insider-based perspective on the subject of Black crime problem, but that mainstream white criminology has systematically ignored it. This neglect, whether intentional or inadvertent, observe Young and Sulton, has deprived the field of American criminology from a much needed insider-based perspective.

Young and Sulton also stress on the explanatory power of structural inequalities in relation to the etiology of inner-city crime, most of which is of an *intra*, rather than, *inter* racial nature, a phenomenon well documented in criminology research as, for example, by Samuel Walker et al., to which reference has been made in previous chapter. Acknowledging the fact that a significant generic relationship exists between structural inequalities and inner-city crime, Young and Sulton, however, do not attribute a kind of society-made-me-do-it blame mentality to the insider-based perspective. They note that this perspective does not dismiss the role of the individuals in crime commission either.[47] The insider-based perspective, however, reminds us that although most African-Americans are law-abiding citizens, the etiology of Black crime problem ought to be taken in its holistic and social context implying that crime is a complex and multidimensional social product. Thus the traditional approach based on official statistics of the Uniform Crime Reports (the UCR.) or the National Crime Victimization Survey (NCVS) alone is not of much value for the etiology of Black crime problem. The insider-based perspective also assails the disproportionate paradigm, discussed below.

The Insider-Based Paradigm versus Disproportionate Paradigm

The disproportionate incarceration paradigm, a product of the critical criminology utilizes, among others, official statistics and maintains that the African-American share of crime and delinquency is disproportionate to its size in the general population. The insider-based perspective rejects this paradigm arguing that with the debilitating and wide range of criminogenic conditions surrounding life in inner-city American ghettoes, barrios and slums, the present level of black crime not only is not disproportionate, but in fact is much less than what it ought to be. The disproportionate paradigm is premised on "every thing is being equal," which is a false premise, argue Young and Sulton. Disproportionate paradigm would become valid only if all the relevant factors were indeed equal among White and Black Americas; such factors not only are not equal but indeed are manifestly unequal, further maintain Young and Sulton. The socioeconomic, political, and

---

46   Young, V., Sulton, A.T., (1996), "Excluded: The Current Status of African-American Scholars in the Field of Criminology and Criminal Justice" p. 1, in A.T. Sulton (ed.), *African-American Perspectives: On Crime Causation, Criminal Justice Administration, and Crime Prevention*, (Newton, MA, Butterworth-Heinemann), pp. 1–15.

47   Young and Sulton, Ibid., p. 3.

legal factors are distributed unequally among social strata in the United States being manifestly unequal when it comes to the realities of inner-city life.

In sum, the proponents of an insider-based perspective argue that because there is no comparable base between White and Black Americas in terms of social, economic, political and legal indices, the crime comparison is meaningless. To meaningfully assail the problem of crime and juvenile delinquency within the African-American community, Young and Sulton suggest that criminologists have to address the differential contributory impacts of nine factors that they have identified quoted below:

1. Equal and just administration of criminal laws
2. Equal access to education opportunities
3. Economic revitalization of African-American neighborhoods
4. Community control of institutions and agencies providing services to African-American neighborhoods
5. Improvement in African-American's quality of life
6. Teaching African-Americans conflict resolution skills
7. Providing productive activities for African-American youngsters
8. Enacting legislation aimed at curbing handgun sales
9. Improving African-Americans' racial identity[48]

The list is a comprehensive one which implies that those who adhere to an insider-based perspective consider the black crime problem a direct outcome of social, economic, political and legal inequalities that have permeated American racial relationships for a long time. In fact, there are those social critics such as Jonathan Kozol who has argued that the inequalities between the Black and White Americas are of a "savage" nature.[49] One of the most disturbing among these inequalities relates to inner-city poverty and its impact on children. The Joint Center for Political and Economic Studies web page, citing the United States Census Bureau reported that:

> In 2001, 16.3% of the children in the United States lived in households with incomes below the federal poverty line of $18,104 for a family of four. In 2001, African American and Hispanic children (about 30.2%) were more than twice as likely to be poor as white children (13.4%).

> In 2001, 28.2% of all young children (ages 0 to 6) lived in near poverty. From 1977 to 2001, the poverty rate for children less than six years of age grew from 18% to 19.3%. In 2001, nearly half (56%) of African American and 45.5 of Hispanic children in this age group lived below 125 percent of the poverty line

---

48   Young and Sulton, Ibid., p. 5.
49   Kozol, Jonathan, (1991), *Savage Inequalities: Children in America's Schools*, New York, Crown Publishers, Inc.

Two thirds of all poor young children (66.1 percent) live with at least one parent who is employed. The comparable percentage for young Hispanic children (71.1%) is higher than that of white (64.8%) and black (62.4%) children.[50]

These statistics show a strong correlation between poverty and traditional minority status (Black and Hispanic) in the United States. Other inequalities relate to education, housing, health care, justice and a host of other factors that comprise social quality of life in inner-city ghettoes, barrios and slums.

A Critique

The factors enumerated by Young and Sulton are important for a more comprehensive analysis of the etiology and epidemiology of Black crime problem that has led, among others, to Disappearance syndrome. Delineation of the contributory role of these factors could help policy makers in their reform efforts, be it in formulating or implementing a more humane and equitable penal measures, or in stamping out the root causes of crime and violence in inner city neighborhoods. It is in these neighborhoods that the bulk of the predatory crimes such as robbery, aggravated assault and gang-related homicide take place. However, the thrust of the insider-based perspective is not much different from that of the mainstream critical approach in criminology, an approach based on the notion that to stamp out crime we need to improve the social and economic conditions of life in inner-city neighborhoods. Thus, if we take these demands as the building-blocks of the insider-based perspective, Young and Sulton seem to be saying that the resolution of the crime problem eventuates if both federal and state governments were to allocate enough money, time and energy to inner-city problem areas. In fact, Young and Sulton are very explicit on the social policy implications of the insider-based perspective as they conclude:

> Thus, any sincere effort to deal with the crime problem must address the problems of unemployment, substandard housing, inadequate health care, physical deterioration, teenage pregnancy, economic development, self-esteem, drugs, family deterioration, racism and discrimination, plus other social and economic ills.[51]

There are two major problems with the insider-based perspective as formulated by Young and Sulton. First, there is a bulky literature on American social reform initiatives, including those that Young and Sulton have identified above, in relation

---

50   "Children Living in Poverty" cited in the Joint Center for Economic and Political web page at: http://www.jointcenter.org/DB/factsheet/chilpovt.htm.

51   Young and Sulton, "Excluded: The Current Status of African-American Scholars in the Field of Criminology and Criminal Justice" Ibid., p. 5.

to larger public remedial expenditures from 1960s to present. For example, the Great Society initiatives of the President Lyndon B. Johnson (1963–1968) undertook a number of important socioeconomic and legal remedial initiatives among which one could mention: (1) The Civil Rights Act of 1964 that forbade race-based job and public accommodation discrimination; (2) The Social Security Act of 1965 that authorized the federal funding of the Medicare; (3) The Economic Opportunity Act of 1964 that provided a measure of economic equity for all; (4) The Voting Rights Act of 1965 that guaranteed minority registration and voting rights; (5) The Elementary and Secondary Education Act of 1965 that allowed federal funding in public education; (6) The Higher Education Act of 1965 that increased federal funding to universities and low-interests loans for needy students attending colleges and universities; (7) Title XIX of the Social Security Act of 1966 that created the Medicaid to improve health care costs of the economically challenged. Similar Congressional Acts followed suit in the next decades that we need not repeat here. There is an extensive research literature showing that some of these initiatives improved the general quality of social life for Black America and some others failed to do so. Thus, the etiology and/or the epidemiology of Black crime problem are continually being addressed in the academe as well as among government policy makers at both federal and state levels. The advocates of the insider-based perspective may find these efforts inefficacious, but they can't argue that these issues have not been addressed since the mid 1960s to present.

The second problem is that Young and Sulton sound as if no positive changes have taken place in the overall quality of social and economic life of the African-American community from the time of the Civil Rights Movement (1955–1968) to present. Black America is no longer subjected to the debilitating and highly insidious job, housing and educational segregation schemes of the pre-Civil Rights Era. Nor black citizens are being subjected to Jim Crow type of vigilantism, institutionalized racism and overt discrimination of the past. Again, we can approach these positive changes from the perspective of both American media and academe. For example, the Newsweek magazine reported that in the 1990s the following positive changes took place:

> Black employment and home ownership are up. Murders and other violent crimes are down. Reading and math proficiency are climbing. Out-of- wed-lock births are at their lowest rate in four decades. Fewer blacks are on welfare than at any point in recent memory. More are in college than at any point in history. And the percentage of black families living below the poverty line is the lowest it has been since the Census Bureau began keeping separate black statistics in 1967. Even for some of the most persistently unfortunate-uneducated black men between 16 and 24-jobs are opening up, according to a just-released study of

hard-luck cases in 322 urban areas by researchers at Harvard University and the College of William and Mary.[52]

The article was based on some of the findings of the Joint Center for Political and Economic Studies which the Newsweek magazine described it as "the Nation's premier think tank on blacks and politics." Some of these advances were as follows:

According to the Center, the number of blacks elected officials has nearly sextupled since 1970, and now stands nearly 9,000. In a poll late last year by the Center, blacks were more likely than whites–for the first time in the history of this survey–to say they were better off financially than in the previous year (51 percent compared with 31.5 percent). A new Newsweek Poll confirms that the finding is not a fluke. Seventy-one percent of blacks (compared with 59 percent of whites told Newsweek's pollsters that they expected their family incomes to rise during the next 10 years. Fifty-seven percent of blacks (compared with 48 percent of whites) foresaw better job opportunities ahead.[53]

There is, however, another side to the story that Newsweek magazine also reported. In the same manner that a relatively small scale middle-class Black America was emerging in the 1990s, there was and remains a much larger segment living in America's inner-city slums, ghettoes and barrios that putatively seem almost left to their perpetual demise. The voice of this large segment can be heard in the lamenting of the likes of Malik Burns, a resident of South Central Los Angeles who, reported the Newsweek magazine, did not buy the above rosy picture about this improvement saying, "this society does not want us to make it." Malik Burn's socioeconomic status was described by the Newsweek magazine:

In a small, spotless one-bedroom apartment he shares with his wife and three children, posters of Malcolm X share wall space with a pair of food stamps, reminders of the family's battles with dire poverty. There are times, he says, when he has skipped meals so that his children can eat. Burns jabs the air with a finger. "If a few blacks are succeeding, it's only because they ... have been let in through the cracks to pacify the rest of us. But if they haven't been able to help their own people, what good does it do?"[54]

This deep-rooted cynicism of the likes of Malik Burns, who live by the millions in America's inner-city neighborhoods, stems from one core factor that surrounds life in the ghettoes: the sense of continually being victimized despite the fact that

52 "The Special Report: The Good News About America," p. 30, in *Newsweek*, June 7, 1999, pp. 30–40.
53 "The Special Report: The Good News About America," Ibid., p. 30.
54 The Special Report, Ibid., p. 38.

African-American community has historically been used to hard and honest work with a strong belief in family, faith in God and abiding by law. The Newsweek magazine reflected Malik Burns's sense of victimization in these words:

> For all their work, the family remains below the poverty line, a counterpoint to the national statistics of the black progress. "I wouldn't say things are positive right now," says Malik, "if the only way we can survive is work two or three minimum-wage jobs–assuming you can get them." The legacy of inequality, he says, is not resolved by a momentary upturn in the economy. Rather, it is in the weave of the American tapestry. "It's a myth to think things are better for black families right now," he says. "In many ways, they are worse than ever."[55]

The sentiments expressed in the above paragraph very likely represent the concerns of the socially and economically disenfranchised inner-city African-American males whose cynicism towards this state of affairs is reaffirmed routinely by being exposed to the phenomenon of *intra-racial* crime and violence which has become the permanent feature of daily life in ghettoes; it is this *intra-racial* (aka black on black) crime and violence which links, quite negatively, the minority communities with the criminal justice agencies be it the police, courts or corrections. To give an example, from 1980s to present, most states have been on the side of the law and order philosophy in the administration of justice. This is despite the fact that as of July, 1999, the U.S. Department of Justice's Bureau of Justice Statistics (BJS) reported that:

- The nation's violent crime rate fell 7 percent last year and was 27 percent lower than in 1993, the Justice Department's Bureau of Justice Statistics (BJS) announced today. The property crime fell 12 percent during 1998 and was 32 percent lower than in 1993.
- Both violent crimes (rape, sexual assault, robbery and assault) and property crimes (burglary, theft and motor vehicle theft) were at their lowest level since BJS began its National Crime Victimization Survey in 1973. In 1998 there were an estimated 37 violent victimization per 1,000 U.S. residents 12 years old and older, and an estimated 217 completed or attempted property crimes per 1,000 U.S. households.
- Murders in the United States declined by 8 percent in 1998, according to preliminary data from the Federal Bureau of Investigation's Uniform Crime Report.
- During 1993–1998 period, there were significant decreases in every major type of violent and property crimes the survey measures, and virtually every demographic group experienced substantial drops in violent victimization. For example, in 1998 the rates for males and females were 32 percent lower than in 1993, and victimization against blacks decreased by 42 percent. Property

---

55   The Special Report, Ibid., p. 38.

crime rates during the 6-year period also decreased for all demographic groups examined.[56]

Was there a causal relationship between disproportionate incarceration and the subsequent noticeable fall in every major violent and property crime in the 1990s? In theory, one could make a logical case by arguing that general incarceration, as a crime control strategy, not only incapacitates those who commit crime; it is also capable of general deterrence and thereby of reducing crime. Thus, the high general incarceration rates of the 1990s, although may look unjust, ought to have helped the overall reduction in the commission of both violent and property crimes as shown by the above Bureau of Justice Statistics data. But this is a misleading conclusion because as discussed in previous chapters, it has been established that excepting for aggravated rape and homicide, the bulk of the violent and property crime is being committed by economically challenged white males. So what is the core problem? Why it is that the male disappearance syndrome is manifestly operating in the African-American community and not in any other traditional minority communities (e.g. Hispanic, Asian American, Middle Eastern)?

Male Authority and Patriarchy

Historically and throughout the world it has been the male (father), rather than the female (mother), who has been portrayed as the primary authority figure whose main responsibility is to inculcate discipline in the mind and the daily routines of juveniles (be at home, school or society at large). The male (father) figure has also been portrayed as the "protector" of the juveniles—from social harm or criminal elements—charged with the responsibility of "winning bread" for the family. In addition, it is the male figure who inculcates the proper masculine traits in his male offspring so as to enable him to face up to his responsibilities. In other words, it takes a father to raise a young man in his own image, regardless of race, ethnicity or social class affiliations.

The female figure on the other hand has all along been given a secondary role whose main function has been nurturing both the male and female offspring in accordance with the functional prerequisites of the patriarchal societies. Despite the fact that modern patriarchal societies have gone through decades of democratization processes that have allowed for the application of gender equity, at home, nonetheless, the centuries-old sexual division of labor has remained almost intact: the mother plays the role of nurturer and the father that of the provider-discipliner.

The same male-oriented view applies in the province of crime and justice to the effect that even in modern legal institutions the main authority figures

56   The U.S. Department of Justice, Bureau of Justice Statistic, "U.S. Violent Crime Rate Fell 7 Percent in 1998 27 Percent Lower than 1993: Violent and Property Crimes at Lowest Levels Since Survey Began."

are by and large males (police, courts and corrections) who conscientiously or inadvertently perpetuate a male-perspective in relation to law, crime and justice. Critical criminologists maintain that there is a direct correlation between crime and masculinity as evinced by the fact that the bulk of both property and violent crimes is being committed by males in modern patriarchal societies, including the USA. Instead of seeking the etiology of crime within the social dynamics of patriarchy, the general trend in American criminology has been one of biological and/or sociobiological nature whereby male criminality is being theorized within the construct of biological differences between males and females. Accordingly: on the average males are bigger, more muscular, more aggressive and more violent than females. Thus, males commit more crimes than females and therefore, have to face its penal consequences. However, there is also the contributory role of the family within which the socialization processes unfolds. Instead, the thrust of feminist literature on crime and masculinity is that in modern patriarchal societies the socialization of young boys is qualitatively different than that of the young girls. The former is socialized for assuming the role of the bread-winner whereas the latter is socialized for assuming the role of the home-maker. Radical feminist scholars and criminologists argue that the biological differences notwithstanding, it is the glorification of the culture of violence that desensitizes young boys to crime and violence.[57] The crime differences are due to the construct of power-differentials that gradually emerges as patriarchal societies reproduce their structures and social relations of production. Thus the construct of power-differentials perpetuates a state of affairs between the sexes that is historical at the same time that it is a universally male-designed, maintained, and propagated system of domination, marginalization and exploitation of the females' body and soul within the patriarchal societies, be it medieval-agrarian or modern capitalist. Family is one such structure within whose social, economic, political and ideological parameters the construct of power-differentials has historically been created, refurbished and propagated. There is a bulky literature on this subject to which reference shall be made as such occasion arises.

Reconsideration of the Fatherhood

The merits of Radical feminism notwithstanding, it is the premise of this book that no matter how one approaches the history of the rise of power-differentials (be it in matriarchal or patriarchal societies) there has been and remains a universally and historically validated perception as to what constitutes the core of legitimacy in any construct of power: morality. This book contends that throughout history, legitimate authority has always denoted a moral, upright and positive image as against non-legitimate authority; legitimate authority by necessity has to denote positivity in each and every constituents of it. For example, we tend to believe

---

57   See for example, Messerschmidt, James W., *Masculinities and Crime: Critique and Reconceptualization of Theory*, Rowman & Littlefield Publishers, Inc., 1993.

that a "good" judge is one whose goodness is not because he/she is good in taking bribes, but that the goodness is because he/she is a decent, fair-minded person of legally sound mind and judgment in whose impartiality and logic a case can be trusted so as to garner justice in the application of law. Likewise, a "good" police officer is one whose "goodness" stems from the fact that he/she upholds the law and enforces it without malice and prejudice. One could extend this logic to all aspects of law, police and corrections.

But what are the essential ingredients of a good father? How do we gauge the elements of goodness in a father? How does the goodness of a father help the positive up-bringing of the male offspring (considering the subject matter), and how does it impede male youngsters' road to experimentation with law-infracting behavior, delinquency or criminality? One could ask the same questions about the positive role of the mother figure. How do we determine the characteristics of a good mother as against a bad mother? One could provide logical answers to these questions by reference to much research that scholars have done in the field of family and its dynamics (e.g., its economic base and relations between parents and offspring) as well as in the fields of social psychology, and juvenile delinquency. The name of the game is the socialization process whose most important formative phases take place at home. It is this home-based socialization process that puts the construct of morality in its proper social and historical context. It is from this perspective that incarceration creates its own standards of socialization within the American penal institutions and philosophy, to be critiqued shortly in this chapter. The Black Muslim challenge is that the American penal philosophy does not follow its own penance ideals thus prison-based socialization standards don't help inmate rehabilitation within the penitentiaries. Once released from prison, an ex-convict is neither mentally, nor temperamentally, ready or able for positive re-incorporation in society.

Enter the Socialization Process

From the bulk of studies done on juvenile delinquency, there is consensus in the field that the family plays a central role in proper socialization of the youngsters. The institution of family, from time immemorial, has played a central role in the formation as well as in the enhancement and perpetuation of a set of basic values, norms and mores which putatively steer juveniles through both childhood and adolescence. What are these basic values and how do we successfully inculcate them in our youngsters? Scholars in the field of juvenile delinquency have become more aware of the importance of both pre- and post-puberty socialization processes under the hegemonic control of the father-figure, a long and arduous process during which youngsters learn the propriety in the usage of the language, as well as in acquiring positive personality traits in conjunction with internalization of proper social norms of conduct at home and in public. It goes without saying that proper socialization of the juveniles is multifaceted and takes within the family under the parental love, care, protection, and control of both parents. However, the fact that we are far from having reached ideal family structure, in globalized patriarchal families the role of the father is indispensable despite its complementary nature that we would want to achieve in ideal family settings. We have already covered some of these issues in previous chapters.

The Central Role of Discipline in the Socialization Process

The bulk of the criminological studies on the cause of juvenile crime and delinquency leading to gang formation have stressed on the central role of discipline, arguing that juveniles who get entangled with criminal justice agencies—at an early age— manifestly show signs of lack of discipline next to manifest contempt for law and authority. There is also this general consensus in the field that the seed of the problem is sown most probably within the family. In the past, it was in the paradigm of the so-called "dysfunctional family" that the causes of juvenile crime and delinquency were theorized. Accordingly, a dysfunctional family, headed by one divorcee parent was wrought with all kind of economic, social and disciplinary problems. This perspective is now being gradually replaced with a much more sophisticated one that tries to relate the causes of juvenile crime and delinquency to the putative role of the family, school, community and juvenile justice system. The gist of this new paradigm is that juvenile crime and delinquency is not a simple event but a complex and multifaceted process that centers on a dynamic set of interlocutors whose operational dynamics, of dialectical relations to one another, contextualize the process. For example, a juvenile's incessant exposure to violent and sexually explicit television shows, video games and Internet is capable of negatively influencing the youngster's view of sexuality whereby the seed of an unconscious linkage between violence and sex is sown in his/her thoughts and personality. However, the conduct of the parents at home next to school curriculum that stresses a different approach to love and sexuality may offset the media's negative influences.

The same applies to our depiction of a set of social relationships in which stress is placed on respect for others as against a stress for "looking for number one"; similarly, the role of social and communal institutions next to those of the juvenile justice agencies play important roles in this complex process, to be further expounded upon later in this chapter. It goes without saying that Radical feminist criminologists argue that the general socialization process takes place within modern patriarchal societies in which the male figure has played a central role as the primary authority figure be at home or in society at large. Thus for both male and female offspring the concept of "functionality" of the family is universally centered around the presence of the male figure who by necessity is a good provider, loving and caring husband; in addition, there is this universal perception that such a role-model is not in trouble with law, especially criminal law.

Disproportionate Incarceration: A Two-Pronged Deprivation Process

The gradual disappearance of black males from inner-city African-American life is the end result of a two-pronged socioeconomic and legal deprivation processes that operate as follows. First, disproportionate incarceration systematically deprives the community from its adult male constituents; as fathers/husbands this duo is consistently expected to act as the legitimate provider of goods and services for the self, the family and the community thus for the legitimate socioeconomic success of the community. Second, disproportionate incarceration also deprives the community from its legitimate male power-block. As a result of the two-prong deprivation, inner-city life is open and vulnerable to various forms of criminal predation by a wide range of unsavory characters be it petty criminals, or major criminal gangs with their distinct criminogenic lifestyle. It is noteworthy that disproportionate incarceration is also capable of leading to the rise of the legitimate female power-bloc, a synergy of both material and psychosomatically manifest power construct that arises due to the very presence of adult females doing what its counterpart does. In fact, it is no exaggeration to suggest that from 1960s to present, the dynamics of life in the inner-city is moving in the direction of the replacement of the male power-bloc by female power-bloc. The problem is not this displacement *per se*, but the fact that socioeconomic success in modern patriarchal societies requires the synergy of both rather than one replacing the other.

The above notwithstanding, there is another issue that we need to address at the expense of some digression from our main topic. The American educational system is a manifest middle class complex structure perpetuating middle class norms and values of success. It is this system that functions as the main purveyor of upward social mobility in modern open-ended class societies of which the USA is the prime example in many respects. The American education system has historically been set up to perpetuate patriarchal norms and values. Through socialization processes, youngsters gradually internalize these normative values as they go through developmental stages at home, in school and in communal institutions in becoming young adults. It is the adult males that by and large act as the gate keeper of the American family, education, and socioeconomic and legal organizations that putatively comprise the American market economy.

This modern patriarchal giant, what we call the Americana, owes a lot to its feminine counterpart who has historically been delegated the role of the nurturer be at home, in school or at work. The same applies to other patriarchal societies be it in the developing or developed part of the world. Thus from a macro perspective, one could argue that because modern class societies are patriarchal, it is the Male Power-Bloc—regardless of its denominational categories (e.g., age, race, ethnicity and SES categories) that acts as the gate keeper of both success and failure; this constellation of male power is also capable of promoting legitimate as well as illegitimate role models for the youths. However, within the Male Power Bloc there are different layers of power due to the fact that modern patriarchal societies are built upon modern capitalism which allows various degrees of socioeconomic mobility. In essence, the American Male Power-Bloc is comprised of different denominational categories as aforementioned, therefore the size, and the coherence of competing male power-blocs is of prime significance as they compete with one another for a segment of the economic pie in a society that despite all its advances in both race and gender equity still remains a major patriarchal culture.

The Male Power Bloc and Patriarchy

By this term, I do not mean the physical prowess of the male figure per se, but a synergy of both material and psychosomatically manifest power construct that arises due to the very presence of adult males who earn a decent and law abiding life for themselves and their families; it is this constellation of good guys in any community who can mentor the youths for success in the American society and economy. The significance of the male-power bloc has historically stemmed from the fact that it is capable of functioning as the originator/purveyor of power wherewithal, be it legitimate (law, mores, values and norms) or illegitimate (war, crime, slavery and other forms of violence and exploitation). Because power wherewithal has its concrete socioeconomic and legal and religious parameters to its articulation, the central function of the male power-bloc is the formulation, procurement and safeguarding of its share of power that translates into its share of economic goods, services and privileges within the prevailing power structure. In medieval times, the patriarchy was the power structure shaped, formed in relation to the operational functions of agricultural mode of production, whereas modern patriarchy is built upon modern capitalism as, for example, in the United States of America. American society is endowed with a wide range of socioeconomic and as well as human-capital resources that putatively have created a thriving market economy, democracy and a complex educational system whose motto is that education is a universal right. This constellation of dynamic forces has created an open-ended class structure that allows both upward and downward social mobility for social classes that are composed of different racial and ethnic groups. However, because of differential access to power wherewithal, the success and/or stagnation-failure in the American modern market economy has been divergent. In addition, success or failure has also been dependent on factors such as group consciousness, homogeneity and solidarity. Thus it is logical to argue that the more cohesive, politically active, and economically engaged a group is, or has been in the past, the higher is, or has been, the chances for success and vice versa.

Who Succeeds in American Society and Market Economy?

It is this book's contention that in modern patriarchal societies, as in the past, it is the Male Power Bloc that is the purveyor of power wherewithal; it is this power bloc that defines, interprets the constituents of success as well as institutionalizing differential access to such wherewithal. An example is the concept of the standard of living which has concrete social, economic, legal and consumptive parameters to its articulation next to a set of powerful symbols that accompany it within its American cultural context. However, the standard of living is not a fixed, but a fluxing construct, one that differs inter-socially as well as generationally. Standard of living, however, is a power wherewithal because it has enticed both individuals, social strata, social classes and even states to enter into fierce competition with one another throughout human history. The question is how do we define standard of living? Who defines it and for what purposes? An example is the United States of America whereby a wide range of social, economic, legal and cultural factors have been utilized for creating one of the most complex and heterogeneous living standards. The problem is that next to high standards of living, the persistence of rampant poverty, discontentment and sense of injustice still prevails throughout inner-city neighborhoods despite reform measures that both state and federal governments have initiated intermittently from 1960s to present to revitalize inner city social and economic life in the United States.

It has been and remain within this epistemology of success-failure that various racial and or ethnic male power-blocs that compete with one another steering and enabling the next generations to follow suit. This does not mean, nor should it be construed that, the legitimate female power-bloc does not play important role in this process, it does; however, not in the manner that its male counterpart has historically been allowed to function due to what is known as the operational functions of the power-differentials in the feminist literature. Thus the actual power-base of each social groups (within open modern class societies and their social strata) is dependent upon 1) the actual number of men and women who are socioeconomically viable, and 2) the number of men and women who are actively involved in the politics of power, a multifaceted complex process through which each social groups' share of economic pie and its overall relation to the state is determined. In the same manner that the White Anglo Saxon and Protestants, the so-called WASPS, have historically comprised the White male power-bloc in the USA, other racial and ethnic minorities have tried to build their respective legitimate male power-blocs (e.g., the Latino, the Hispanic, the Italian, the Arab, the Iranian, the Indian etc.) so as to get their representation in the political foray. None has faced their share of male disappearance syndrome. It is this disappearance that I argue in the rest of this book comprises one of the most significant challenges to American penology. It is this strategic void created by disproportionate incarceration that is now being addressed by Black Islam within American penal institutions. This does not mean that the issue of power has not been addressed by African-American intellectuals or revolutionary groups in the past. In fact, the Civil Rights Era literature is inundated with a wide range of black intellectuals and movements that tried to address this issue. What they ignored was the simple fact that none paid much attention to the power of faith in its ability to focus the issue of personal responsibility to self, family and community in the manner that a new brand of Islamic faith is doing in American penitentiaries, the focus of this chapter.

In short, these factors in conjunction with the criminal justice remedies sought from the mid-1960s to present have led to the black male disappearance syndrome. One remedy sought in the 1980s was the revitalization of the socioeconomic base of the inner-city life, a subject that is beyond the scope of this book. The other was various revolutionary attempts to revitalize Black Power and Consciousness as, for example, in the mantle of Black Panthers, or the more academic Afro-centrism in Black Studies. However, despite all these reform measures costing huge expenditures, American penal institutions not only have not measured up to the ideal of rehabilitation, but now are becoming suitable grounds for a new form of religious radicalization. To remind the reader, the thrust of this book is that prison-bound Islam is a challenge to modern American penology. However my core argument is that it is not the religion of Islam that is radicalizing, but the prison conditions that is the main culprit; in fact, one could analogize American penal institutions to life in large inner city ghettoes, barrios and slums. A large number of American penal institutions are now moving towards replicating the socioeconomic conditions and cultural norms of inner cities. Although it is true that American cities have never been walled in the manner that penal institutions are, but a wide variety of socioeconomic and racial walls have historically separated the inner-city life from its affluent suburbanite counterpart. Modern American penal institutions have historically been classified based on security levels and threats ranging from minimum to maximum housing inmates that drastically differ in terms of their crime. Inmate classification has intrinsically been connected to their socioeconomic lot and psychosomatic and psychiatric typologies. Put together, American penal institutions comprise one of the most complex walled residential conglomerates that house a wide range of inmates as their clienteles. This complexity is due to a number of important reform measures that American Corrections went through during the past half century.

Thus the question arises: how do we correct one who has not been subjected to the multifaceted corrective influences of the family, the education and communal structures and norms during childhood or adolescence; or conversely, how do we correct one who has been subjected to all such corrective processes in the past and yet has chosen crime as a profession? We do have both groups in both federal and state penal institutions as, for example, hate groups next to Norco-terrorism prison gangs? Or take the case of serial killers, rapists, child-molesters, psychopath and bipolar schizophrenic. It is hard to fathom that these inmate categories entertain any degree of culpability whose cognition is the first step for criminal catharsis thus for meaningful engagement with behavioral modification programs that are administered. However, crime commission is not a simple matter of free choice, but one that has a number of important contributory elements in its formation and engenderment. Except for professional thieves, contract killers, and drug dealers, the raison d'être of much of the inner city criminal activities is of a socioeconomic deprivation/reaction nature.

Chapter 6
Islam in American Prisons

Most of the information concerning the spread of the faith of Islam in North American penal institutions is of a rudimentary and anecdotal nature. However, since post 9/11 terrorism events there is now a growing body of scholarly research on the subject of faith-based prison rehabilitation showing conversion to Islam is a hard core reality among prison inmates, especially African-Americans. This chapter first gives a brief history of the Muslim immigration to the United States of America and then discusses the dynamics of Islam's spread in American penal intuitions.

Muslim Immigration to North America

The history of Islam's spread in North America is yet to be studied in a comprehensive and nonpartisan manner in the academia. Fareed Numan, however, argues that there are historical documents showing that America was a known entity to Muslim sailors. An example is a number of Chinese documents that according to Fareed Numan are indicative of the fact that as far back the year of 1178 CE. Muslim sailors regularly traveled to Mu-Lan-Pi, identified as what we consider today's America.[1] Other dates given by Numan include the year 1310 whence the Muslim king of Malian Empire conducted trade in the Gulf of Mexico, followed by the arrival of the African Muslims in 1312.[2] Next is the arrival of a large number of African slaves in 1530. The estimated number of African slaves given is "more than 10 million … uprooted from their homes and brought to American shores."[3] However, one of the most important modern dates is the year 1807 whence Congress prohibited the importation of the African slaves into the mainland US. Despite this prohibition, the trade in African slave did not stop, and in fact reached a new height during 1840–1860, accordingly.[4]

Some studies show that the first modern wave of Muslim immigration to North America took place in the 1870s, according to Yvonne Haddad.[5] Most of these

---

1 Fareed H. Numan, "A Chronological Observation" pp. 1–7 on the website at http://www.Islam.101.com/history/muslim_us_hist.html.

2 Ibid.

3 Ibid.

4 Ibid.

5 "Islam in the United States: A Tentative Ascent: A Conversation with Yvonne Haddad" at website: http://www.usinfo.state.gov/journals/itsv/0397/ijse/hadad.html.

immigrants emigrated from the Ottoman Empire Provinces of Syria, Lebanon, Jordan and Palestine and were from different ethnic groups such as Arabs, Kurds, Turks and Albanians. The second wave of Muslim immigration took place in the aftermath of the disintegration of the Ottoman Empire which followed the conclusion of the Great War (1914–1919). Devastated by the war, a large number of Muslims from different locales of the Middle East, formerly under the Ottoman Empire, immigrated to the United States to the effect that in 1924 a specifically anti-Muslim immigration law was passed by Congress which put a decisive stop to this second wave of Muslim immigration. The Act severely restricted immigration of persons on the bases of "country" or "area of birth" enforcing a racial-ethnic quota regime. Most African, Asian, and Middle Eastern countries were given a quota of 100 immigrants per annum, whereas White Europeans got the lion's share of immigration. The preferential treatment gave the lowest quota to Spain (131) and the highest to Germany (51,227), followed by Great Britain and Northern Ireland (combined quota of 34,007), Free Irish State (26,567).[6]

Jane I. Smith observes that following World War II, a new wave of Muslim immigration to this country took place that continued intermittently until 1960s. Accordingly, this cycle of immigration was partially engendered due to the passing of the US Immigration and Nationality Act of 1953 which dismantled the quota regime of the 1924. Additionally, the American Civil Rights Movement ushered in a new and more liberal perspective into the American race and ethnic relations. The third wave went beyond the mostly Arab-Muslims of the Middle East immigrants, but covered immigrants from other Muslim countries in Asia and Africa.[7]

The fourth wave started in mid 1960s, partially due to a wholesale change in the American immigration law and partially due to the post WWII era of modernization and development schemes in the Middle East, Africa, and Asia, schemes which created a relatively well-educated, upwardly mobile, and modernized intelligentsia in the Islamic world—a segment of which sought better life and economic opportunity in the USA. It was for the first time in the US history of immigration that, not the national origin, but immigrant's educational and technical know-how and expertise that became the deciding factor for admittance into this country. In contrast, as Europe, economically, politically, and socially became stabilized, thanks to the post-WWII reconstruction under the Marshall Plan, a noticeable decline in the number of European immigrants to the USA took place.[8]

From the 1980s to present, two main events have led to the fifth wave of Muslim immigration into the USA. One was the Iranian Revolution in 1979 which toppled the pro-Western Pahlavi monarchy (r.1925–1979). The second was the demise of the Soviet Union in early 1990s. The power-vacuum created by the

---

6   See Comprehensive Immigration Law (1924) at website http://www.occawlonline.pearsoned.com.

7   Jane I. Smith, "Patterns of Muslim Immigration," pp. 1–6 on the web page of US Department of State at http://usinfo.state.gov.

8   Jane I. Smith, Ibid.

Iranian Revolution led to eight years of devastating war with Iraq (1980–1988), the rise of Islamic fundamentalism, and state sponsored terrorism all of which forced an unprecedented exodus of large segments of Iran's upper and middle classes to Europe and North America. In addition, the Iranian Revolution had a precipitous destabilizing impact on the Middle East region as, for instance, in the radicalization of the Palestinian-Israeli conflict which inadvertently led to other regional wars. In other words, the Iranian Revolution perpetuated the turmoil in the Middle East resulting in an unprecedented population dislocation.

The fall of the Soviet Union in 1991 led to much social and political changes and turmoil in the ex-Muslim republics of the Soviet Union most of which were located in Central Asia. Whether the fall of the Soviet Union will have a discernible impact on Muslim emigration to US is yet to materialize. The resulting social and political instability in Caucasia (e.g. between ex-Soviet Republics of Armenia and Azerbaijan) and Central Asia, however, is having a discernible centripetal impact on the whole region. For example, a new and deadly form of Islamic fundamentalism movement emerging in Afghanistan under the ex-Taliban regime now turned into the full fledged terror networks of the *Al-Qaida* may drastically alter the future of emigration of Muslims from many Islamic countries to the USA.

American Muslim Community

American Muslim community is comprised of diverse racial and ethnic groups with different social, economic and educational statuses. The majority of North American Muslims adhere to Sunni Islam—which is also the dominant branch in the Islamic world—followed by those who adhere to Shiite Islam. The Wahhabi, an orthodox Sunni minority view of Islam adhered to in the Kingdom of Saudi Arabia, has a certain following among North American Muslims. Finally there is a specifically African-American view of Islam whose main representative is the Nation of Islam (NOI). This version of Islam is practiced among a segment of the African-American community as well as inmates. The Nation of Islam is a controversial Islamic movement some of whose beliefs are radically different than those of the mainstream Islam practiced among the larger immigrant American Muslim communities. For example, in the Nation of Islam's official website, under the title "The Honorable Elijah Muhammad," it is stated that "We Thank Allah, Who Came in the Person of Master Fard Muhammad For Raising Up His Last and Greatest Messenger, The Honorable Elijah Muhammad!!"[9] The claim that Allah, the Universal God in the vernacular of the Qur'an, has appeared in the persona of Master Fard Muhammad runs against the very core of traditional Islam's representation of Allah. The Qur'an in cxii, 1 thru 3, declares that Allah is One Who Is, and Always has been. Allah, declares the Qur'an unequivocally,

9   See the website of the nation of Islam at http://www.muhammadspeaks.com/ MessengerHistory.html. The exclamations in the quote are original.

neither begets, nor was begotten, and that there is none who is comparable to Allah. In addition, the Qur'an rejects any allusion to Allah's need for reincarnation in any human form. The idea that Allah has reincarnated in the persona of a Master Fard who has chosen Mr. Elijah Muhammad as his "Last Messenger," is antithetical to both the Qur'an and to the core dogma of Islam namely, that it was Muhammad Ibn Abdullah (570–632 CE) who personifies Allah's Last Messenger, the *Khatam al-Anbiyaa* in the vernacular of the Qur'an. This said, there is no doubt that the Nation of Islam plays an important historical role in converting African-American inmates to its version of Islam. Islamic proselytizing in American state and federal penitentiaries is a convoluted subject to be discussed in some details in this chapter; the precursor of it is, however, the Nation of Islam discussed in some details in this chapter.

How Many Muslims Are There in the United States?

American Constitution prohibits religious-based census. Therefore, the question as to how many Americans adhere to Islam inside or outside of the penal institutions is not an issue that can be resolved through referral to census or inmate population data released by Department of Corrections in each State of the Union, or the Federal Bureau of Prisons. There are different studies, however, that have tried to scientifically determine the proximate number of Muslims residing in this country as well as studies that guesstimate Muslim inmates. For example, concerning the actual number of American Muslim, a study conducted by The Graduate Center of the City University of New York titled, "The American Religious Identification Survey 2001" (ARIS 2001) in its "Profile of the US Muslim Population," has concluded that the total number of Muslims living in this country is less than 3 million. The methodology for data collection is explained as follows:

> The American Religious Identification Survey 2001 was based on a random digit-dialled telephone survey of 50,281 American residential households in the continental USA (48 states). The methodology largely replicates the widely reported and pioneering 1990 National Survey of Religious Identification (NSRI) carried out at the Graduate Center of the City University of New York. ARIS 2001thus provides a unique time series of information concerning the religious identification choices of American adults.[10]

The ARIS study was based on a central question: "what is your religion, if any?" Out of more than 50,000 who responded to the telephone surveys of the ARIS 2001, we are told, 219 identified their religion as Islam. This number, then,

---

10   Barry A. Kosmin and Egon Mayer, "American Religious Identification Survey 2001" pp. 1–6, at web page of The Graduate Center, CUNY, at http://www.gc.cuny.edu/studies/aris_part_two.htm.

served as the base for national identification of American Muslim population in this country. The authors maintain that:

> The ARIS 2001 total in Table 1, which shows 1,104,000 Muslim adults, is smaller than the figures in current circulation. Yet it is twice the number reported in the NSRI survey in 1990. Allowing for a sampling error of +/-0.5 percent, the ARIS 2001 figure may be adjusted upwards to its maximum range of 1.0 percent of all 208 million American adults.with such an adjustment, the total national figure of U.S. Muslims is 2.2 million, giving a total national population (including children) of just under 3 million. By comparison, the CUNY National Survey of Religious Identification 1990 found that 0.3 percent of respondents adhere to Islam.[11]

The authors also caution the readers that American Muslims should not be confused with American Arabs whose number is estimated at around 3.5 million by the Arab American Institute. Of this number, 75 percent adhere to Christianity, and 25 percent to Islam, accordingly. The authors argue that by taking the 25 percent—which corresponds to 850,000 Muslim Arab-Americans, as a base for determining the total number of American Muslims, one reaches a total number for the American Muslim population which can't be more than 3.4 million.[12] Other sources and studies give different estimates of the total number of American Muslims living in this country. One Internet site by the name of "Islam For Today" puts the number at 4 million.[13] Another Islamic site puts the number at 5.7 million.[14] The Council on American-Islamic Relations (CAIR) puts the number at the round figure of 7 million.[15] Another method to identify the estimated number of American Muslims is through the study of the institution of the American Mosque. As to the number of Muslim inmates, there are studies to which reference shall be made later in the chapter as the proselytizing role of the Nation of Islam in American penal institutions is discussed.

---

11   Kosmin and Mayer, Ibid., p. 2.

12   Kosmin and Mayer, Ibid.

13   See "Expression of Islam in America" (anonymous) in Islam For Today website at: http://www.islamfortoday.com/america11.htm.

14   See the section of Muslims: the facts at New Internationalist 345 at website http://www.newint.org/issue345/facts.htm.

15   See "What about the American Muslim community?" at the web page of the Council on Islamic-American Relations at http://www.cair-net.org/asp/aboutislam.asp. The directly quoted above information is from a larger study titled, "Faith Communities Today," which was conducted by the Hartford Institute of Religious Research in Hartford, Connecticut.

American Muslim Mosque

It is plausible to propose that the growth of the American Muslim community is discernable through the growth of the American Muslim Mosque; it is also plausible to argue that the growth of the Mosque, as a religious institution, is a sign of the spread of the Islamic faith in the US. As of April 2001, the US Department of State's Office of International Information Programs gave the following information gathered through a survey titled, "Mosque in America: A National Portrait":

- Mosques in the United States: 1,209
- American Muslims associated with a mosque: 2 million
- Increase in number of mosques since 1994: 25 percent
- Proportion of mosques founded since 1980: 62 percent
- Average number of Muslims associated with one mosque in the United States: 1,625
- U.S. mosque participants who are converts: 30 percent
- American Muslims who "strongly agree" that they should participate in American institutions and the political process: 70 percent
- U.S. mosques attended by a single ethnic group: 7 percent
- U.S. mosques that have some Asian, African-American, and Arab members: nearly 90 percent
- Ethnic origins of regular participants in U.S. mosques:
  - South Asian (Pakistani, Indian, Bangladeshi, Afghani) = 33 percent
  - African-American = 30 percent
  - Arab = 25 percent
  - Sub-Saharan African = 3.4 percent
  - European (Bosnian, Tartar, Kosovar, etc.) = 2.1 percent
  - White American = 1.6 percent
  - Southeast Asian (Malaysian, Indonesian, Filipino) = 1.3 percent
  - Caribbean = 1.2 percent
  - Turkish = 1.1 percent
  - Iranian = 0.7 percent
  - Hispanic/Latino = 0.6 percent
- U.S. mosques that feel they strictly follow the Koran and Sunnah: more than 90 percent
- U.S. mosques that feel the Koran should be interpreted with consideration of its purposes and modern circumstances: 71 percent
- U.S. mosques that provide some assistance to the needy: nearly 70 percent
- U.S. mosques with a full-time school: more than 20 percent[16]

---

16   Muslim Life in America at U.S. Department of State: International Information Programs web page at: http://www.usinfo.state.gov/products/pubs/muslimlife.

A typical Muslim mosque in the US, as is discernible from the above bulleted items, seems neither racially-ethnically, nor denominationally, restricted institution of worship but one that functions as a communal hub of congregation and of social activism open to all who profess an affinity with Islam. From 1994 to present , the American Muslim Mosque has increased in number and are scattered in all states, including Alaska. The largest number of Muslim Mosques are located in California (227), followed by New York (140), New Jersey (86), Michigan (73), Pennsylvania and Texas (67 in each), Ohio (66), Illinois and Florida (57 in each), Georgia (41), North Carolina (34), Washington (24), Arizona and Alabama (23 in each), Missouri (21), Wisconsin (19), Colorado and West Virginia (17 in each), Tennessee and South Carolina (15 in each), Louisiana and Iowa (14 in each). The remaining states have mosques which range in number between 10 and 1.[17] These mosques provide a wide range of service to the faithful that we shall discuss shortly. A similar growth trend can be observed in Canada, England, and France too.

In 2001, a comprehensive study of the American Mosque was published, sponsored by four American Muslim organizations. These were: the Council on American-Islamic Relations based in Washington, D.C.; the Islamic Society of North America; the Ministry of Imam W. Deen Muhammad; and the Islamic Circle of North America. Affiliated with these organizations, researchers studied eight subject areas in relation to the proliferation of the Muslim mosques in this country.[18] The main areas covered were: (a) basic characteristics, (b) worship, (c) history, mission, programs, organizational dynamics and finances of the Muslim mosque in North America. According to the report's findings, the following dynamic picture emerged concerning American Muslim Mosque:

> The number of mosques and mosque participants are experiencing tremendous growth. On average there are over 1,625 Muslims associated in some way with the religious life of each mosque. Half of the mosques have 500 or more Muslims associated with them. The average attendance at Friday prayer is 292 persons. Median attendance is 135.[19]

The 2001 study also revealed the following in comparison to data of the 1994 study:

---

17   Muslim Communities: Number of Mosques in the United States by State, Ibid.

18   Bagby, Ihsan, Paul M. Perl and Bryan T. Froehle, (2001) "The Mosque in America: A National Portrait", A Report from the Mosque Study Project, *Council on American-Islamic Relations*, Washington, D.C.

19   Bagby et al, Ibid.

Table 6.1 The growth of Muslim mosques in USA, 1994–2000

	2000 Study	**1994 Study**	**Increase (%)**
Number of Mosques	1209	962	25%
Average Jum'ah attendance	292	150	94%
Total Associate per Mosque	1625	485	235%
Total Associated with all Mosques	2 million	500,000	300%

This report, in conjunction with similar studies, showed that: (a) Islam is a fast growing faith in the US; (b) the mosque is an important institution in the life of American Muslim communities; (c) the mosque plays a central functional role in the spread of the Islamic faith in the nation; and (d) the question of the number of American Muslims is relatively difficult to determine with precision. There are different social, political and demographic factors that complicate impartial scientific research of this issue especially in the aftermath of terrorism events of 11 September, 2001.

Post 9/11 Sensibilities to Islam and Muslim Mosque

In the aftermath of 11 September, 2001 terrorism events which shook the US's taken for granted sense of immunity from the long arms of international terrorism, an activist and radical identification with Islam is not without its negative repercussions as documented by the Council on American-Islamic Relations. In a report titled, "The Status of Muslim Civil Rights in the United States 2002," it is stated that:

> Data gathered for this report demonstrate that Muslims in the United States are more apprehensive than ever about discrimination and intolerance. U.S. Government actions after September 11, 2001 alone impacted more than 60,000 individuals. Muslims have charged that the government's actions violated the First and Fourth Amendments to the U.S. Constitution because they included ethnically and religiously-based interrogations, detentions, raids, and closures of charities.[20]

The report, then, goes into the details of a number of areas in which post 9/11 anti-Muslim policies have been implemented as, for example, in profiling American Muslims as potential terrorists in airports, ports of entry, and local mosques; Muslim community-based services such as charity institutions have also come under close scrutiny of both federal and state law enforcement agencies throughout

---

20   The Status of Muslim Civil Rights in the United States 2002: Stereotypes and Civil Liberties, (Council on American-Islamic Relations Research Center, Washington, D.C.). p. 1.

the nation. Similar profiling has been utilized in screening international students who have applied to American colleges and universities. This state of affairs has taken place despite the fact that the official position of the federal government, expressed by the President George W. Bush, has been that:

> When we think of Islam we think of a faith that brings comfort to a billion people around the world. Millions of people find comfort and solace and peace. And that's made brothers and sisters out of every race. America counts millions of Muslims amongst our citizens, and Muslims make an incredibly valuable contribution to our country. Muslims are doctors, lawyers, law professors, members of the military, entrepreneurs, shopkeepers, moms and dads. And they need to be treated with respect. In our anger and emotion, our fellow Americans must treat each other with respect.[21]

In addition to the above positive attitude expressed by the President George W. Bush, the report on the "Status of Muslim Civil Liberties in the United States 2002" notes that the American Muslim communities do not consider the American police and courts as two monolithic anti-Muslim structures bent on disregarding civil liberties of the American Muslims cautioning that, "In this time of crisis, the judiciary has taken actions in favor of Muslim complaints."[22] Invasion of Iraq by the multinational forces spearheaded by the US Armed Forces in 2003, and the subsequent stages of the war against Islamic terrorist groups in that country and around the world, has added apprehension among immigrant Arab and Muslim American communities. Prior to the outbreak of the actual hostilities, the Council on American-Islamic Relations (CAIR) published and distributed a "Step-by-step to community safety if America attacks Iraq," in which the concerns of the Muslim communities were expressed warning that:

> As it becomes increasingly clear that America will attack Iraq in next few days, CA put together a "Muslim Community Safety Kit" for Muslims, Arab-Americans and those perceived to be Middle "Eastern" who may by targeted by religious or ethnic profiling or bias-related hate crimes. According to the FBI "A U.S. war with Iraq or another terrorist could trigger a wave of hate crimes against Muslims and Arab-Americans in the United States."[23]

---

21   "In the Words of the President George W. Bush," on the website of the U.S. Department of State, International Information Programs at http://usinfo.state.gov/products/pubs/muslimlife/bushword.htm.
22   The Status of Muslim Civil Rights in the United States 2002: Stereotypes and Civil Liberties, p. 17.
23   See "Step-by-step guide to community safety if America attacks Iraq" on the web page of Council on American-Islamic Relations at http://www.cair-net.org/asp/article.asp?id=138&page=AA.

The document then provided a long list of what to do in case hate crimes were to be directed against those who may become the potential victims of such crimes. As of yet, we don't have a comprehensive study showing whether the war in Iraq is having a discernible deleterious impact on Arab-American and/or American Muslim communities in this country. Besides scattered acts of violence committed against individuals, or small businesses perceived of having some Middle Eastern connection, none of the pre-war dramatic anti-Muslim, or anti-Arab-American, scenarios fathomed by doomsday political pundits, have taken place to this date. Neither mass deportation nor internment of the American-Iraqis or Muslims has taken place, neither is there any indication that American Muslims are being fired en masse from their places of employment, be it at the state or federal agencies, or at corporate America. In fact, from the US President down to those in the position of authority at the state and federal levels, all have tried to alleviate such fears among both Arab and non-Arab Muslim immigrant communities throughout the Nation.

Demographic Characteristics of American Muslim Community

The Pew Research Center in its 2007 survey, titled "Muslim Americans: Middle Class and Mostly Mainstream," maintained that, "Muslims constitute a growing and increasing segment of American society. Yet there is surprisingly little quantitative research about the attitudes and opinions of this segment of the public."[24] Citing the constitutional prohibition against a religious-based census and the relatively small number of the Muslim population in the US as the two main reasons for this state of affairs, it was stated further that, "The Pew Muslim American survey estimates that Muslims constitute 0.6% of the U.S. adult population. This projects to 1.4 million Muslims 18 years old or older currently living in the United States."[25] The Pew 2007 report cautioned that this number could indeed be "higher" considering the fact that the survey was conducted exclusively over regular telephones, but did not include cell phones. In addition, an estimated 13.5% of the general public does not have any "phone service" according to the report thus the rationale for the higher estimates.[26] The most significant results of the Pew 2007 report was not its attempts to determine the actual number of the American Muslim population *per se*, but the fact that from a socioeconomic perspective, the American Muslim community is of a "middle class" status with a "mainstream" perspective. According to the Pew 2007 report, "The Muslim American population is youthful, racially diverse, generally well-educated, and financially about as well-off as the

---

24   Muslim Americans: Middle Class and Mostly Mainstream, Pew Research Center, May 22, 2007. Foreword.
25   Muslim Americans, Ibid., p. 9.
26   Muslim Americans, Ibid., p. 9.

rest of the US public. Nearly two-thirds (65%) are immigrants while 35% were born in the United States."[27]

Interestingly, Muslims who have immigrated to the United States within the past three decades (1980-2007) have given four main reasons for emigration: educational opportunity (26%), economic opportunity (24%), family reasons (24%), conflict/persecution (20%), other (3%), don't know (3%). It is remarkable that despite all the media hype that Muslims hate America and are about to cause Armageddon, those who have immigrated to the United States seek socioeconomic opportunities for bettering their lots. In fact, one scholar of the subject has characterized American democracy as the most ideal for the blossoming of Islam's core teachings of peace and progress with an eye on social justice and the other on law and order.[28] It is not ironic that, "Although Muslim Americans have distinctive beliefs and practices," as specified by the Pew 2007 report, "their religiosity is similar to American Christians in many respects." The Pew 2007 report concluded that, "American Islam resembles the mainstream of American religious life."[29] Does this mean that there is no potential terrorism threat to American national interests from radical Islamic groups with their sympathizers who might be called into action as, for example, in 1993 bombing of the World Trade Center, the precursor to 9/11 terrorism? This threat is within the realms of probabilities to which reference has already been made in previous chapters of this book. However, to the rhetorical question as to whether Islam is compatible with the American ideals expressed in the American Constitution and the Bill of Rights, different answers have been provided by Muslim institutions and community leaders especially after September 11, 2001 terrorism events. For example, the Muslim Public Affairs Council (MPAC), in an article titled, "The Islamic Foundations of Patriotism," argues that being an American Muslim not only is not antithetical to American notion of patriotism, but in fact is complementary because:

> Our thesis is that the relationship is indeed synergistic: that within the central dogma of Islam, the intellectual development of Islamic thinking and jurisprudence, as well as Islamic history, there are many tenets consistent with, and supportive of, the sentiment of patriotism to the United States.[30]

Starting with this thesis, the article expounds on five major factors to argue that these factors are intrinsic to both American and Islamic teachings in relation to the essential ingredients of an ideal life; it is these factors that make Islam quite compatible with the mainstream American notion of love for one's country. These factors are (1) sanctity of life, (2) liberty as an essential value, (3) justice as

27   Muslim Americans, Ibid., p. 15.
28   Kusha, Hamid R., *The Sacred Law of Islam*.
29   Muslim Americans, Ibid., p. 27.
30   "The Islamic Foundations of Patriotism" pp. 1–11, at the web page of the Muslim Public Affairs Council at http://www.mpac.org/popa_article_display.aspx?ITEM=48.

equality before law, (4) justice as due process, and (5) the pursuit of happiness.[31] The article defends these factors by citing different verses from the Qur'an and from the words and deeds attributed to the Prophet Muhammad. For example, on Islam's position on the sanctity of life, the article cites the verse 32 in chapter v of the Qur'an. The verse, originally vouchsafed upon the Children of Israel, advises the believer if an innocent person were to be murdered, it is as if the whole humanity has been murdered. By the same token, if a life were to be saved, it is as if the life of the humankind has been saved. This premise of the Qur'an, the articles maintains, is quite reflective of the value of life in Islam making the faith quite compatible with the American Declaration of Independence's sanctity of life premise.

On the issue of liberty as an essential value, the article cites one of the most cited verses, verse 256 in chapter ii in the Qur'an, which states unequivocally that in matters of religion, compulsion shall not be resorted to because the route to both salvation and damnation has been warned to faithful. Because no one can be compelled to accept or to reject a religion, this premise of the Qur'an, argues the article, is compatible with the American Founding Fathers' stress on liberty as it applies to one's choice for religion.[32] Insofar as justice and equality before law is concerned, the article stresses on the fact that the thrust of Islam, as a monotheistic faith, is justice for to argue otherwise would invalidate other proclamations of the faith. For example, the Qur'an is adamant that Allah is Justice par excellence whose every deed are based on justice. Justice and liberty are intrinsically connected to one another because liberty without just laws is hard to sustain. Citing the preamble to the US Constitution, the article maintains that the American constitutional stress on justice goes parallel with the Qur'an's stress on the same as, for instance, in verse 25 of chapter 57 of the Qur'an. This verse reads, "We sent aforetime our apostles with clear signs and sent with them the book and the balance (of right and wrong) that human beings may establish justice."[33]

Islam in American Penal Institutions, 1930–2008

There are scholars who have observed that the history to establish Islam in American penal institutions dates back to the 1930s, and in relation to the incarceration of the first Black Muslims[34] who belonged to the Nation of Islam.[35] It is constructive to give a brief history of the Nation of Islam (NOI) before embarking on its prison-bound rehabilitative activities.

---

31   Ibid.

32   Ibid.

33   Ibid., p. 6.

34   Philip, Jenkins, "Islam in America" pp. 1–6 on the Foreign Policy Research Institute website at http://www.fpri.org/0404.200307.jenkins.islaminamerica.html, p. 3.

35   Philip Jenkins, Ibid., p. 3; Robert Dannin, "Island in a Sea of Ignorance" p. 6.

A Brief History of the Nation of Islam

Based on its official web page and publications, the Nation of Islam was founded by a mysterious A. Wallace D. Fard Muhammad in 1930s in Detroit, Michigan. There is not much information about his background including his alleged mastery of Islamic teachings. The Nation of Islam has accorded Mr. Fard Muhammad the ultimate divine status stating that:

> We believe that Allah (God) appeared in the Person of Master W. Fard Muhammad, July, 1930; the long-awaited "Messiah" of the Christians and "Mahdi" of the Muslims. We believe further that Allah is God and besides HIM there is no god and He will bring about a universal government of peace wherein we all can live in peace together.[36]

This claim to divinity is, despite the fact that in the early accounts of the rise of the Nation of Islam, as rendered by some scholars of the subject, Mr. Fard is portrayed as a silk peddler born in the Holy city of Mecca in the 1870s who migrated to the United States and founded some sort of a "voodoo" religious cult among migrant black workers in Detroit.[37] It is beyond the scope of this book to delve into Mr. Fard's life details which is almost non-existent; what is certain is that his claim to divinity was enthusiastically embraced by one Elijah Poole, the would-be next leader of the NOI, the Honorable Elijah Muhammad. The Nation of Islam's official website states that, On July 4, 1930, the long awaited 'Saviour' of the Black man and woman, Master W. Fard Muhammad appeared in this city. He announced and preached that God is One, and it was now time for Blacks to return to the religion of their ancestors, Islam .... In the autumn of 1931, Elijah Poole attended his first lecture by Master Fard Muhammad and was overwhelmed by the message and immediately accepted it.[38] Upon recommendation of Mater Fard, Mr. Elijah Poole, we are told, changed his name to "Karriem" and assumed the position of a minister in The Temple of Islam, the precursor to the NOI. Later, Master Fard elevated Mr. Karriem to the position of the "Supreme Minister," advising him once again to change his name from Karriem, to Muhammad. Mr. Elijah Muhammad is on record that he never considered his Christian name as his own, writing, "The name Poole was never my name nor was it my father's name,"

---

36   The Muslim Program at http://www.noi/orgmuslims_program.htm. Retrieved on 6/20/2008.

37   Benyon, Erdmann D., "The Voodoo Cult among Negro Migrants of Detroit," *American Journal of Sociology* 43 (July 1937–May 1938), pp. 894–907.

38   A Man who Raised a Nation at http://finalcall.com/national/savioursday2k/htm_ nation.htm. Retrieved on 6/23/2008.

because "It was the name the white slave master of my grandfather after the so-called freedom of my fathers."[39]

Robert Dannin (who has done much research on the history of the Nation of Islam as well as on Muslim converts in American prisons) maintains that Master Fard was reported of having had already claimed that he was the true reincarnation of one Noble Drew Ali, another mysterious figure who, based on some accounts, preceded Master Fard in claiming reincarnation of Allah. Dannin cautions his readers that in analyzing the veracity of these bombastic reincarnation claims and their impacts on the Nation of Islam not only do we have to go back to its precursor, the Moorish American Science Temple, but also to the nineteenth century Black Freemasonry movement. These religious-fraternal organizations represented black aspirations within the late nineteenth century American social and political atmosphere. Dannin observes that:

> By the turn of the century thousands of fraternal lodges existed throughout the country. The most important African-American lodges established before the Great Migration were the Prince Hall Masons, Odd Fellows, Elks, True Reformers, United Brethren, Knights of Pythias, Mysterious Ten and Good Samaritans, and the Grand United Order of True Reformers, founded in 1881 by Rev. W.W. Brown in Richmond, Virginia.[40]

The black fraternal lodges performed various social functions similar to what their white counterparts did for the weaklings and downtrodden of the society. The lodges also engaged in secretive rituals that Dannin argues helped black social and cultural solidarity at a time that a large segment of the black population lived in abject poverty in rural America.[41] With the onset of the full fledged urbanization in the first decades of the twentieth century, the black lodges and fraternities became social service providers for the large segments of the black population that had migrated to large cities in search of their share of the American Dream. This migration (of a large segment of both black and white masses) from the rural into the urban America created both problems and opportunities for the American manufacturing industries which integrated the migrants as cheap wage laborers; however, there were radical labor unions which also tried to recruit them into their ranks and files. The black churches, synagogues as well as lodges and fraternal organizations were also involved in these integration efforts.

Dannin seems to be suggesting that one way these fraternal black organizations could attract part of this sea of immigrants to their ranks and file was through religion, be it Christianity, Judaism or, in the case of the Moorish American Science

---

39   A Man who Raised a Nation at http://finalcall.com/national/savioursday2k/htm_nation.htm. Retrieved on 6/23/2008.

40   Dannin, Robert (2000), *Black Pilgrimage to Islam*, New York: Oxford University Press, pp. 24–25.

41   Dannin, Ibid., p. 25.

Temple, Islam.[42] However, one should not assume that the Moorish Temple's view of Islam had much ideological affinity with the mainstream Islam whose genesis had emerged in the seventh century Hejaz region (the old name of what is known as today's Saudi Arabia). The primordial Islam that emerged in Hejaz region went through much social and cultural refinement as it became a world religion during fourteen centuries of its history until it landed on the North American shores. The same caveat applies to the Nation of Islam's version of the faith especially during the movement's "Resurrection" phase that corresponds to the 1930s in Detroit and later in Chicago. Writing on Noble Drew Ali's views, Dannin states that, "In his amalgamation of Islam, Christianity, and Eastern religion, he drew on the unchurched folk beliefs of slavery in which Old and New Testament prophets could be fused into a singular and powerful symbol of resistance to oppression."[43] By the term "unchurched," Dannin means religious views that do not correspond to the canonized view of the three monotheistic religions and especially of Christianity that was prevalent among the nineteenth century black churches and synagogues. This view applies to the Nation of Islam's formative stages under its most prominent spiritual leader, Elijah Muhammad.

Enter Elijah Muhammad, 1930–1975

With the exit of the mysterious Mr. Fard Muhammad, the leadership mantles of the Nation of Islam we are told were assumed by his most devout disciple, Mr. Elijah Muhammad. He is on record that he never entertained any doubt about Mr. Fard's divinity. Elijah Muhammad was a man of humble origins, but undoubtedly was endowed with remarkable leadership abilities according to the Nation of Islam's literature that has praised him in extraordinary terms claiming that due to his accomplishments, "The Honorable Elijah Muhammad, in the dawning of the 21st century, remains a pivotal world policy maker and key figure whose program and position will shape the destiny of the new century and millennium. His supporters have determined."[44] It is also claimed that under his leadership Muslims, "achieved dramatic, never before seen results in the areas of religion, politics, social interaction, economic development, and international affairs of the so-called American Negro at that time."[45] Whatever the merits of these spectacular claims, what is certain is that unlike other faith-based organizations that preceded the NOI by at least a century, the Nation of Islam's proselytizing efforts had a provocative antiestablishment tone and gist to its denominational articulation. That is why during the 1930s–1970s, the Federal Bureau of Investigation (FBI)

---

42   Dannin, Ibid.

43   Dannin, Ibid., p. 26.

44   70 Year Commemorative of the Nation of Islam in North America: Master Fard Muhammad Taught the Hon. Elijah Muhammad A man who Raised a Nation at http://finalcall.com/national/savioursday2k/hem_nation.htm. Retrieved on 6/19/2008.

45   70 Year Commemorative of the Nation of Islam in North America, Ibid.

under J Edgar Hoover, closely monitored the NOI and especially its leader, Mr. Elijah Muhammad.

The official bibliography of Mr. Elijah Muhammad states that from 1930s until 1975, the Nation of Islam under the leadership of the "Last Messenger of Allah," took a leading role in the struggle of the Black people for justice and equality. During these years the Nation of Islam's proselytizing rationale centered on the notion that America was the land of oppression and injustice at the apex of which stood the legacy of Transatlantic Slavery. Islam was a solution to all injustices that Black America had suffered under White America, thus Mr. Elijah Muhammad in his numerous sermons and writings argued a core message that comprised the Nation of Islam ideological thrust of Islamic proselytizing, be it inside or outside of American penal institutions:

> Because of slavery in America, separations occurred; fathers from families, mothers from daughters and sons– Beatings, killings, tortures. Life for Black men in America was suffering, shame and death. The Emancipation Proclamation, after Civil War brought about the Black man becoming a WILLING servant for his former slave master, NOT a return to his name, language or God … after the Civil War, the Black began calling himself in the names of his slave-master. Practicing the religion of slave-master, speaking the language of the slave-master. He was given nothing by the slave-master to go for self. Slavery, suffering and death was, now, the lifestyle for the Blackman of America, now called: Negro, nigger, coon, pickininny, shine, boy, uncle, etc…. [46]

The Nation of Islam further claims that the appearance of Elijah Muhammad has been foretold in the Bible (Deuteronomy 18:18) thus his life story is recounted from his very meager beginning to his becoming one of the most acclaimed leaders of Black America to the effect that:

> At the announcement of death of Messenger Elijah Muhammad (peace be upon him)–on February 25, 1979, at the age of 78, in a Chicago hospital, reportedly, of congestive heart failure, he left behind, an empire, estimated to be worth $60,000,000, which included LAND and cattle holdings in Michigan, Georgia and Alabama, along with grocery stores, restaurants, mosques, schools and newspapers, homes, clothing stores and many other things that a NATION must have to survive.[47]

The Nation of Islam has credited Mr. Elijah Muhammad with many accomplishments as mentioned above. However, The Federal Bureau of Investigation, in its early investigation of the Nation of Islam, gave a different

46   See "The Honorable Elijah Muhammad: Last Messenger of Allah" at the Nation of Islam's official web page: http://www.muhammadspeaks.com/MessengerHistory.html.
47   The Honorable Elijah Muhammad, Ibid.

picture of Mr. Elijah Muhammad depicting him as the founder of the "Muslim Cult of Islam" (MCI) with its military wing called the "Fruit of Islam" (FOI). According to the unclassified and published FBI file:

> The MCI is an organization composed entirely of Negroes which was reportedly originated around 1930 in Detroit, Michigan. The national leader and founder is ELIJAH MOHAMMAD, who claims to have been sent by Allah, the Supreme Being, to lead the Negroes out of slavery in the United States. Members fanatically follow the alleged teachings of Allah as interpreted by MOHAMMAD, and disavow allegiance to the United States. Members pledge allegiance to Allah and Islam and believe that any civil law which conflicts with Muslim law should be disobeyed. The Cult teaches that members of the dark skinned race cannot be considered citizens of the United States since they are in slavery in this country and, therefore, must free themselves by destroying non-Muslims and Christianity in the "War of Armageddon". For this purpose the Cult has a military branch called the Fruit of Islam (FOI), composed of all male, able bodied members, who participate in military drill and judo training.[48]

The FBI files on the NOI show that Mr. Elijah Muhammad was arrested on 20 September, 1942, in Chicago, IL, charged with the crime of sedition. He was subsequently interrogated by the FBI agents. The unsigned interrogation document purports that Mr. Elijah Muhammad was of firm convictions that in 1930 he had met Allah reincarnated in the persona of the aforementioned A. Wallace Fard Muhammad. Accordingly, during 1930–1933 Mr. Fard, residing in Detroit, held general meetings with an audience numbering around 800 to 900 to teach a religion that was "called Islam." He is reported of having had regular meetings with Mr. Elijah Muhammad instructing him on Islam's teachings for a period of nine months and subsequently disappeared altogether never to be heard from again.[49] What were the contents of these teachings of an Islam that "Allah" had personally instructed to the future leader of the NOI? Under the caption of the "Principles," the FBI interrogatory document has quoted Mr. Elijah Muhammad as having enumerated the following to comprise the principles of Islam:

- Belief in Allah
- Belief in the prophets
- Belief in the scriptures that the prophets bring
  a. The Bible
  b. The Holy Quran

---

48   Federal Bureau of Investigation, "Elijah Muhammad" File: CG 25-20607, p. 2. The FBI's files on the NOI and its leaders have been released pursuant to the Freedom of Information Act which gives this basic right to American citizens to learn about the nature and contents of any file that the FBI may have on them.

49   Elijah Muhammad File, Ibid., pp. 3–4.

- Prayer
- Charity.[50]

Apparently, there was no mention of the Hajj, the obligatory pilgrimage to Mecca that every Muslim has to perform at least once in his/her life time. Neither was there any mention of principle of *Ma'ad* which stands for the Day of Resurrection, one of Islam's central beliefs. Missing from this view of Islam was also the *Saum* which stands for the obligatory dawn-to-dusk fasting during the holy moth of Ramadan. These principles, not mentioned above, have been adhered to in all major and minor sects of Islam, including in the present NOI under the leadership of Mr. Louis Farrakhan (1975–2005). However, in the early 1930s, as the very Allah was giving instructions to his "Last Messenger," Elijah Muhammad, three pillars of Islam were missing. This is absurd on several grounds. First, it is the unequivocal premise of the Qur'an that the Prophet Muhammad was the Last Messenger of Allah and the faith unequivocally teaches that with the passing of Muhammad (in Summer 632 C.E., in the city of Medina), the gate to divine revelations has been sealed until the Day of Resurrection, *Yaoum al-Qiyama*. In mainstream Islam, be it the Sunnite or the Shiite, it is considered blasphemy to deny this status of the Prophet Muhammad let alone to suggest that there is another "Last Prophet of God" to whom a reincarnated Allah has given the above principles some of which contradict original Islam's principles. In addition, it is a principal belief in Islam that Allah does not appear to mortal souls through reincarnation, a concept that has its roots in Hinduism, and is patently anti-Qur'an. Allah, as depicted by the Qur'an, is an entity beyond human capacity to fathom, let alone to be spoken to in a reincarnated nature as claimed by the NOI.

The Nation of Islam is on record that the Federal Bureau of Investigation's renditions and accounts in relation to the top leadership of the movement can't be trusted because most of such accounts are of a concocted nature designed to give a bad impression of the NOI. There is no doubt that the FBI, from the inception of the NOI in 1930 to present, has never had a positive view of the NOI. In the Red Scare atmosphere of the 1930s, the NOI was considered as a dangerous seditious cult bent on creating anti-American sentiments among the larger African-American community. Thus NOI had a prominent place on the FBI list of those who engaged in "anti-American" activities. Therefore, it is very likely that the FBI agents neither cared, nor could really understand, to which Islamic principles the NOI adhered to in such an atmosphere of fear, suspicion and resentment. By the same token, some of the arguments and claims of the NOI concerning Islam is very controversial as for example the notion that "The purpose of Islam is to clean up the dark people physically and spiritually so they will be respected by the other civilized people of the earth."[51] The purpose of Islam—like other religions in the line of Abraham, Judaism and Christianity—from its inception to present has

---

50   Elijah Muhammad File, Ibid., p. 5.
51   Elijah Muhammad File, Ibid.

been purification of the soul and body of the faithful from crime, violence, greed and excesses of life so that one could submit oneself to the ideals of a healthy and balanced life in which human dignity and honor is preserved. To that end, Mr. Elijah Muhammad's observation is correct when he said that, "Islam desires to eliminate prostitution, gambling and drinking among the dark people so they can be respected." However, this is not a desire which the Qur'an expresses for Black people *per se*, but for all faithful and, in fact, for the humanity regardless of race, class, ethnic origins or gender. Islam, like its Judeo-Christian counterparts, is race neutral in its core teachings in contrast to some of the most vile and racists remarks that religious extremists (be it Muslim, Christian, or Jew) have thrown against one another in the name of the "purity" of faith.

The Qur'an reminds Muslims time and again that Jews and Christians are People of the Book (*Ahal al-Kitaab*) to whom Allah has sent his most beloved Prophets, Moses and Jesus, the Christ, for guidance, redemption and salvation. In fact, the Qur'an is adamant that a "true" Jew or Christian is as much a "true" Muslim as a "true" Muslim is a "true" Jew or Christian. Why? Because all men and women of true faith "submit" to one God, that the Qur'an portrays it as Allah. This "submission," however, is not one of coerced nature that Muslim fundamentalist circles advocate, but is one of ecumenical nature that transcends time and culture. In short, a true Muslim is not a racist, neither is he or she a religious bigot bent on waging Jihad against the rest of the civilized world; a true Muslim can find God in the Muslim Mosque, the Jewish Synagogue, or the Christian Church. This is the meaning of religion in the line of Abraham, a concept that has a millennia of tradition behind its prevalence among enlightened Jews, Christians and Muslims, a school of thought to which this author belongs.

In the FBI documents, Mr. Elijah Muhammad is reported of having claimed that during his sojourn Allah issued "approximately" 35,000 registration cards to his followers prior to his disappearance in 1934. Those who registered with Allah were allegedly given divine immunity from the Selective Service Act of 1940 through which able bodied men were mandated to register with the United States Armed Forces.[52] However, the Act's provisions did not apply to the members of the NOI, claimed Mr. Elijah Muhammad saying:

> I realize that failure by me to register constitutes a violation of Federal Law but the reason I did not register is that in 1931 Allah told me I was registered as a Moslem and belonged to him. At this time Allah also told me that he did not want me to associate in any way with fighting or military service. Allah has told all Moslems that they should remain righteous and not engage in fighting or military service of any kind. Allah gave to all of us of registered Moslems names this teaching himself when he gave out the identification cards with our holy

---

52   Elijah Muhammad File, Ibid.

name[s] on, that you shall not take any part in fighting or anything pertaining to fighting. This also applied to prostitution and all kinds of gambling.[53]

It is true that Islam teaches against violence, unprovoked aggression and war against others and, in fact, stresses on peaceful settlement of conflicts. However, the United State's active involvement in WWII can't be regarded as a war of aggression considering how she was dragged into the war in the first place. Not to mention the fact that the WWII was a global effort against Fascism and Nazism, two ideologies of hatred and violence that had to be stopped. In any case, Mr. Elijah Muhammad's refusal to register based on religious grounds did not endear him to the FBI and other local and state law enforcement agencies. Internally, however, Mr. Elijah Muhammad attracted to his cause a cadre of energetic and ambitious African-American Muslim converts. The NOI literature not only praises Mr. Elijah Muhammad for his organizational prowess, but also for his unique abilities in assessing the leadership qualities of the younger men who surrounded him, the likes of Malcolm X, and Louis Farrakhan.

Enter Malcolm X 1925–1965

One of the most famous among early converts to Nation of Islam's social and political cause was Malcolm X (1925–1965) who played an important role in the early stages of the movement to convert African-American inmates to Islam.[54] Prior to his own conversion to Islam which took place in 1947, whence he chose the name of Malcolm X, he was known by his Christian name of Malcolm Little, born into a devout Baptist home in Omaha, Nebraska. Malcolm Little, the story goes, was of exceptional intelligence and self-discipline from early boyhood. He graduated from junior high at the top of his class, but dropped-out, we are told, once his most favored teacher at the senior high rudely awakened him to the fact that his ambitions for becoming a lawyer was never going to materialize because of his race. Later, Malcolm went to Boston, MA, in search of his good fortunes that never materialized in a number of odd jobs that he performed there. Upon moving to Harlem, New York, he was gradually dragged into a life of petty crime to the effect that by the early 1940s, Malcolm Little was reported of having had set up a number of gambling, drugs, and prostitution rings in Harlem.[55]

In 1946, and back in Boston, Malcolm and his associate (known as the "Shorty" Jarvis) were arrested charged with having committed burglary. Upon conviction, Malcolm was sentenced to 10 years in Charlestown, MA State Prison. We are

---

53   Elijah Muhammad File, Ibid.

54   See William L. Van Deburg, *New Day in Babylon: The Black Power Movement and American Culture, 1965–1975*, Chicago, IL, The University of Chicago Press, 1993, pp. 16–107.

55   See "About Malcolm X: Biography" at website: http://www.cmgww.com/historic/malcolm/about/bio.htm.

told that it was during his incarceration years that Malcolm became acquainted with the Nation of Islam's charismatic leader, Elijah Muhammad's teachings and thus converted to Islam. The conversion to Islam was an event that must have had lasting moral and psychological impacts on Malcolm as evinced through his writings, sermons and interviews that he gave to different print and news media. Apparently, Malcolm believed in the moral and spiritual power of Islam to inculcate the requisite elements for the rejuvenation of the Black sense of self-worth and identity, both of which he proposed African-Americans had lost to the North American institution of slavery. However Malcolm later splintered from the Nation of Islam in 1964 and created his own organization named Muslim Mosque, Inc. There are different stated reasons for Malcolm's splinter from the Nation of Islam. Some argue that it was over the issue of strategy, some argue that it was due to personality clashes between Malcolm and Elijah Muhammad, or with other young disciples of Mr. Elijah Muhammad as, for example, Mr. Louis Farrakhan. However, a look at Malcolm's "A Declaration of Independence" of March 12, 1964, shows that the splinter was due to deeply rooted differences between Malcolm and Elijah Muhammad over long-term plans of the NOI.

In his Declaration of Independence Document, Malcolm, after giving homage to Islam and after reiterating his respect and admiration for Mr. Elijah Muhammad, noted that although he had been and remained Muslim, did not agree with the Nation of Islam's top leadership thus was forced out of the organization. This was despite the fact that he believed in Mr. Elijah Muhammad's core teachings including his thesis of "complete separation" as the best solution for Black America. However, he cautioned that the time was not ripe for the actual implementation of the plan because there were then 22 million blacks who, warned Malcolm, were living in America with dire social, economic and political needs and aspirations that had not materialized yet. He also stressed on the importance of working in unison with other Black leaders announcing his intentions to create a new mosque in New York City that he named Muslim Mosque Inc. Malcolm also idealized the meaning of the "political philosophy of black nationalism," as one that had to be indigenous. Accordingly, the mandate of the new Black leadership had to be one of serving the needs of the Black community rather than being subservient to White America's tunes and orders. As to the range and reach of the new Black political activism of the Muslim Mosque Inc., Malcolm's plan was to create an atmosphere of inclusiveness so that the Muslim Mosque remained open to all, be it white or black on the grounds that, "There can be no-black—white unity until first there is some black unity. There can be no worker's unity until there is first some racial solidarity...."[56]

As to the nature of the main problem facing Black America, Malcolm opined that it was Black political disunity thus urging Black leaders to put aside their personal difference and concentrate on a common cause. He also rejected the

---

56   A Declaration of Independence, Malcolm X, March 12, 1964 at website: http://www.teachingamericanhistory.org/library/index.asp?document=1148.

nonviolence strategy advised by a cadre of Black religious and political leaders
(e.g., Dr. Martin Luther King, Jr.), who sought social and legal equality through
nonviolent political activism. Malcolm rejected this strategy declaring that,
"Concerning nonviolence: it is criminal to teach a man not to defend himself
when he is the constant victim of brutal attacks. It is legal and lawful to own a
shotgun or a rifle. We believe in obeying the law."[57] Another important feature
of Malcolm's Declaration of Independence was its targeted audience, a new
generation of post Civil Rights era Black youths who were not content with the
pace of reform and change in American race relationship. Targeting this dynamic
yet disgruntled audience, Malcolm declared that, "Our accent will be upon youth:
we need new ideas, new methods, and new approaches. We will call upon young
students of political science throughout the nation to help us."[58] Malcolm's stress
upon youths and especially politically activists, did not bode well for generations
of Black activists, be it among the ranks and files of the Civil Rights, or Black
Churches and Synagogues, including that of the Nation of Islam. Malcolm's
disdain for the older generation of Black politicians and reformists was reflected
in his following remark, "We are completely disenchanted with the old, adult,
established politicians. We want to see some new faces—more militant faces."[59]
On February 21, 1965, Malcolm was assassinated as he was giving a speech at the
Audubon Ballroom in New York City. There was a lot of speculation as to whether
his remarks concerning President John F. Kennedy's assassination had anything
to do with his own assassination. Malcolm's assassination is a controversial issue
that has not been settled as of yet despite the many denials that the Nation of
Islam has published to that effect. In any case, the ideas, speeches, and charismatic
personality of Malcolm X have played significant roles in the 1960s version of the
Black consciousness. Having had personally experienced the horrors of prison life
and its devastating mental and moral impacts on inmates, Malcolm must have had
realized the rehabilitative role of Islam for African-American community at large
and prison inmates in particular.[60] However, his assassination deprived African-
American community from one of its most charismatic young leaders at a critical
time in the progression of the Civil Rights era.

Enter Louis Farrakhan 1975–2005

Louis Farrakhan is the next person who has played an important yet controversial
role in Islamic proselytizing efforts during his sojourn as the second leader of the
Nation of Islam. Born as Louis Eugene Walcott on May 11, 1933 in Roxbury,
MA, Farrakhan converted to Islam in 1955 and gradually rose in the leadership
cadre that Mr. Elijah Muhammad had built around his charismatic personality. He

---

57   A Declaration of Independence, Ibid.
58   A Declaration of Independence, Ibid
59   A Declaration of Independence, Ibid.
60   See *The Autobiography of Malcolm X*, New York, NY, Ballantine Books, 1965.

collaborated with Malcolm X for sometime, but later was appointed as the Minister of the Muhammad Temple when Malcolm left the Nation of Islam over unsettled ideological/organizational issues with Mr. Elijah Muhammad. Reading Malcolm X's Declaration of Independence, one gets a distinct impression that the difference between the two was deeply political in nature: Malcolm's view of Islam was more of a revolutionary and progressive nature as compared to the more convoluted and bombastic view upon which Mr. Elijah Muhammad had built the Nation of Islam. Once Malcolm X fell out of favor with the top leader, it was time for the highly ambitious Farrakhan to step in. It is noteworthy that Malcolm's split with the NOI was not as devastating to the NOI as when W.D. Wallace Muhammad, the son of Mr. Elijah Muhammad was elected as the next leader of the NOI in 1975. This was ironic considering the fact that the son did not agree with his father's views as to what the faith of Islam stood for, neither with his father's belief that Allah had reincarnated in the person of Master Fard, a core belief of the NOI which sets it diametrically opposed to mainstream Islam's view of deity. It is very likely that Malcolm X and his followers also did not believe in Elijah Muhammad's reincarnation views, thus one main reason for his split from the NOI. In any case, the NOI literature has given homage to Mr. Farrakhan praising him with a series of accomplishments during his leadership tenure. From 1975 onwards, Mr. Farrakhan assumed de facto leadership position of the NOI although Mr. Elijah Muhammad was still alive, but did not run the day-to-day affairs of the NOI. He passed away in 1978. During the past three decades (1978–2008) that the Nation of Islam has been under the leadership of Mr. Farrakhan, he has been praised by his followers and loathed by his detractors to be discussed shortly.

Nation of Islam's Community Building Activities

The Nation of Islam in its official declarations and publications has credited its two top leaders, Elijah Muhammad and Louis Farrakhan, for having succeeded in establishing NOI-affiliated networks which have effectively cleansed the housing projects and prisons from the scourge of addiction to, and pushing of, illicit drugs, gambling, prostitution as well as prison-bound gang violence and forced-homosexuality. There is evidence to back up this claim. For example, in the early 1990s, the Department of Housing and Urban Development (HUD) signed a contract with an NOI-affiliated security company. The stated purpose of the contract was to help The Baltimore Housing Authority to remove from the housing projects drug-pushing gangs known for their perpetration of much violence throughout the projects. In November, 1995, the HUD terminated the contract on technical grounds. However, the Anti-Defamation League (ADL) claimed that, "There are indications that these companies have used public funds to proselytize, spread their parent organization's racist and anti-Semitic doctrines, and recruit new members for the Nation of Islam."[61] The ADL in its communiqué urged the HUD to act decisively so as " ... to ensure that other Nation of Islam-affiliated security firms are in compliance with the full range of civil rights and equal employment laws."[62] No mention was made as to how the NOI-affiliated security companies had misappropriated public funds to proselytize, or to spread anti-Semitic messages.

The communal networks of the Nation of Islam, notwithstanding their alleged anti-Semitic messages, are financed by a number of business ventures such as restaurants, grocery shops, clothing stores, farms and donations that the Nation of Islam is reported of having had built during Mr. Elijah Muhammad's sojourn (1930–1975). For example, the Nation of Islam operates farming ventures named Muhammad Farms, a project whose initial finances came through the "Three Year Economic Saving Program" originally initiated by Elijah Muhammad in 1964.[63] Accordingly, the members of the organization were asked to donate $10 each month for a period of three years and thus the name of the program. With the proceeds, the NOI bought 1,556 acres of farm land located in Brownwood of Terrell County, Georgia. Called Muhammad Farm, the land was utilized for planting watermelons, cantaloupes, sweet corn, snap beans, okra, and yellow squash and sold to large national food markets for a profit. The official line of the NOI is that it is through these types of economic ventures that the NOI is financing its operations within or without the penal institutions. However, there are also large sums of money, gifts and donations that the NOI has acknowledge to have received from Muslim countries as well as controversial foreign heads of state as, for example, the Colonel Muammar Qaddafi of Libya.

Other community-building projects of the Nation of Islam include its mosque and charity building as well as prison-bound rehabilitative activities. For example, in his 7 September, 2007 sermon to the inmates of the Statesville Penal Institution in Joliet, IL, Mr. Farrakhan is reported of having said: "Let peace reign in. Don't shed each other's blood. Find ways to dispel conflict; resolve it peacefully, and make your stay here as good as it could possibly be, then the walls have to come down because you are too big. You've grown too much to be held in a prison."[64] The sermon's main points, conciliatory in tone, try to inculcate a sense of rehabilitative empowerment in the inmates encouraging them to consider incarceration as a challenge against each inmate's resolve not to succumb to prison's criminogenic impulses, a point to be discussed in some detail shortly.

Finally, there is the Nation of Islam's mass-oriented communal consciousness-building activity (that is now incorporated as The Million Man March, Inc.) whose

---

61   The Anti Defamation League web page at http://www.antidefemationleague.org.

62   Ibid.

63   See the article, "The Three Year Economic Savings Program" in the Nation of Islam's electronic web page at: http://www.noi.org/3year-econ.html.

64   Farrakhan, L. "Development to outgrow confinement," at the web page: http://www.finalcall.com/artman/publish/article_4457.shtml. Retrieved on 6/16/2008.

stated objective is black conscientious-building, be it inside or outside the penal institutions. It goes without saying that these mass-mobilization activities are organized in a way so as to raise the stature of the Nation of Islam as the "main voice" of Black Islam in North America. There is no doubt that this stance of the NOI does not bode well with other established Civil Rights organizations as for example, the National Association for the Advancement of the Colored People (NAACP). Congruent with its stated objectives, the NOI strives for enhancing patriarchal family structure under a new breed of Black legitimate male authority figure, the father. The NOI is on record that Mr. Farrakhan is now at the forefront of this resurgent Black Muslim movement despite the fact that he has been vociferously criticized by a wide range of circles and personalities including the President of the United States. For example, on 16 October, 1995, CNN reported that, "—Nation of Islam leader Minister Louis Farrakhan spoke for over two hours at Monday's Million Man March, telling hundreds of thousands on the Mall in Washington that White supremacy is the root of the country's suffering."[65] The same report quoted the President Bill Clinton (1992–2000) as having had characterized Mr. Farrakhan's speech as, "one man's message of malice and division"; the reporter observed that, "Farrakhan has angered Jews, Catholics, gays, feminists and others with his comments over the years. He has called Judaism a 'gutter religion' and recently defended his use of the term 'bloodsuckers' to describe Jews, Asians and others who open business in minority communities and take the profit elsewhere."[66]

Reacting to Mr. Farrakhan's speech at the One Million Man March, Senator Bob Dole is reported as having had said, "If you want to talk about anti-Semitism, it's written all over Louis Farrakhan. That's his message of hate …. There are a lot of well-intentioned people coming to Washington. And I like the talk about self-reliance, about picking yourself up, cleaning our cities and getting kids off drugs, but I don't think Farrakhan should be the leader of the march."[67] Angela Davis was reported as having observed that, "No march, movement or agenda that defines manhood in the narrowest terms and seeks to make women lesser partners in this quest for equality can be considered as a positive step."[68] However, there were also praises for the One Million Man March and its organizers, but not necessarily for Mr. Farrakhan. Mr. Jesse Jackson was reported as having said, "It's important we have such a march to focus attention on the urban crisis and move from the negative urban policy of chasing welfare mothers, chasing their fathers and locking

---

65   "Farrakhan revels in the spotlight of Million Man March" -Oct. 16, 1995 on the CNN webpage at: http://www.-cgi.cnn.com/US/9510/megamarch/10-16/update/index. html. Retrieved on 9/29/2008.

66   Farrakhan revels in the spotlight of Million Man March, Ibid.

67   On the March…CNN-Quotes from the crowd at the web page: http://www-cgi. cnn.com/US/9510/megamarch/quotes.html. Retrieved on 9/29/2008.

68   On the March…CNN-Quotes from the crowd, Ibid.

children up to some real commitment of reindustrialization of urban America."[69] A Muslim participant in the march by the name of Bilal Hasan was quoted as having said, "I think the march is important in terms of awakening us to what needs to be done. But this has nothing to (do) with Farrakhan. I grew up in Mississippi. Since that hasn't gotten me to hate white folks, Farrakhan certainly can't get me to hate them."[70] Another marcher, Bruce Cornelius from Macon, GA, was reported as having said, "My hope is that the men who are in attendance will go home with a change of mind and a change of heart. I'm using this to begin a whole new stage of development in my life. I don't expect my life to be the same from this day forward."[71] Another marcher, Earl Shinhoster, the Acting Executive Director of the National Association for the Advancement of the Colored People (NAACP), was reported as having said, "In this situation, the message is more important than the messenger."[72] In short, both supporters and detractors of Mr. Farrakhan thought the message of the One Million Man March was important notwithstanding the tone and or the language of the messenger. The primary purpose of this book is to delineate the Nation of Islam's faith-based rehabilitative activities rather than psychoanalysis of the Nation's leadership.

How Many Muslim Inmates Are There in American Prisons?

The question of the actual number of Muslim inmates in American penal institutions is as elusive as the question of the actual number of Muslims living in North America. However, there are different estimates of the rate of conversion to various denominations of Islam including to that of the Nation of Islam. For example, The Media Guide to Islam is on record that, "The National Islamic Prison Foundation claims to convert an average of 135,000 prisoners a year and federal prison statistics estimate that 10 to 20 percent of prisoners in America are Muslims."[73] In a comprehensive study of the spread of the Islamic faith in the US, Jane I. Smith has estimated the number of prison conversion to Islam at 300,000.[74] Another scholar, Sulayman Nyang has estimated that prison-bound conversion to Islam is a fast growing phenomenon among African-American Muslim community to the effect that one of every 10 African-American conversions to Islam takes place within the prison settings.[75] In her September 1999 article in the Wall Street

---

69   On the March...CNN-Quotes from the crowd, Ibid.

70   On the March...CNN-Quotes from the crowd, Ibid.

71   On the March...CNN-Quotes from the crowd, Ibid.

72   On the March...CNN-Quotes from the crowd, Ibid.

73   See "Converts: Conversion in U.S. Prisons" pp. 1-2 at: http://www. mediaguidetoislam.sfus.edu/intheus/06_converts.htm.

74   Jane I. Smith, *Islam in America*, New York, NY, Columbia University Press, 1999.

75   See Sulayman S, Nyang, *Islam in the United States of America*, ABC International Group Inc., 1999.

Journal, Lisa Miller observed that, " … The growth of Islam in US prisons is creating anxiety among some Christian ministers. While the vast majority of inmates in the federal prison are still Christian, the number of Muslim inmates has nearly tripled over the last six years to 6,500."[76] Miller, citing data from American Correctional Association, guesstimates that Muslim inmates comprise about 20% of inmate population in Maryland, New York and Pennsylvania. Robert Dannin who has conducted primary research in a number of prisons in New York State— known for housing a large number of African-American Muslims inmates—has come up with some interesting data on the number of African-American converts during the 1980s and 1990s tabulated in Tables 6.1 and 6.2 below.[77]

Table 6.2 African American inmates professing Islam in NY prisons

Year	Inmate Population	Muslim Inmates	Percentile Change
1989	50,000	7,554	15%
1992	60,000	10,186	16.9%

The following prisons in New York State house Muslim inmates according to Dannin whose relevant data tabulated in Table 6.2 below:

Table 6.3 New York prisons housing African-American Muslims

Prisons	1989	1992	Percentile Change
Attica	327	388	119% increase
Auburn	234	310	132% increase
Eastern	135	175	139% increase
Green Haven	286	348	122% increase
Wende	74	135	182% increase

Dannin also argues that one should not lose sight of the fact that "[his] study does not account of the numerous Muslims at the New York's municipal Rikers Island prison, a massive facility holding over 15,000 prisoners where there has been a very active (missionary) da'wa program for many years, apparently under

---

76   Miller, Lisa, "Inside the Competitive New World of Prison Ministries," *The Wall Street Journal*, September 7, 1999, p. B1.

77   Robert Dannin, "Island in a Sea of Ignorance" pp. 1–31 on the website: http://www.nyu.edu/classes/crisis/prison.html.

the auspices of a group of Muslim corrections officers."[78] It is highly probable that a similar trend is observable for the first decade of the twenty-first century.

Prison-bound conversion to Islam is also noticeable in other Western democratic societies as, for instance, in Britain. Comparing Islamic-based with traditionally Christian-based conversion in British penal institutions, Basia Spalek and David Wilson stated that, "Christianity, in particular the Church of England, had traditionally provided religious care to prisoners. In the last 25 years, however, the religious affiliations of the prisoners have been changing, with the number of prisoners significantly increasing while the number of prisoners registered as Christian steadily declining."[79] In fact, there has emerged a prison cottage industry in Britain advising Muslim converts how to how legally confront negative feelings against Islam in British penal institutions. This cottage industry includes, among others, various British-Muslim support groups working with Muslim prisoners since 1994. Among their noticeable services are the following: (1) how to make a complaint against prisons abuse; (2) how to make a complaint against secret service agencies; (3) how to make a police complaint; (4) list of Muslim campaign and care organizations; (5) list of human rights law and civil liberties lawyers; (6) list of human rights organizations.[80]

Demographic Characteristics of Muslim Inmates

Prison-bound conversion to Islam is a male phenomenon. Felecia Dix-Richardson in her research has shown that although African-American male inmates convert to Islam on regular basis, there is marked resistance to Islam among female African-American inmates. Accordingly, "For over the past 60 years, it has been common practice for African-American male inmates to convert to Islam as part of the prison experience. The yearly number of prison converts is estimated at 30,000. However, Islamic conversion among African-American female inmates is not seen as common."[81] Taking this study's estimates of conversion to Islam for the past 60 years at its face value, one reaches the number of 1,800,000 African-American male who have converted to Islam during the past six decades. This, of course, is an estimated number of conversions to Islam on a longitudinal basis subject to the dynamics of demographic change within the prison settings. However, it is

78   Robert, Dannin, Ibid., p. 3.

79   Basia Spalek and David Wilson, "Racism and Religious Discrimination in Prison: The Marginalisation of Imams in Their Work with Prisoners" p. 96 in Basia Spalek (ed.), *Islam and Criminal Justice*, Portland, OR: Willan Publishing, 2002, pp. 96–112.

80   See Muslim Prisoner Support Group webpage at http://www.mulimprionersupportgroup.com.

81   Dix-Richardson, Felecia, (2002) "Resistance to Conversion to Islam Among African-American Women Inmates," pp. 109–126, Journal of Offender Rehabilitation, vol. 35, no.3/4.

an important indicator of the prevalence of Islamic conversion among African-American male inmates in this country. Why female inmates do not convert to Islam with the same enthusiasm and frequency that male convicts do? One main reason is because Islam, like other monotheistic religions in the line of Abraham (Judaism and Christianity), is of a patriarchal nature despite a number of important social, economic and legal rights that the Qur'an has recognized for women. There is a voluminous literature on this subject that the reader may consult concerning Islam's approach to women's rights.

Based on the available literature some of which were discussed above, it seems that prison-bound conversion to Islam is the first step for the mostly poor and/or socioeconomically challenged inmates to connect with a protective network of the like-minded co-religionists that the Nation of Islam has created with organizational capabilities of giving inside protection to its followers including converts. Once released from the prison, those who have "succeeded" in making good and reliable converts out of themselves can further benefit from the Nation of Islam's social and communal reward system, accordingly. In fact the claim of the Nation of Islam is that it has now expended its rehabilitative outreach and agenda to embrace all inmates and not just Muslim African-Americans. For example, in its 18 January, 2000 document titled, "Nation of Islam Calls on All Prisoners," addressed to an inmate gathering at the Manchester, Kentucky, Federal Correctional Institution, a Muslim chaplain, Minister Benjamin, retorted that, "Some of you thought that the Nation of Islam was just concerned with Black people. Yes, we are concerned with Black people, but you cannot be concerned with Black people and not be concerned with all people. In truth, no race, no people are going to survive this planet alone; no ideology of supremacy is going to work."[82]

Nation of Islam's Faith-Based Rehabilitation Activities

Prison-bound rehabilitation activities of the Nation of Islam include its effective campaign for the recognition of right to the so-called Free Exercise of Religion in American penitentiaries. These include: the right to hold religious sermons and/or services; the right to wear religious emblems; the right to correspond with religious leaders; the right to proselytize.[83] These are important achievements for the NOI considering the post 9/11 American public's apprehension over the possibility of inmate radicalization; it is important to point out that the exercise of this right is not absolute and has to be balanced against the security concerns of the prison administrators. Thus, American state and federal courts have responded differently to what is inflammatory Islamic literature. For example, in *Northern v. Nelson*

---

82   Muhammad, Mujaddid R., "Nation of Islam Calls on All Prisoners" website http://www.november.org/razorwire/razold/17/17001.html.

83   Palmer, John W. (2006), *Constitutional Rights of Prisoners*, 8th ed., LexisNexis, pp. 120–124.

(1970), the court did not agree with the Muslim inmates' contention that they were entitled to access to the copies of the Qur'an, but allowed access to *Muhammad Speaks*, a controversial NOI literature.[84] It is noteworthy that *Muhammad Speaks* is a collection of Mr. Elijah Muhammad's words of wisdom, public declarations and religious views that included, among others, religious sermons whose thrust was that incarceration was a divine test of one's strength of faith against injustice, a theme that Elijah Muhammad vociferously proclaimed.

From the available literature on the Nation of Islam's prison-bound proselytizing activities, one gets the impression that converts are encouraged to pray on a daily basis; observe the Nation of Islam's religious holidays that include the traditional Islamic month of Ramadan. However, there are non-traditional and specifically NOI-affiliated ones, the likes of Savior's Day and Holy Day of Atonement/ Reconciliation. Black Muslim inmates are also encouraged to identify with the so-called "religious items" that are either of a personal or of a congregate nature, to apply for membership by adhering to its requirements, to disclose one's medical prohibitions, and to voluntarily observe the Nation of Islam's dietary standards, burial rituals and reading its sacred texts that include both the Qur'an and the Bible. The most interesting among these items is the Nation of Islam's Day of Atonement/Reconciliation that is observed on October 16 of each year. We are told that it was the Reverend Farrakhan who outlined atonement's eight steps on 16 October, 1995, a day which corresponds to the One Million Man March in Washington D.C. The rationale for atonement is as follows quoted below from a nation of Islam pamphlet:

> Point out the wrong. Often, people need to be told when they are wrong, because they don't always see it themselves.
>
> The next step is to personally admit the wrong.
>
> The third step involves confession of the wrong. The first confession is made to Allah and then to the individual who has been wronged.
>
> The fourth step is repentance. In repentance a feeling of remorse or regret for the deed takes place.
>
> Atonement, the fifth step, involves a willingness to do something, to make amends for the wrong done.
>
> The next step then becomes forgiveness. Through forgiveness one grants pardon for the wrong done, in essence to declare the individual innocent of the wrong done.

---

84   Palmer, Ibid., p. 127.

The seventh step is reconciliation and restoration

The original place of restoration is perfect union with Allah.[85]

The pamphlet further advises its members that, "For Nation of Islam (NOI) members, personal prayer is required five times a day."[86] It then proscribes prayer-related rituals that include: washing the face, feet and hands as well as the cleanliness prerequisite of the place of actual prayer, be it of an individual or congregate nature.

Black Islam's Challenge to American Penology: A Critique

The question here is whether the Nation of Islam's prison-bound activities are capable of manifesting Islam's redemptive powers within penal settings? Do Muslim inmates (be it black or otherwise) with strong religious beliefs refrain from committing criminal acts while incarcerated? In other words, is there a relationship between the strength of belief and the number of prison-bound infractions? The literature on the subject of the redemptive power of religion in prison is extensive but mostly of a speculative nature, according to Todd Clear and Melvina T. Sumter.[87] Clear and Sumter maintain that, "During the twentieth century there has been much speculation by scholars in the United States about the relationship between religion and prisoners." Despite these efforts, " … we know little about religion in prison, particularly as it relates to the psychological adjustment of offenders to the prison environment."[88] Clear and Sumter conclude that their research—based on self-report questionnaire of a non-random sample of 769 inmates under incarceration in 20 prisons scattered in 20 states—has shown, "that a significant relationship exists between inmate religiousness and multiple measures of inmate adjustment to the prison environment."[89] There are similar studies albeit with different methodological approaches that have reached similar results as, for example, O'Connor and Perreyclear. They studied the relationship between prison-bound religious sermons and offender rehabilitation. They concluded that, after controlling for relevant demographic and criminal record factors, the study found that, "As religious involvement increased the number

---

85 "Nation of Islam," undated and unspecified education pamphlet retrieved from NOI affiliated website.

86 "Nation of Islam," undated and unspecified education pamphlet retrieved from NOI affiliated website.

87 Todd R. Clear and Melvina T. Sumter, "Prisoners, Prison and Religion: Religion and Adjustment to Prison, *Journal of Offender Rehabilitation*, volume 35, no. 3/4, pp. 125–156.

88 Clear and Sumter, Ibid.

89 Clear and Sumter, Ibid.

of inmates with infractions decreased."[90] Thus it is plausible to argue that those who possess strong religious faith are psychosomatically in a more advantageous position to those who do not.

Studies on Muslim prisoners have reached similar conclusions as, for example a recent study done by Nawal H. Ammar, Robert R. Weaver and Sam Saxon. Basing their research on sample questionnaires sent to close to 4,000 Muslim males in Ohio State prisons to assess reasons for conversion to Islam while incarcerated, Ammar et al., found demographic, ideological as well as ethnographic reasons for conversion. One Muslim chaplain, report Ammar et al., gave following reasons as to why African-American inmates converted to Islam, "From, my personal experience as a chaplain in the U.S. Federal Penal system, Islam is most impressive for prison inmates because of its simplicity, comprehensiveness, universal egalitarianism and the brotherhood of its community."[91] The study quotes an inmate's rejoicing of the fact that he has converted to Islam stating that, "... How many guys got 50-years-to-life and can smile and laugh every day? We are physically slaves and Allah has made us winners."[92]

It is noteworthy that Ammar et al., did not consider the Nation of Islam as a prominent movement in the area of prison-bound conversion to Islam, stating that their data showed that, "most of the Muslims affiliate with the American Muslim Mission rather than with the Nation of Islam, irrespective of when they identified themselves with Islam...."[93] However, The Office of the Inspector General in its April 2004 report titled, "A Review of the Federal Bureau of Prison's Selection of Muslim Religious Services Providers," had a somewhat different view in relation to the Nation of Islam's role in prisons. The Report's section B, "Islam in Federal Prisons" stated:

> The BOP houses approximately 150,000 inmates in 105 BOP facilities nationwide. According to the chief of the BOP's Chaplaincy Services Branch, approximately 9,000 inmates, or about 6 percent of the inmate population, seek Islamic religious services. While Muslim inmates are not required to report which sect of Islam they identify with, inmate self-reporting indicates that Muslim inmates can generally be classified into four groups: Sunni, Shiite, Nation of

---

90   Thomas P. O'Connor and Michael Perreyclear, "Prison Religion in Action and Its Influence on Offender Rehabilitation," *Journal of Offender Rehabilitation*, volume 35, no. 3/4, pp. 11–33.

91   Ammar, Nawal H., Robert R. Weaver and Sam Saxton, "Muslim in Prison: A Case Study from Ohio State Prisons" p. 420 in *International Journal of Offender Therapy and Comparative Criminology*, 48(4), 2004, pp. 414–428.

92   Ammar et al., Ibid., p. 420.

93   Ammar et al., Ibid., p. 421.

Islam and Moore Science Temple of America. Approximately 85 percent of BOP inmates who identify themselves as Muslim are Sunni or Nation of Islam.[94]

In any case, prison-bound conversion to Islam is a fact, be it in relation to the Nation of Islam's or the more mainstream immigrant Islam's perspectives upon which they carry out their faith-based proselytizing activities in American penal institutions. One advantage of religious belief is that it could organizationally link the convict with the respective church, synagogue, and mosque in the surrounding community as well as with the regional and/or national headquarters of that denomination(s). Once linked up with the larger religious organizations, the whole dynamics of incarceration changes depending on the overall linkage that a religious denomination has established with its inmate faithful in state and/ or federal penitentiaries or both. It is in this respect that the Nation of Islam's prison-bound activities have provided a powerful challenge to American penal philosophy.

Prison-bound conversion to Islam is also a powerful mechanism at the service of the Nation of Islam in giving credence to its historical claim that White America has been unjust to Black America despite the fact that Black America has contributed to the formation and accumulation of the wealth of White America. The NOI from its inception to present has been adamant that that White American has to compensate Black America for a wide range of injustices that it has inflicted on blacks by subjugating African-American community to four centuries of slavery and socioeconomic exploitation. The compensation that the NOI has sought is not one of solely financial nature, but one that is of a multifaceted nature having social, political, and legal dimensions to its remedial eventuation; this can be discerned from a ten point manifesto of the NOI titled "The Muslim Program." Under the caption of "What the Muslims Want" the NOI states that:

We want freedom. We want a full and complete freedom.

We want justice. Equal justice under the law. We want justice under the law. We want justice applied equally to all, regardless of the creed or class or color.

We want equality of opportunity. We want equal membership in society with the best in civilized society.

We want our people in America whose parents or grandparents were descendants from slaves, to be allowed to establish a separate state or territory of their own–either on this continent or elsewhere. We believe that our former slave masters are obliged to provide such land and that the area must be fertile and

94   See "A Review of the Federal Bureau of Prisons' Selection of Muslim Religious Services Providers" p. 5, published by the Office of the Inspector General, April 2004, U.S. Department of Justice.

minerally rich. We believe that our former slave masters are obliged to maintain and supply our needs in this separate territory for the next 20 to 25 years– until we are able to produce and apply our own needs. Since we cannot get along with them in peace and equality, after giving them 400 years of our sweat and blood and receiving in turn some of the worst treatment that human beings have ever experienced, we believe our contribution to this land and the suffering forced upon us by white America, justifies our demand for complete separation in a state or territory of our own.

We want freedom for all Believers of Islam now held in federal prisons. We want freedom for all black men and women now under death sentence in innumerable prisons in the North as well as the South. We want every black man and woman to have the freedom to accept or reject being separated from the slave master's children and establish a land of their own. We know that the above plan for the solution of the black and white conflict is best and only answer to the problem between two people.

We want an immediate end to the police brutality and mob attacks against the so-called Negro throughout the United States. We believe that the Federal government should intercede to see that black men and women tried in white courts receive justice in accordance with the laws of the land – or allow us to build a new nation for ourselves, dedicated to justice, freedom and liberty.

As long as we are not allowed to establish a state or territory of our own, we demand not only equal justice under the laws of the United States, but equal employment opportunities-NOW! We do not believe that after 400 years of free or nearly free labor, sweat and blood, which has helped America become rich and powerful, so many thousands of black people should to subsist on relief or charity or live in poor houses.

We want the government of the United States to exempt our people from ALL taxation as long as we are deprived of equal justice under the laws of the land.

We want equal education – but separate schools up to 16 for boys and 18 for girls on the condition that the girls be sent to women's colleges and universities. We want all black children educated, taught and trained by their own teachers. Under such schooling system we believe we will make a better nation of people. The United States government should provide, free, all necessary text books and equipment, schools and college buildings. The Muslim teachers shall be left free to teach and train their people in the way of righteousness and decency and self respect.

We believe that intermarriage or race mixing should be prohibited. We want the religion of Islam taught without hindrance or suppression.[95]

These demands (quoted verbatim from NOI Muslim Program) notwithstanding as to what one might think of their bases of legitimacy, have comprised the Nation of Islam's tripartite call for freedom, justice and racial equality being propagated in the African-American community as well as in American penal institutions to which reference has already been made above.

The Nation of Islam's demands for justice, equal opportunity and equal protection under law are commendable; some other ones enumerated in the Muslim Program are quite radical such as the demand for the provision of a separate state, or territory for the African-Americans who are scattered all over the country; some are holding positions of authority in the state and federal government bureaucracies as well as holding positions in corporate America. There are other prominent African-American personalities who have run for high offices at the national level. Besides Black Governors, Mayors, Chiefs of Police, there are Black entrepreneurs, business leaders and executives, entertainers, vocalists, opera singers, artists, poets, philosophers, and university professors who have reached fame and notoriety; there are also the likes of Dr. Condoleezza Rice who has served as the first Black woman National Security Advisor to, as well as the Secretary of State of, the President George W. Bush. Finally, there was one Black Senator, Barack Obama (Democrat), who competed for the 2008 Presidential elections in the United States America as the Democratic Party's nominee having defeated among other White contenders, Senator Hillary Rodham Clinton, one of the most astute female political stars of the Democratic Party in the US. He won the Office of the President of the United States of America and assumed office on January 20, 2009. This level of advancement may not be enough for a community that comprises close to thirteen percent of the US population, but it hardly represents a racially segregated society either.

However, there is no doubt a large segment of the inner-city residents who are not content with the operational functions of American society and economy and especially the administration of penal justice. For example, Niles Lathem, a New York Post Correspondent, has filed the following story about the remarks made by a prominent African-American Muslim chaplain, "March 9, 2006—Washington – The head of Islamic chaplains in the New York City Department of Corrections said in a recent speech that the 'greatest terrorists in the world occupy the White House,' Jews control the media, and Muslims are being tortured in Manhattan jails."[96] These remarks of a Muslim chaplain, notes the author of the article, were

---

95   See "The Muslim Program" in the Nation of Islam's electronic web page at: http://www.noi.org/program.html.

96   Lathem, Niles, "NYC Prison Imam's Anti-US, Anti-Semitic Rant" cited on http://sweetness-light.com/archive/top-nyc-imams-anti-us-anti-semitic-rant retrieved on 6/1/2008.

secretly recorded by one counterterrorism organization, The Investigative Project. Although the chaplain, notes the article further, denied having uttered these remarks, "but later admitted to The Post that the tape was most likely accurate and said his word are being 'taken out of context.'"[97] Whatever the merits of these observations, what is certain is that the prison settings is by and large not amenable to much brotherly love that inmates are capable of showing one another on a regular basis; it is for this reason that penal institutions are vulnerable to many forms of pseudo-radicalization. The remedy is to move to a more comprehensive humanization of penal settings, a point that this book stresses. However, there are other Muslim chaplains and inmates who have shown respect to their fellow inmates regardless of their faith and or race-ethnic orientations. For example, The New York Times in its 23 May, 2008 issue published a piece titled, "Prison Has the Body, but Allah Has the Spirit" which depicted the attitudes of one African-American convict, Mr. Hamzah Abdul Aziz, sentenced to a minimum of between 10 to 20 years of imprisonment for the crime of murder. However, imprisonment does not seem to have altered his positive view of life saying, "This is only a place that keeps you locked up spatially. I don't have bars and razor wire blocking my mental life. I'm in a state of peace."[98] This is perhaps because Mr. Aziz has found peace and contentment through prison-bound conversion to Islam. In fact, reading the article one get this distinct impression that Black Islam is gaining momentum in American penal institutions a fact testified by Dean R. Riley, the superintendent of the Fishkill state prison in New York whom the New York Times article quotes saying, "When I started in this department 32 years ago, there weren't many Muslims in the prison system and they were unrecognized."[99] He continues, "Today, there are probably one of the most supportive groups among themselves and within the system, too. They take care of their own. It certainly has been in the department's interest to recognize them."[100]

The Nation of Islam's ten point demands is not unique; a multitude of the Black forces and movements have made similar demands during the past century. For example, the Black Panthers, a radical and nationalistic movement that rose to prominence in the 1970s among inner city ghettoes of New York City, published a ten-point plan of action demanding social, political, economic and legal equity. Under the motto of *Black Power*, the Panthers advocated a quasi-conspiratorial view as to how the White America has systematically been scheming and conspiring to destroy the soul and body of the Black America. In the Black Panther literature, this destruction was depicted as deliberate, engineered through sinister and pernicious plans to dragging the Black community to addiction to illicit drugs, hard liquor,

97   Lathem, Ibid.
98   New York Times, Friday, May 23, 2008, "Prison Has the Body, but Allah Has the Spirit. Retrieved on September 8, 2008 from http://query.nytimes.com/gst/fullpage.html?res=9E0CE3DF153DF931A35754C0A964958.
99   New York Times, Ibid.
100   New York times, Ibid.

and crime and vice. The Panthers believed that the White establishment wanted to systematically destroy the Black community and deprive it from its share of socioeconomic and educational achievements. The remedy that the Panthers suggested was to regain the power for Black America by neutralizing these conspiracies. As long as Black America accepted its second class status, it would be impossible to successfully stand up against, and neutralize, the conspiratorial schemes of the White America was the thrust of this literature in the 1970s and 1980s. Unlike the Nation of Islam that considered conversion to Islam as a remedy for retrieving Black man's dignity, the Panthers sought a revolutionary path for gaining power, a path that put them at extreme odds not only with the police but also with traditional Black civil rights advocates as, for example, The National Association for the Advancement of the Colored People (NAACP), the Urban League, etc., who found the Panthers too radical in politics and too conspiratorial in their perception of the operational functions of the American government.

Another attractive feature of the Nation of Islam (to those who convert to its version of the faith be it within or without the prison setting) has perhaps something to do with the movement's stress on the central role of the family and especially on the role of the father figure in confronting some of the core problems that African-American community faces. One purpose of the "One Million Man March" organized by the NOI in 1995 in Washington D.C. was to stress on the fact that the Black Family, as an institution, has been in a multifaceted crisis, a crisis that requires urgent attention of both White and Black politicians and social critiques. The NOI is on record that the problem of Black family not only has not been resolved, but in fact it is deepening because both White and Black politicians have failed to address the root causes of this problem. In contrast, the NOI literature portrays Mr. Farrakhan as the new *sin qua non* Black Leader comparable to Dr. Martin Luther King, Jr., capable of resolving this problem by calling on the larger African-American community and especially black males to get them into action. During the One Million Man March, pledges were made to the effect that from that day onwards the marchers, be it the followers of the Nation of Islam or non-followers, will not engage in self-destructive behavior. Marchers were asked to pledge that they will "…love my brother as I love myself; strive to improve myself spiritually, morally, mentally, socially, politically and economically myself, my family and my people." In addition, pledges against illicit-drug induced violence against women and children were made, including those against crime.[101] The organizers also made a pledge to continue working to improve African-American community and especially the status of the black male.

On the tenth anniversary of the One Million Man March on 16 October, 2005, ten similar pledges were made concerning the issues of black unity, spirituality, education, economic development, political power, reparation, prison industrial

---

101   See the MMM Pledge on the AFRO-Americ@: The Million Man March at the web page: http://www.afro.com/history/million/pledge.html; retrieved on September 29, 2008.

complex, health, artistic/cultural development and peace. There is no doubt that for the followers of the Nation of Islam, Mr. Farrakhan has heralded a new era for the resurrection of Black soul and body politic. Thus the appeal of the Nation of Islam to a segment of the African-American community as well as inmates can be explained as the by-product of disproportionate incarceration of the black males that this book proposes is the root cause of the many problems that inner-city African-American communities have faced from 1960s to present.

Chapter 7
Islam's Challenge to American Penology

The justice parameters of Islam's challenge to American penology is based on the notion that the American penitentiaries have structurally and procedurally evolved as oppressive institutions that dehumanize mostly socioeconomically disenfranchised inner-city petty criminals and drug users and pushers. These negative aspects of incarceration deprive Black America from its ability to compete with other racial and ethnic minorities and especially with White America. The Nation of Islam, representing a segment of the African-American community, has published its ten-point Muslim Program that, as discussed in Chapter 6, gives the reader an idea about its deep-seated negative view of the American race and ethnic relationships[1] notwithstanding some of the important reforms and positive developments that have taken place in this important arena. In a segment of The Muslim Program titled "What We Believe," the Nation of Islam has rejected integration stating that:

> WE BELIEVE that the offer of integration is hypocritical and is made by those who are trying to deceive the black peoples into believing that their 400-year-old open enemies of freedom, justice and equality are, all of a sudden, their "friends." Furthermore, we believe that such deception is intended to prevent black people from realizing that the time in history has arrived for the separation from the whites of this nation.[2]

From the standpoint of the Nation of Islam, the main remedial challenge facing African-American community is not reintegration into mainstream American economy and society, but total segregation from it. Thus, Black Islam's challenge to American penology is philosophically permeated on the notion that it is through segregation that true justice would prevail. Integration with White America is but a "ploy" by those who want to keep African-Americans in bondage. The battle cry of the Nation of Islam is to liberate Black America from this bondage whose one, among a multitude of other penalizing instruments, is the penal institutions that every year unjustly and disproportionately incarcerates hundreds of thousands of black males. The fact that American justice system is unjust in dispensing penal justice is not coincidental; it is part of a grand conspiracy. And here is the crux of the problem: American criminal justice system dispenses penal justice not on the

---

1   See "The Muslim Program" in the Nation of Islam's electronic web page at: http://www.noi.org/program.html.

2   The Muslim Program, Ibid.

basis of conspiratorial agendas deliberately designed to keep minorities in bondage, but upon legal as well as socioeconomic priorities and proclivities of the American Justice Market, an integral part of the much larger American socioeconomic and legal system. American penal justice has become, *mutatis mutandis*, a tangible legal product with different degrees of fairness to its articulation that can be *procured* rather than served to all and on equal footing regardless of race, gender, ethnicity and socioeconomic differences of those who get entangled with crime. In modern and globalized free-market economies, of which the United States is a major constituent, much lip service is regularly given to the notion that justice is blind served upon those who deserve it as a matter of legal justice. The thrust of this book is that that in modern and globalized free-market economies, justice is *procured* with different degrees of fairness to its application. It is also a central premise of this book that the Nation of Islam's challenge to American penology should be directed to engendering a positive and crime free lifestyle in American penitentiaries, rather than promoting racial discord and segregation. In fact, segregation from mainstream America is no longer a viable alternative now that the President, is a black man who has won the 2008 US Presidential Election running against Senator John McCain, a white prominent Senator from the State of Arizona with a long list of accomplishments in the United States Senate, the main power base of the American white political establishment. The President, Mr. Barack Hussein Obama, would hardly agree with the above cited demand of the Nation of Islam; however, he perhaps would agree with the thrust of the Nation of Islam's demand for comprehensive justice.

Procuring Legal Justice

Legal justice within the Anglo-American legal system is an ideal whose core has historically been formed within the Judeo-Christian principle of procedural fairness in both civil and criminal trials; it is a fair trail that in the most abstract sense determines a defendant's perception as to whether or not the conviction has been garnered through legitimate means. It is one thing to believe that one deserves a punishment that has been garnered through the operational functions of a justice system that avails all the requisite means so that one could mount a viable defense against the charges of criminality. It is quite a different thing if the defendant believes that the whole just process is a sham, thus unjust from the time of arrest all the way down to the time of conviction. Thus, in the most abstract sense, it is the defendant's perception of the fairness of any justice system that may adversely or otherwise impact the punishment phase as well as the efficacy of the rehabilitation. It is hard to imagine that an unjust system is capable of rehabilitating offenders as against a just one. It was upon this notion that rehabilitative penance became an ideal of the colonial penitentiaries as discussed in previous chapters. The colonial penal system and philosophy was simple in both theory and application: those who committed capital crimes were subjected to capital punishment and those who committed lesser serious crimes were given a second chance for penance in colonial penitentiaries.

With the rise of modern capitalism and the tumultuous processes of industrialization and urbanization, American view of the etiology as well as the epidemiology of crime changed. It is no longer conceivable, let alone legally permissible, to apply punishment without the thorough and complicated legal procedure that modern justice systems have devised. Colonial penologists could not conceive of such complexity let alone be able to apply it as is regularly done in modern justice systems In fact, establishing legal guilt is becoming a daunting task thanks to advances in every branch of the Science of Exculpation. Thanks to the mindboggling technological advances in forensic sciences, both the prosecution and defense attorneys are in a position to challenge the veracity of every piece of evidence utilized in determining legal guilt. This ability has its own procurement cost that subjects criminal defendants to its adverse impacts. Thus, the establishment of legal guilt is to a large extent related to the socioeconomic status of those who get entangled with the American criminal justice system.

In colonial America, the main function of punishment was restoration of society's mechanical solidarity that, French sociologist, Emile Durkheim opined, shattered every time that a crime was committed; in the mechanical type of societies, the social solidarity rested on sociocultural homogeneity that was due to general agreement on norms of behavior and social mores. Crime, argued Durkheim shattered this homogeneity thus had to be harshly punished so as to show a common solidarity against crime and deviance. Modern American society has long since transformed itself from a simple mechanical into a culturally heterogenic open-ended class society that in many respects is the envy of the world, including in its ability to make justice procurable for those who can afford its huge cost. As a general rule, those who commit crime but cannot afford the procurement cost, find themselves behind prison bars and, sometimes, for the rest of their lives thanks to such "marvels" of modern legal thinking that produces the likes of the Three Strikes Law. Not to mention Possession Laws that since the passing of the Harrison Act of 1914, have led to the creation of immense wealth for drug cartels and Norco-terrorist gangs around the world at the same time that it has been instrumental in the overcrowding of the American prisons by petty drugs addicts and pushers who not surprisingly reside and work in the inner-city ghettoes, slums and barrios by the millions.

The procurement of penal justice is also related to factors such as age, race and ethnicity, educational and even ecological variables all of which play differing roles and impacts in this complex process; not to mention the fact that procurement of justice is also dependent on the dynamics of local politics in relation to factors such as race, gender, ethnicity as well as religious sensibilities that differ in local, state and federal jurisdictions throughout the nation. In sum, because of the historical transformation of an "ideal" into a "tangible" procurable product, a manifestly disquieting factor has entered into the arena of the American Legal Justice Market: the socioeconomic prowess. Those criminal defendants who are unable to pay for the services of a wide range of expertise utilized in criminal prosecution (be it against or for plaintiff/defendant) to establish legal, rather than actual, guilt in court, are left with the adverse and punitive aspects of the American criminal prosecution. By and large, the negative aspects of prosecution apply to those criminal defendants that come from socioeconomically challenged social strata. A large segment of this population belongs to racial and ethnic minorities living and working in inner-city neighborhoods. It is this segment that is more vulnerable to the system's adverse punitive processes that include among others, disproportionate incarceration, and death penalty. It is this segment that is also being victimized by the overall negative conditions of social and economic life of the inner-city to be discussed shortly.

Enter the Redemptive Power of Religions

As previously discussed, the strategic remedy sought by the Nation of Islam is complete segregation from White America. In the absence of this radical solution, the Nation of Islam has sought the application of the redemptive power of Islam to resolving prison-bound ailments that inmates face. Generally speaking, the redemptive power of religious faith has been subjected to debate in social sciences. As discussed in Chapter 6, there are studies that have shown both the positive and negative aspects of monotheistic faiths, be it Christianity, Judaism or Islam. For example, based on a preliminary study of the National Criminal Justice Reference Service database, the following has been observed by those who have studied the issue of conversion to Islam in English penitentiaries:

> The main findings indicated that inmates who converted to Islam while within prison fared better at prison adjustment and community reintegration because Islam provided a moral framework from which inmates could rebuild their lives.[3]

This is important considering the fact that as observed by the Human Rights Watch as of June 2008, incarceration figures show that, "US incarceration rates are climbing even higher, with racial minorities greatly overrepresented in prisons and jails...."[4] It is not just the high incarceration rates that is disturbing, but the fact that, as observed by David Fathi of the American branch of the Human Rights Watch, "The new statistics also show large racial disparities, with black males

---

3 Basia, Spalek and Saleh El-Hassan (2007), "Muslim Converts in Prison" *Howard Journal of Criminal Justice*, volume 46, no.2, pp. 99–114.

4 See the Human Rights Watch entry, "US: Prison Numbers Hit High: Blacks Hardest Hit by Incarceration Policy," at the website: http://www.hrw.org/English/docs/2008/06/06/usdom19035.htm. Retrieved on 7/4/2008.

incarcerated at per capita rate six times that of white males. Nearly 11 percent of all black men ages 30 to 34 were behind bars as of June 30, 2007."[5]

Prison-bound conversion to Islam is a fact, be it in relation to the Nation of Islam's proselytizing activities or other immigrant-based Muslim denominations' similar activities in North America. One advantage of religious belief is that it could organizationally link the convict with the respective church, synagogue and mosque in the surrounding community as well as with the regional and/or national headquarters of that denomination(s). Once linked up with the larger religious organizations, the whole dynamics of incarceration changes depending on the overall linkage that a religious denomination has established with its inmate faithful in state and/or federal penitentiaries. It is in this respect that the Nation of Islam's prison-bound activities have provided a powerful challenge to American penal philosophy. However, there is another facade to Black Islam's challenge to American penology being shaped within the confessional parameters of the motto that America is the Land of Opportunity. The rest of this chapter argues that in the same manner that prison-bound Islam seems capable of rehabilitating inmates in American penal institutions, it is plausible to suggest that adhering to a modern and progressive reading of Islam is also capable of improving the social and economic status of those who adhere to the faith's core teachings, including African-Americans. The main arguments of this chapter are framed within the America, the Land of Opportunity motto of modern American popular culture.

America, the Land of Opportunity

Modern American popular culture conscientiously portrays the US as the Land of Opportunity, a land that is built on the ideals of freedom, justice and equal opportunity. Accordingly, America takes to its embrace anyone that is fleeing oppression, discrimination and injustice. Once in America, those who have earnestly embraced these ideals would succeed in achieving their American dream. What is this dream? It is the dream of success, a dream that the American popular culture depicts as of being universal, but only achievable in the USA. This ability of the US is because American society functions like a cultural melting pot wherein opportunities are availed to all who have immigrated to America in search of freedom, justice and a better way of life. Success or failure in America is a matter of choice, ability and willingness to utilize a wide range of social, economic and political opportunities that exist in America. Thus, the higher a group's ability is to utilize these opportunities for success, the higher shall be that group's share of the wealth, prestige, and power that this melting pot is capable of garnering. The rationale as to why some groups fare better than others is because they adapt better to American success criteria making positive contribution to American society and economy, and therefore get compensated handsomely in comparison

---

5   Human Rights Watch entry, Ibid.

to lesser successful groups. In reality, American society and way of life has, by and large, been dominated by one social group, the White, Anglo-Saxon and Protestant, known collectively as the WASP; this is the main group that played an important part in the colonization of the North America gradually ascending to the apex of post-colonial USA's social and economic structures, despite the fact that non-WASP groups have also played important contributory roles in the creation of American culture and society from colonial times to present. However, this does not mean that other racial and/or ethnic groups have not been able to make a niche for themselves. In fact, as shown in this book, different immigrant groups from South East Asia and the Islamic Middle East have been quite successful in achieving their shares of the American dream.

African-Americans in the Land of Opportunity

Unlike the majority of other ethnic and racial groups who have immigrated to America—most of the time voluntarily due to political and religious repression and persecution in their native lands—to fulfill their American dream, the entrance of the African element into America's melting pot has been of a coerced nature organized and executed through slavery, an institution whose logic, history and legacy runs against the very eschatological essence of the Judeo-Christian constituents of America, the Land of Opportunity. It is noteworthy that according to Jeffery C. Stewart, "It is a myth that most Africans who became slaves in America were captured by Europeans in slaved raids. Most of the Africans who became slaves were sold into slavery by other Africans."[6] This fact notwithstanding, in the midst of the construction of the North American culture and societies based on the ideals of justice and equity, the institution of slavery found a central place for itself gradually being legitimated through a set of elaborate, and yet, pseudo-religious and pseudo-scientific theories all of which were contradictory to the liberating messages of monotheistic faiths in the line of Abraham. How did slavery impact the African-Americans' ability to efficaciously compete in America's melting pot so as to achieve their share of the American dream? The thrust of the voluminous literature on the Transatlantic Slavery Trade is that it left its deep socioeconomic and psychosomatic scars on Black America. This wounding and scarring was despite the fact that as observed by Herbert Aptheker, "The Negro people have fought like tigers for freedom, and in doing so have enhanced the freedom struggle of all other people."[7] Basing his arguments on a number of historical documents that show "Early Negro Petitions for Freedom, 1661–1726," Aptheker argues that, "Individual Negroes quite frequently petitioned governmental bodies for freedom

---

6 Stewart, Jeffery C., (1996), *1001 Things Everyone Should Know about African American History*, New York, NY, Random House, p. 10.

7 Aptheker, Herbert (ed.), A Documentary History of the Negro People in the United States: From Colonial Times Through The Civil War, Vol.1, Introduction, Carol Publishing Group, 1990.

prior to American Revolution."[8] These documents include, but are not limited to, New Netherlands Petition, 1661; Virginia Petition, 1675; and North Carolina Petition, 1726.[9]

Colonial Slave Petitions for Freedom and Justice

In the New Netherlands document, two free African-Americans married to one another, petition the Director-General of the Netherlands to grant free status to their adopted baptized son. According to Aptheker, the petition was based on the logic that since the petitioners themselves enjoyed the status of "free Negroes" and have reared their adopted son without any outside help and especially without any burden to the West Indian Company they deserve such granting. In the Virginia document, a "Negro" servant to a deceased Mrs. Anny Beazley of "James City County" petitions the Governor General of Virginia to grant him, Phillip Coven, freedom. The petition was apparently requested on the grounds that Coven's deceased master had expressed her decision to grant him freedom provided that he perform eight years of services for one Mrs. Humphrey Stafford, a cousin to Mrs. Beazley.[10] The document indicates that Coven not only performed such services but that he had also been sublet by Beazley to her relatives for additional services to render. The petition is indicative of the fact that original indentured servitude could drag African-Americans into the clutches of multiple long-term servitude even though the original master might have deceased long ago.

In the North Carolina document, as shown by Aptheker, the complainant, Peter Vantrump, a "free Negro," petitions the Chief Justice of the General Court [of North Carolina] to adjudicate and declare him as one with a free status so as to prevent false claim of servitude be placed on him by one Edmund Porter.[11] Other slave petitions for freedom pertain to 1773–1779 that have been categorized as freedom petitions of the Revolutionary War. These include the following: Felix petition to the "Province of the Massachusetts Bay To His Excellency Thomas Hutchinson, Esq; Governor ... " January 6, 1773; petition signed by Peter Bestes, Sambo Freeman, Felix Holbrook, and Chester Jolie "For the Representative of the town of Thompson" April 20, 1773; a general petition "To his Excellency Thomas Gage Esq. Captain General and Governor in Chief ... " of Massachusetts, May 25, 1774; Petition "To the Honorable Counsel & House of [Representa] tives for the State of Massachusetts Bay in General Court assembled," January 13, 1777; petition "To Honbl. General Assembly of the State of Connecticut ... " May, 1779.[12] In these and similar freedom petitions the slaves show utmost respect to the prevailing social, legal, and religious norms wrapping their arguments in the

---

8   Aptheker, Ibid., p. 1.
9   Aptheker, Ibid., pp. 1–4.
10 Aptheker, Ibid., pp. 2–3.
11 Aptheker, Ibid., pp. 3–4.
12 Aptheker, Ibid., pp. 5–12.

context of justice as promised by both law of the land and the Christianity's basic moral tenets namely, that a master has to do justice to his slaves when they have done him good; the plea for justice is premised on the notion that the slaves have been true to these premises asking the master(s) to reciprocate by granting freedom to those slaves who rightly deserve it. In the Felix petition it is stated that:

> We desire to bless God, who sent his Son die for their Salvation, and who is no respecter Persons; that he hath lately put it into the Heart of Multitudes on both sides of the Water, to bear our Burthens, some of whom are Men of great Note and Influence; who have pleaded our Cause with Arguments which we hope will have their weight with this Honorable Court.[13]

Interestingly, the Felix petition noted that some slaves did not deserve freedom because of being involved in destructive riots, a reference perhaps to the past slave revolts and destructive acts (such as vandalism and arson) that took place in 1712, 1739 and 1741. Among these, the revolt of 1712, one of the bloodiest, resulted in the passage of the Slave Act of 1712 in New York. In a letter to his British superiors in London, dated June 23, 1712, New York Governor, Robert Hunter, gave a detailed account of the causes of this bloody event. Accordingly, the rioters, comprised of twenty-three Africans, must have been quite unhappy with both their living conditions and the rough treatment at the hands of their masters on a routine basis. The rioters, equipped with guns, swords, and hatchets got together and marched to midtown and set ablaze certain quarters. In the confrontation that ensued, nine white colonists were killed and about six were injured. The militia units were called to the scene who arrested twenty-seven Africans of whom twenty-one were executed, and the rest were set free for lack of evidence. Thus, the Slavery Act of 1712 was passed for a more stringent regime of slave control. It compensated the colony for the cost of executions, restricted night time movement of the slaves above the age of fourteen, and prohibited African slaves and Native Americans from carrying weapons or congregating in numbers more than three.[14]

Other colonies followed suit as other revolts erupted in the South as, for example, the revolt of 1739 which took place near the Stono River in South Carolina. Thus, it has come to be known as the Stono Rebellion. It resulted in the death of several whites by twelve slaves who subsequently tried to escape to Florida. In the end, The State of South Carolina passed anti-slave importation laws and other colonies followed suit. All in all, despite all the conscientious efforts of the slaves, no respite came until the abolition of the slavery, to be discussed shortly.

---

13   Aptheker, Felix petition, Ibid., p. 6.
14   See Callaghan, E.B. (1885), Documents Relative to the Colonial History of the State of New York. Vol. V, pp. 341–342.

Unjust and Immoral Subjugation

This subjugation was unjust from the standpoint of both the law and morality in a society that whose motto for justice is unique in modern times proclaiming that:

> We the people of the United States, in Order to form a more perfect Union, establish Justice, insure domestic Tranquility, provide for common defence, promote the general Welfare, and secure the Blessings of Liberty to ourselves and our Posterity, do ordain and establish this Constitution for the United States of America.[15]

The same ideals have also been expressed in the Declaration of Independence. The first paragraph of the document presented to Congress of the United States on July 4, 1776, stated that, "We hold these Truths to be self-evident, that all Men are created equal, that they are endowed by their Creator with certain unalienable rights that among these are Life, Liberty, and the Pursuit of Happiness ...."[16] It then proceeds in articulating the reasons as to why the colonies ought to declare their independence from the Great Britain. The rationale for independence has a lot to do with the tyrannical reign of the sovereign, King George III, whose conduct is described as, "The History of the present King of Great Britain is of repeated Injuries and Usurpations, all having direct Object the Establishment of an absolute Tyranny over these States. To prove this, let facts be submitted to a candid world.[17] The Document lays out thirteen "facts" concerning the despotic and unjust conduct of the sovereign towards the colonies. The thrust of these facts is that the sovereign has either unjustly utilized the law to impose his despotism on the colonies, or has failed to respond to the just grievances of the colonies. Simply put it, the Declaration of Independence stresses upon the notion that law is more than an instrument of power *per se*, but a *sui generis* province of common good whose instrumentality ought to be safeguarded jealously by men of good conscience and moral integrity.[18]

Slavery and Due Process

Although enslavement of the African constituent of America's melting pot started in 1610, it took more than two centuries for its official end that eventuated through the ratification of the 13th Amendment to the Constitution of United States on

---

15   Cited in Edwards, G. C., Wattenberg M. P., and Lineberry, R. L. (eds), (1997), *Government in America: People, Politics, and Policy*, New York, NY, Longman, p. 322.

16   Lawrence, D. G., (1999)., *America: The Politics of Diversity,* Belmont. CA, Wadsworth Publishing Company p. 441.

17   Lawrence, Ibid.

18   Lawrence, Ibid., p. 442.

6 December, 1865. The 13th Amendment to the US constitution is known as "Slavery" and maintains that:

> *Section 1.* Neither slavery nor involuntary servitude, except as a punishment for crime whereof the party shall have been duly convicted, shall exist within the United States, or any place subject to their jurisdiction.
>
> *Section 2.* Congress shall have power to enforce this article by appropriate legislation.[19]

The 13th Amendment was followed by yet another important and complementary one, the 14th which is known as the "Citizenship, Due Process, and Equal Protection of the Law" Amendment, ratified on 8 July, 1868. It consists of five sections of which, section one is of interest to our discussion. It reads:

> *Section 1.* All persons born or naturalized in the United States, and subject to the jurisdiction thereof, are citizens of the United States and of the State wherein they reside. No State shall make or enforce any law which shall abridge the privileges or immunities of citizens of the United States; nor shall any State deprive any person of life, liberty, or property, without due process of law; nor deny to any person within its jurisdiction the equal protection of the laws.[20]

Put together, these two Amendments were to give to the ex-slaves the status of free citizens to gradually incorporate them in the mainstream American social and political life.

In reality, however, it took almost a century for integration process to take shape. Anti-slavery law freed the slaves from *de jure* bondage, but not from *de facto* ones that re-emerged in various forms in the context of Jim Crow Laws that under the guise of the so-called separate but equal doctrine led to segregation and a wide range of discriminatory practices until the rise of the Civil Rights Movement in mid 1950s. It has been observed that as early as 1880, the United States Supreme Court rendered a judgment on the 14th Amendment, arguing that the Amendment:

> ... was designed to assure to the colored race the enjoyment of all the civil rights that under the law are enjoyed by white persons, and to give to that race the protection of the general government, in that enjoyment, whenever it should be denied by the States. It not only gave citizenship and the privileges of citizenship to persons of color, but it denied to any State the power to withhold

---

19   Edwards, Wattenberg and Lineberry, *Government in America*, p. 329.
20   Edwards et al, Ibid., p. 330.

from them the equal protection of the laws, and authorized Congress to enforce its provisions... [21]

It took almost a century for the American society at large to accept the notion that a freed slave deserved all the affinities of the civil rights both at the state and federal level. The first stumbling block was a series of state-based laws and regulations that circumvented the clauses of not only the 13th and 14th Amendments, but also those of the 15th Amendment, "The Right to Vote" which was ratified on February 8, 1870.[22] Following these developments, the freed-slaves gradually migrated from Southern States to Western and industrial Northern States settling mostly in the already overcrowded inner city neighborhoods during the so-called Great Migration.

Enter Ghetto Life in the Land of Opportunity

The defining characteristics of ghettoes that differentiates them from their medieval European counterparts has a lot to do with the permanence of a set of socioeconomic and psychosomatic parameters that engender the sense of unjust deprivation within the inner-city in America whose motto is being the Land of Opportunity. On the one hand this land is the envy of the world in its ability to creating opportunities to get wealthy and pass it on to next generations. On the other hand, it has created within the inner-city ghettoes, barrios and slums the phenomenon of underclass whose sense of being permanently left out of the generated-wealth is in sharp contrast to the defining characteristics of the medieval ghettos. Louis Wirth, in his seminal paper, "The Ghetto," published in 1927, identified this sense as one of isolation. Wirth identified ghetto as a medieval European identification of an area of the city that was characterized by its Jewish settlers. It was not the medieval city that enticed the process, but the other way around, "The ghetto, the modern Jewish immigrant settlement in the Western world, has arisen out of the medieval urban institution by means of which the Jews were effectually separated from the rest of the population."[23] From a sociological perspective opined Wirth:

> ... the ghetto as an institution ... represents a prolonged case study in isolation. It may be regarded as a form of accommodation through which a minority has effectually been subordinated to a dominant group. The ghetto exhibits at

21   Cited in Witt, E. (ed) (1979), *Congressional Quarterly's Guide to the U.S. Supreme Court*, Washington, D.C., Congressional Quarterly Inc., p. 587.

22   Edwards et al., *Government in America*, p. 330.

23   Wirth, Louis, "The Ghetto", in *The American Journal of Sociology*, p. 57, Vol. 33, No.1. (Jul., 1927), pp. 57–71.

least one historical form of dealing with a dissenting minority within a larger population, and as such has served as an instrument of control.[24]

American ghettoes, accordingly, are no longer just places where poor immigrant Jews reside, but places that represent "Little Sicilies, Little Polands, Chinatowns, and Black Belts."[25] These little towns—of what one might characterize as islands of socioeconomic and cultural otherness—once left to their own devices gradually go through deleterious processes mentioned above. The irony is that modern American ghettoes have not been designated as places for isolating any specific race, ethnic or religious group, but they have functioned as places that the immigrant groups have settled in as they have arrived in America and, then, have moved from inner-city to suburban America by climbing the ladder of social mobility, including a segment of the African and Hispanic Americans. It is not coincidental that we come across the political phenomenon of Barack Obama, who has been elected as the next president of the United States of America to assume the Office of the Presidency in 20 January, 2009.

However, despite success stories, several decades of research have shown that ghetto life is marred with a wide range of debilitating and dysfunctional structures that differentiate the quality of ghetto life from its suburbanite counterparts where the bulk of America's middle and upper class strata live. These include high rates of chronic unemployment; high number of persons addicted to illicit drugs and alcohol; the prevalence of bad diet or under-nutriment; the presence of large number of deviant and psychologically maladjusted indigent and transient individuals. These factors permeate anger, frustration, apathy, despair and negative disposition towards the police and other government agencies. In addition, due to intra-racial violence, ghettoes regularly lose a large number of their adult males to either violent untimely death or to correctional institutions. Therefore, intra-racial inner-city violence in conjunction with disproportional incarceration is the main driving force depriving inner city Black communities from their shares of the success stories including the father/husband factor. This systemic deprivation, of course, does not automatically translate to the wholesale and inevitable road to early delinquency for the inner-city youths thus to full-blown criminality, thanks to the combined and positive role of other mentors of the youths such as the mother as well as the religious institutions. However, as discussed in Chapter 4, the gradual disappearance of the adult male from the institution of the black family and community at large is having deleterious effects on the youth socialization by exposing them to a higher chance and level of vulnerability to early experimentation with, sex, alcohol and illicit drugs, dropping out of high school, as well as involvement with delinquent and criminal gangs, all ingredients that may lead to an early onset of criminality.

---

24 Wirth, Ibid., pp. 57–58.
25 Wirth, Ibid, p. 58.

Quality of Social Life in American Ghettoes

The quality of social life in urban settings is measured by three intertwined indicators, according to Ed Diener and Eunkook Suh. These are "health and levels of crime, subjective well-being measures ... and economic indices."[26] For example, basing his study on the 1990 US census, Paul A. Jargowsky, studied the relationship between poverty, family and schooling in America's major metropolitan areas (covering slums, ghettos and barrios) during 1970–1990. The study indicated that poverty stricken inner-city neighborhoods not only had more single mothers, but also less educated adults to the effect that one could find a definite regression between the levels of poverty and availability of educated males in inner-city slums, ghettos and barrios.[27] Regardless of the poverty level of the neighborhoods in the inner-city, the percentage of the households headed by females was shown by the study of being much higher among African-American families in comparison to other racial and ethnic groups. Through a multi-variant analysis of the poverty rates applied to different inner-city neighborhoods, Jargawski reached the conclusion that this relationship is applicable to the entire metropolitan areas throughout the USA. Other studies have articulated the relationship between welfare and unemployment to determine if the two have led to the deterioration of family life in the ghettos.

Reforming American Ghettoes

To improve ghetto life many reform measures have been undertaken during the past century as, for instance, the Greater Society Initiatives, during President Lyndon B. Johnson (1963–1968). Ironically, it is the stated wisdom that it was with these initiatives that the conditions of the poverty stricken families and especially those residing in the inner-city ghettoes started to deteriorate. One main reason was that some of the Great Society initiatives encouraged a debilitating form of social and economic dependency on social welfare programs from which a large segment of the African-American families have not been able to recover. It is ironic that whereas the two main objectives of this initiative was the elimination of poverty and racial injustice, the end result was so overwhelmingly negative for the intended target as reflected in the late New York Senator Daniel Patrick Moynihan's, "The Negro Family: The Case for National Action" report. Released in March, 1965, the Moynihan report covered issues related to different aspects of the Black family, its problems, and the remedies that the report advised for improving the institution of the Black family. For example, in Chapter I of the report titled, "The Negro American Revolution," Senator Moynihan praised black

26   Diener, Ed and Suh, E. (1997), "Measuring Quality of Life: Economic, Social and Subjective Indicators", p. 189 in *Social Indicators Research* 40: pp. 189–216.

27   Jargowsky, Paul A., (1997), *Poverty and place: Ghettos, barrios, and the American city*, New York, NY: Russell Sage Publications.

struggle for equality and gave homage to its leadership for choosing nonviolent
tactics and philosophy to achieving equality in America. However, he characterized
the "fundamental problem" of the movement as one of asking for both equality
and liberty. He reasoned that these were two very different ideals that could not be
achieved simultaneously. Accordingly, "Liberty and Equality are the twin ideals of
the American Democracy. But they are not the same thing. Nor, most importantly,
are they equally attractive to all groups at any given time nor yet are they always
compatible, one with the other."[28]

Moynihan also praised the Great Society initiatives as a set of effective
programs designed to improve the general quality of social life through inner-city
neighborhoods at the same time that he devoted pages arguing that, "At the heart
of the deterioration of the fabric of Negro society is the deterioration of the Negro
family."[29] Comparing the white family with the black family, Moynihan argued that,
"The white family has achieved a high degree of stability and is maintaining that
stability. By contrast, the family structure of lower class Negroes is highly unstable
and in many urban centers is approaching complete breakdown."[30] Moynihan also
cautioned the readers that the success of the Black middle class does not mean that
all is good through the whole social ladder of the black community and especially
of lower strata and groups giving four reasons for this state of affairs that included:
(1) high divorce rates; (2) high rate of out of wed-lock births; (3) high rate of
female-headed families; and (4) high rate of welfare dependency.[31]

On the topic of slavery, Moynihan report found American slavery one of the
worst examples in the annals of human history that inflicted much injustice on
the African slaves, but argued that with the post-Civil War Reconstruction efforts
slaves were emancipated, but were not given equality. Among other deleterious
impacts on the emerging Black family, one of the most enduring was the lack
of a strong father figure. It was for this very reason that Moynihan opined, "The
Negro family made little progress toward the middle class pattern of the present
time."[32] Then going through subjects such as urbanization, the American wage
system, unemployment and poverty he tried to show that the American economy,
notwithstanding its structural shortcomings, had been beneficent to all who were
well adjusted to its work, education and behavior prerequisites for success. The
seeds of failure were sown within the family and its dynamics thus the reasons
for the abject failure of life within inner-city ghettoes. The Moynihan report
came under sever criticism for its blaming the victim rather than analyzing the
structural factors that led to the overall failure of the Great Society initiatives.

---

28   Moynihan, Daniel P., (1965) "The Negro Family: The Case for National Action," a
report published by the U.S Department of Labor at web page: http://www.dol.gov/oasam/
programs/history/webid-meynihan.htm. Retrieved on 8/27/2007.

29   Moynihan, Ibid.

30   Moynihan, Ibid.

31   Moynihan, Ibid.

32   Moynihan, Ibid.

During the past four decades, state- and federal-initiated and financed reforms and urban revitalization programs were undertaken to revitalize the quality of social life through in inner-city neighborhoods to which reference has been made in this book. Despite all these revitalization efforts the quality of life in inner-city ghettoes, barrios and slums has not improved. What is to be done to break out of this debilitating dependency?

The Nation of Islam's Remedy against Dependency

The Nation of Islam is on record that both the socioeconomic and political position and authority of African-American Black male, family and community has deteriorated progressively due to the long-term deprivation caused by slavery and other injustices that White American has inflicted on Black America. However, the reconstruction of the self, family and community, leading to the eventual efflorescence of Black America, will eventuate if Black America were to embrace Islam. Thus, from a macro perspective the remedy against the debilitating and criminogenic aspects of ghetto life and welfare dependency is through a wholesale conversion to Islam, and from a personal perspective through earnest adherence to the faith's core teaching as articulated by Mr. Elijah Muhammad. What are these core beliefs? The official web page of the Nation of Islam has declared these beliefs as follows quoted below:

(1) WE BELIEVE in the One God whose proper name is Allah.

(2) WE BELIEVE in the Holy Qur'an and in the Scriptures of all the Prophets of God.

(3) WE BELIEVE in the truth of the Bible, but we believe that it has been tempered with and must be reinterpreted so that mankind will not be snared by the falsehoods that have been added to it.

(4) WE BELIEVE in Allah's Prophets and the Scriptures they brought to the people.

(5) WE BELIEVE in the resurrection of the dead–not in physical resurrection– but in mental resurrection. We believe that the so-called Negroes are the most in need of mental resurrection; therefore they will be resurrected first. Furthermore, we believe we are the people of God's choice, as it has been written, that God would choose the rejected and despised. We can find no other person fitting this description in these last days more than the so-called Negroes in America. We believe in the resurrection of the righteous.

(6) WE BELIEVE in the judgment; we believe this first judgment will take place as God revealed in America.

(7) WE BELIEVE this is the time in history for the separation of the so-called Negroes and the so-called white Americans.

By this we mean that he should be freed from the names imposed upon him by his former slave masters. Names which identified him as being the slave master's slave. We believe that if we are free indeed, we would go in our own people's names– the black people of the Earth.

(8) WE BELIEVE in justice for all, whether in God or not; we believe as others, that we are due equal justice as human beings– as a nation–of equals. We do not believe that we are equal with our slave masters in the status of "freed slaves."

We recognize and respect American citizens as independent peoples and we respect their laws which govern this nation.

(9) WE BELIEVE that the offer of integration is hypocritical and is made by those who are trying to deceive black people into believing that their 400-year-old open enemies of freedom, justice and equality are, all of a sudden, their "friends." Furthermore, we believe that such deception is intended to prevent black people from realizing that the time in history has arrived for the separation from the whites of this nation. If the white people are truthful about their professed friendship towards the so-called Negro, they can prove it by dividing up America with their slaves. We do not believe that America will ever be able to furnish enough jobs for her own millions of unemployed, in addition to jobs for the 20,000,000 black people as well.

(10) WE BELIEVE that we who declare ourselves to be righteous Muslims, should not participate in wars which take the lives of humans. We do not believe this nation should force us to take part in such wars, for we have nothing to gain from it unless America agrees to give us the necessary territory wherein we may have something to fight for.

(11) WE BELIEVE that Allah (God) appeared in the Person of Master W. Farad Muhammad, July 1930the long-awaited "Messiah" of the Christians and the "Mahdi" of the Muslims. We believe further and lastly that Allah is God and besides HIM there is no god and He will bring about a universal government of peace wherein we all can live in peace together.[33]

---

33 See "The Muslim Program" in the Nation of Islam's electronic web page at: http://www.noi.org/program.html.

The first six belief items are, *mutatis mutandis*, in accord with traditional Islam's belief system as articulated by the Qur'an and the Hadith. The rest are beliefs related to the Nation of Islam's view of race and ethnic relationship in USA. However, reading the Nation of Islam's literature on the family, one gets a distinct impression that for the NOI top leadership the ideal Black Muslim Family is one that is patriarchal thus under the hegemonic control of the father/husband figure despite a lot of lip service given to the value of Black women. For example, in a 20 August, 2007, sermon titled, "The Value of Female," delivered at the Nation of Islam's Mosque Maryam in Chicago, IL, Mr. Farrakhan is reported of having said the following on the topic of why women are important:

> The Honorable Elijah Muhammad said that the first act of creation after the Self-Creation of God, He studied Himself, knowing that it was painful and difficult. He studied Himself and brought from Himself a second self. The female, according to Bible, is a part of the man. But she is more than a part of man; the woman is the second self of God. Sisters, if you know why you are as you are, it makes better for you to be yourself. [34]

Then, Farrakhan is reported of saying further that,

> You are not the woman of man; you are the woman of God....You are not at peace today. You are very disappointed and hurt by us, because you expected something and did not get what you expected. An illusion attracted you, but reality woke you up. Where you wrong to expect? No. Why do you expect something from a man? The Holy Qur'an deals with the nature of things, because no person can rule unless you understand the nature of that, which you are trying to rule. You must understand your own nature, in order to develop self-mastery. [35]

Following these remarks, to resolve the issue as how men and women are different in their respective nature, and how each category should seek enlightenment on this important question, Farrakhan is reported as referring to Islam's holy text, the Qur'an, saying:

> The Holy Qur'an says, 'Men are the maintainers of women.' It is the natural role of a man to work hard and produce what is necessary to maintain a woman and the children that are produced from that woman. As a maintainer, he is a protector, provider, and he is supposed to guide. You cannot guide a woman with sex, and if a man is dumb enough to think that sex can guide a female, then the marriage falls apart and the relationship tumbles down. Guidance comes from the brain, not from any other part of the body. Guidance must manifest wisdom

34   Farrakhan L. "The Value of the Female" on the web page: http://www.finalcall.com/artman/publish/cat_index_9.shtml. Retrieved on 6/16/2008.
35   Farrakhan L. "The Value of the Female" Ibid.

and truth that is from God, then the man must bring you wisdom and truth that is from God, because the only thing that can maintain the woman of God is the word of God, rightly brought from a man who is in the image and the likeness of God.[36]

Finally, Farrakhan scolded his fellow men for what he characterized as "something" that accordingly has happened to black men and women saying,

> Sisters, something has happened to us, as men, and something has happened to you as women. Something terrible has happened to men because we can attract you, but we cannot hold you. We can give you children, but we do not know how to help you rear them. We can make money, but we are rather selfish. Women have been greatly misused and abused. It is so painful that we live in a world that has raised sex to the level where we get lost in a pleasure that was to create a heavenly existence. The more we get lost in it, the more painful our life becomes. So, having raised sex to the degree that Satanic mind has raised it, men have lost respect for the second self of God and the second self of the self. Men, then, use women for pleasure and discard women as you would a wrapper paper from a cookie, cake or candy. It was sweet to you, but you cannot use the wrapper, so you throw it away.[37]

Reading the above and similar comments of Mr. Farrakhan, one gets a distinct impression as to what the top leadership of the Nation of Islam considers the source of the core problem that has gradually engulfed the African-American community: a dysfunctional and at times complete breakdown of the social bond that unites male-female relationship upon which the institution of family is built. Whereas in an ideal social setting, the bond between the sexes manifests its prowess through love, respect and affection between the two sexes, this is no longer the case according to Farrakhan; it is now the element of "lust" that comprises the main reason that brings the two sexes together. Whereas in the Judeo-Christian and Islamic views, proper sexual activities take place between a duly wed wife and husband within the institution of marriage for the purpose of procreation, this is no longer the case in America at large; sexual relationship is now fulfilling another purpose that is only amenable to the so-called Satanic carnal desire of the opposite sex. In addition, the prevailing division of labor between the two sexes doesn't seem to be performing its intended objectives as articulated by the Heavens and advised by the spiritual leader of the nation of Islam, Mr. Elijah Muhammad. The challenge is to dismantle the practice of Satanic carnal desire of the opposite sex by restoring the institution of marriage; once this rationale of sex for the sake of sake is dismantled, once the relationship between the opposite sexes is revamped in accordance with the divine plan for procreation, and once

---

36   Farrakhan L. "The Value of the Female" Ibid.
37   Farrakhan L. "The Value of the Female" Ibid.

the inner-city Black family is restructured on these purely Islamic bases of sex, gender and household structure, the institution of Black family can be redeemed and gradually get disentangled from the criminogenic clutches of ghetto life and its welfare dependency.

Enter Traditional Islam's View of the Act of Creation and Purpose

Mr. Elijah Muhammad's view of the so-called "act of creation," is patently against the very source to which reference has been made in Mr. Farrakhan's above sermon, the Qur'an. Nowhere in the Qur'an is any allusion to God of having created Himself "after" creating the rest of the cosmos; neither the Qur'an makes any allusion that humankind is a "second" half of God. The Qur'an is adamant that humankind is a creation of Allah as expressed in iv: 1 which reads: "O mankind! Be careful of your duty to your Lord Who created you from a single soul and from it created its mate and from them twain hath spread abroad a multitude of men and women."[38] In other verses, the Qur'an has identified these duties of humankind that include among others, principles of righteousness, good deed, love for ones espouse, children and community as, for example, in ii: 177 which reads:

> It is not righteousness that ye turn your face to the East and the West; but righteous is he who believeth in Allah and theLast Day and angels and the Scripture and the Prophets; and giveth his wealth, for love of Him, to kinsfolk and orphans and the needy and the wayfarer and to those who ask, and to set slaves free; and observeth proper worship and payeth the poor-due. And those who keep their treaty when they make one, and the patient in tribulation and adversity and time of stress. Such are they who are sincere. Such are the God-fearing.[39]

Thus, from the standpoint of the Qur'an, the challenge in front of the humankind is bettering the elements of self, family and community for the purpose of human conditions regardless of sex, race, gender or social class. This is Islam's universal call that articulates its macro as well as micro social and existential level. On a micro level, however, the Qur'an also calls on the primacy of individual responsibility for the betterment of the self through control of one's base and lowly inclinations. Mr. Elijah Muhammad's terminology is poetic in its beauty, but is not in tune with mainstream Islam's view of the purpose of creation of the humankind, neither with the purpose of procreation.

However, what Mr. Farrakhan is trying to convey in relation to the central position of husband/father figure in family has its base in traditional Islamic teachings namely, that family is the core social institution; it is within the family structure that each sex has to adhere to a proscribed division of labor in relation to household chores as well as provision for the family. This division of labor is of

38   *The Glorious Qur'an*, Chapter IV (al-Nisa), p. 74.
39   *The Glorious Qur'an*, Chapter II (al-Baqarah) , p. 27.

a sex and gender-based nature that the faithful must adhere to because not only is it divinely ordained, but also because males and females are created for different yet complementary functions. What are these functions? Males are created for provision, protection and work outside the household, and females for nurturing functions. It is because of this division of labor that the adult male (the father/ husband) assumes the role of the legitimate authority figure entitled to discipline the unruly child with the proviso that the disciplining act is not of an abusing nature. In addition, it is the responsibility of the parental duo to inculcate positive personality traits in the offspring. Mother's role is important, but in traditional Islam her contribution is secondary to that of the father.

Insofar as the rearing of the male offspring is concerned, it is the father who inculcates traditional Islam's proscribed norms of masculinity. These include a wide range of personality traits as well as behavioral patterns and norms of conduct such as dedication to the cause of honesty, hard work, perseverance, love and respect for parents as well as respect for teachers and those in the position of proper authority. It is these norms that help the positive steering of the boys at home and society at large preparing them for a decent, crime-free and moral way of adult life whose purpose is to form family and procreation. The father also plays a central role in the life of the young girls until puberty. As already mentioned, in traditional Islam there is a very distinct sexual division of labor for parents: mothers have been given the role of the nurturer and fathers the role of the provider and setter of discipline. This does not mean that the father should not be a nurturer; he should, but not at the expense of his "God given" role that Muslim traditionalists wholeheartedly believe is biologically and psychosomatically grounded in Islamic traits of masculinity. In other words, in traditional Islam, like its Judeo-Christian counterparts, family is of a patriarchal structure with the father figure as its main legitimate authority figure. This patriarchal ideology appeals to a good number of inmates who, upon entrance into the penal settings, readily recognize the prevalence of prison-bound machismo and its code of conduct some of which were discussed in previous chapters. Ability to defend oneself against various forms of physical violence and forced-homosexuality requires not only physical prowess and agility, but a certain cunning and discipline next to a determined demeanor and ability to look into the eyes of other seasoned convicts in the "belly of the beast" to borrow a famous phrase from Jack Henry Abbot's description of life in American prisons.

Islam's View of Parenting and its Impacts on Personality Development

Traditionally, Islam's view of proper parenting has been that the parental duo, very early on in the developmental stage of their offspring's personality, inculcates the seeds of what is known as *hurmat* which roughly translates as the social boundaries and construct of respect for self and for the parents. The term *hurmat* is a complex one whose root word is *ha.r.m* which connotes (a) acts which are forbidden (*haraam*), (b) places in which solemnity in thoughts and respectful conduct is expected (*haram*), and material that are not to be consumed (e.g., carrion, alcoholic beverages, mind-altering substance etc.), For example, in the Qur'an there are acts which have been forbidden by the Heavens defined as the *Hurmat Allah.* In xxii, 30, the Qur'an declares: "That (is command). And whoso magnifieth the sacred things of Allah, it will be well for him in the sight of his Lord … " What are these acts? There exist a complex traditional view as what constitutes acts that have been specifically sanctioned by Allah and those which are not, a subject which is beyond the scope of this book. What is certain is that some of these acts have been covered under the Islamic notion of *ahkaam* which represent Islam's commandments very similar to the Judeo-Christian version of it; some others are covered under *addab wa akhlaaq* which represent social etiquette, morals and good mannerism; and yet some others are covered under *ibaddat* which stands for fasting and prayer rituals. Parents are responsible for steering their offspring's physical and emotional development at home.

The Islamic notion of responsibility covers other areas such as parental safeguarding of the children against what some Western criminologists have characterized as the pulls and pushes of the street next to allures of deviance and criminality. For example, Travis Hirschi in his social bond theory maintains that one's involvement with, and attachment to, society's conventional norms and institutions successfully contains falling victim to the lure of crime and deviance. This is an important issue that the Nation of Islam has given primacy to its articulation in its literature. It is noteworthy that the bulk of the research on juvenile delinquency and crime has substantiated the general thrust of Hirschi's social bond theory, a subject discussed in some length in previous chapters of this book. As shown in Chapter 4, a whopping 58 percent of this juvenile offending population is coming from African-American youths who live in the impoverished and socially disorganized inner-city communities. Of this percentage of youth officially admitted to prison, 60 percent were held in prison, a percentage that is respectively 3, 5, and 8.5 times as high as White, Hispanic, and Other youth categories held in prison. In other words, not only the socioeconomically challenged African-American youth, as a social category, is being admitted to prison, way disproportional to its demographic share of the US population (12.5 percent), but the percentage held in prison (rather than released early for good behavior, or paroled) is also quite disproportional to all other racial and ethnic youth groups who commit serious crimes. It is in this context that the Nation of Islam's demands for justice as discussed in the Muslim Program cited above, finds its epistemic resonance in the overall failure of the American public education that is now almost devoid of its original functional intent and purposes: to provide a set of positive values and norms for success in American free-market economy. Most important among these are the factors of discipline, personal responsibility and ability to resist against the lures of the street especially that of the violence and narcotic-based road to success.

Instead, American public educational curricula, by and large, promote a strictly secular-materialist perspective that at best explores a mechanistic and process-oriented blueprint for success. The problem is not the sheer inability of the public educational system to inculcate the value of hard and honest work among a large segment of youths of the inner-city, but the very fact that the system has long since become irrelevant to the social and economic realities that surround ghettoes, barrios and slums in many large cities throughout the USA. One of these realities is the prevalence of inner-city narcotic-based subculture of violence and crime that is now capable of recruiting, training and rewarding handsomely youths who are left to their own devices within or without a dysfunctional public educational system that is neither capable of providing vocational instrumentality nor the traditional Judeo-Christian moral values to its clientele, mostly comprised of the lower working class youths in a society that is engulfed with a mind-boggling array of products that has to be consumed, legally or otherwise. The point here is that once an educational system has been subjected to a gradual depletion of its educational philosophy as to what constitutes the value and purpose of life, it can no longer inculcate moral responsibility in the minds of its educational clientele, be it the student or the educator. One wonders, why life seems so cheap in American inner-city neighborhoods as compared to suburban America. Why parochial schools fare so much better in terms of their educational delivery than public schools? Could it be because parochial schools serve student populations that are coming from families that are relatively well endowed in terms of their socioeconomic status? Could it be because parochial schools are disciplinarian in their delivery of their curriculum, a factor that intrinsically reflects the Judeo-Christian and/or Islamic view as to what constitutes purpose of life, the purpose of human existence? Could it be because parochial schools place much stress on personal as well as on parental responsibility in every aspect of education as a complex arena for both learning and behavior modification? Could it be a combination of all these factors is responsible for this success?

Enter Islam's Educational Philosophy

Until very recent times throughout the Islamic world, the prevailing educational philosophy centered on the belief that education meant explanation of, and exploration into, the nature of an exclusively Islamic-Shari'a based world-view, a view that was theocentric in the core. Accordingly, the cosmos, including human affairs, are under the hegemonic control of divine will and power. Thus, the formal educational system, under the purview of Islam's learned-men, the *Ulama*, a category that categorized as the clergy, be it the Sunnite or the Shiite, propagated this theocentrism to every aspect of education, be it public or private. Starting from the mid-nineteenth century to present—under the influence of the developments that have taken place in modern democratic societies in Europe and North America, a gradual reevaluation of the strategic role and function of the Shari'a-based education has taken place in Islamic societies. The gist of this reevaluation has centered on the question of whether with the onslaught of multifaceted forces of modern technology, urbanization and industrialization, a traditional and Shari'a-based education is capable of responding to the modernization and developmental needs and efforts of many Islamic countries. How this issue relates to the Nation of Islam's prison-bound proselytizing efforts as well as its remedial policies for rescuing inner city ghettoes, barrios and slums from welfare dependency and other adverse impacts of ghetto life?

The thrust of the Nation of Islam's literature is that prison's harsh and dehumanizing social environment provides a valuable educational setting for those who earnestly want to remand their crime and violence-ridden past. The same rationale applies to the ghetto life that Malcolm X critiqued in his writings and speeches as discussed in Chapter 6 of this book. To this end, conversion to Islam is the *sin qua non* step for the first step towards emancipation from any form of negative dependency (be it within or without the prison-setting) as it is common knowledge that religions in the line of Abraham (Judaism, Christianity and Islam) allow for repentance provided that one does not return to pre-repentance way of life. This prison-bound education is not just one of how to read and write *per se*, but one of learning how not to give in to the lure of irrational violence and criminality that is engendered by the prison subculture and/or that of the ghetto life with their respective resultant criminal typology as discussed in Chapter 5. It is in this context that the Nation of Islam's demands for justice as discussed in the Muslim Program cited above, finds its epistemic resonance in American public education that is now almost devoid of its original functional purposes for which it was structured in the first place: to provide a set of middle class based values, and norms for success in American free-market economy. The failure of the American public educational system is especially pronounced and deep rooted in inner-city ghettoes, boroughs and barrios; of especial significance is the public education's inability to inculcate discipline, be it educational or interpersonal within the school setting. Next is the content of the educational curricula which promotes a strictly secular-materialist perspective that at best explores a mechanistic and process-oriented epistemology of existence. The problem is not that institutionalized religion has completely been divorced from public education curricula, but the very idea as to why we exist is no longer discussed in any meaningful context other than the fact that we are here to consume a mind-boggling array of products on a gradually reaching mega-monstrosity level. It is consumption that determines the raison d'être of modern and post-modern existence and not the notion that we are here for a sublime purpose as suggested by the three monotheistic religions in the line of Abraham.

From Black Islam to American Islam

Could it be argued that next to the Nation of Islam's perception as to what the faith of Islam represents—a representation that due to the nature of the African-American experience in North America is by necessity of a race-based frame of reference—there is now an emerging American Islam thanks to a large Muslim immigrant population? It could be argued that there have emerged other representations and typologies among Muslim immigrant groups as they have tried to adjust to the tempo of American social and economic life. These can be classified as the modern secularists, traditionalist and fundamentalist representation and typologies. A synopsis of each representation is provided below that the reader can compare and contrast each with that of the Nation of Islam.

Modern Muslims in America

Modern Muslim immigrants argue that the US is a secular and democratic society that is hardly in need of traditional Islamic values and norms thus American Muslim communities ought to abandon the Shari'a-based education and societal order ideals once and for all and try to adjust positively to American education and societal order based on secular laws. The spokepersons of this school of thought are highly educated and modernized in their world view; they defend their position by pointing to the sorry state of affairs of countries that apply the Shari'a Law (e.g., Islamic Republic of Iran, Saudi Arabia, Sudan, and Afghanistan under the ex-Taliban regime). They propose that it is adherence to Islam's Sacred Law that has impeded any attempts to improve these countries' societal order because no matter how approached, a Shari'a-based education and societal order is medievalist antithetical to modern and progressive organization of society and economy. Thus, to modernize and develop, Islamic societies must abandon the Shari'a-based view and structure of societal order and replace it with modern secular constructs, be it the law or correctional institutions. In particular, to accentuate the differences between the two models, modern secularist forces compare and contrast the position of American women with those of Muslim women in many Islamic countries. Women in American society enjoy a wide range of freedoms that Muslim women are deprived of, goes the argument. An important faction is the feminist school that has historically been critical of the American justice system arguing that American justice is a product of America's patriarchal culture that has historically marginalized women, and racial and ethnic minorities in relation to justice, be legal or socioeconomic.

Traditionalist Muslims in America

Muslim traditionalists argue that a Shari'a-based education and social order is capable of enhancing those positive aspects of the Islamic faith that have historically made many Islamic societies relatively free of much crime and deviance. Among Muslim traditionalists, there are those reform-minded politicians, academicians, and segments of the clergy who argue that a Shari'a-based education and social order of many Islamic societies are in dire need of reform. The reformers argue that both the Qur'an and the Prophet Muhammad have advised the believers that the Law of God is for humankind's progress and prosperity as well as tranquility and peace of mind. Thus the Shari'a Law is open to time and social and culturally bound interpretive nuances. The Shari'a Law as the base of education and social order is not, and has never been, a closed system thus reforming a Shari'a-based education and/or societal order does not mean abandoning the positive traditions of Islam, but those which are no longer functional for the vitality of the society and economy in the face of challenges that Islamic societies face in this day and age.

Fundamentalist Muslims in America

Muslim fundamentalists can be looked upon as circles or groups of those who are of the opinion that Islamic societies do not adhere to the letter of the Shari'a Law. Therefore no Islamic society is truly Islamic in the manner Muslim fundamentalist forces would want them to be: a society that is built on an ideal education and societal-order based on a 'total' adherence to the words and spirit of the Shari'a Law that the Prophet Muhammad adhered to during his reign in the City of Medina (622-632 CE). For these fundamentalist forces, the strategic problem of the Islamic world is that it has become too westernized at the expense of the fundamental teachings of the pure Islam of the time of the Prophet Muhammad. Accordingly, the remedy for Islamic societies is a return to the societal-order of Prophetic model of Medina. The most representative of this thought was the Taliban of Afghanistan in the 1990s. This view has given to its relatively small and yet dedicated force, a certain Islamic *Weltaunschuung* whose power stems from its idealized view that the Shari'a Law ought to be adhered to in its strict totality. The Nation of Islam under the leadership of Mr. Louis Farrakhan has identified with a form of Black Islam that shares features with both fundamentalist and traditionalist versions of Islam. For example, the NOI literature gives primacy to a patriarchal reading of the Qur'an, a reading that resonates harmoniously with both fundamentalist and traditionalist reading of the Qur'an notwithstanding each version's claim to purity.

Chapter 8
Conclusions

Historically, the Anglo-American rationale for incarceration has been based on the notion that incarceration neutralizes those who are capable of endangering societal order by committing predatory crime. However, following its Judeo-Christian roots, the thrust of the American penology has been that the efficacy of incarceration, as penal measure, is enhanced when it is utilized in conjunction with the ideals of penance. Simply put, incarceration is a means for rehabilitative purposes and not an end by and of itself. Following this rationale, American penal institutions have ideally been conceived as places for correcting convicts whose congregation within the penal settings is a temporal form of regulated deprivation from civil liberties that ordinary citizens enjoy. This regulated deprivation comprises the proverbial pay-back of one's dues to a society whose laws and functioning order he or she has violated. Thus, by going through a regime of hard work, iron clad discipline, and a Judeo-Christian-based education system in the penitentiaries, the pay-back is materialized. But this is not the end of the process; once released from prison, the ex-convicts, having gone through such an ironclad penance experience, would very likely not recidivate so as to redeem their places in society. As discussed in previous chapters, there was a time that these ideals seemed to be working, but from the 1960s onwards the ensuing prison overcrowding derailed penance ideals by gradually turning penal institutions into convict warehouses to the effect that overcrowding has now become a constitutional issue, some of which we discussed in previous chapters of this book. Despite various reform measures initiated during the post-overcrowding era (1960–to present) to ameliorate prison overcrowding, it remains one of the daunting tasks facing American corrections. The strategic question facing prison administrators has been how to manage limited prison space so that the penitentiaries remain rehabilitative at the same time that they don't lose their justice-punitive edge? Faith-based rehabilitation is one resurging alternative even though it is not a newcomer to American corrections as discussed in previous chapters of this book.

In the 1980s, attempts to privatize penal institutions seemed as a functional remedy for the over-crowing problems, but the so-called Privatization Movement is no longer being pursued as a permanent solution. Instead, a return to the centuries old faith-based rehabilitation is the new trend in post 9/11 America. The strategic aim of faith-based rehabilitation is to help convicts to better cope with adverse impacts of long-term incarceration as well as to prevent them from returning to a life of crime after release from prison. It is hoped that by preventing ex-convicts from recidivating thus preventing return to prisons, a long term solution for prison overcrowding may ensue. In the past, the cost for faith-based rehabilitation would be incurred by various Jewish and Christian organizations and denominations. With the rise of the Nation of Islam in 1930s, Black Islam entered the arena of faith-based rehabilitation. However, due to the First Amendment's Establishment Clause, neither state nor federal government could finance the cost of this type of rehabilitation efforts. In the post 9/11 era, this prohibition has been lifted thanks to legislations such as The Community Solutions Act of 2001, The Savings Opportunity and Charitable Giving Act of 2001, or The Compassion Capital Funds of 2002, as documented by Carol J. De Vita and Sarah Wilson.

One could argue that American penal philosophy has gone through secularization processes thus it is no longer beholden to its Judeo-Christian roots. Put it simply, the hardcore realities of crime have profoundly changed American perception of what constitutes just punishment. Penance is no longer one of the central ideals of the correctional strategies, if it had ever been one. One could also argue that the hardcore reality in most free market economies is that those who commit crime and/or recidivate are being given too many chances for rehabilitation to the effect that now we come across the specter of the so-called Victim's Rights Movement in the USA. The battle cry of this movement is that victims of crime go through several layers of re-victimization at the hands of the American justice system; that criminal defendants have too many rights; that the gap between legal and actual guilt is too far apart giving too many privileges to criminal defendants at the expense of the victim's rights. The list is a long one.

One of the arguments of this book is that the proliferation of faith-based rehabilitative programs in American penitentiaries gives credence to the notion that the secularization attempts have not been able to debunk the significance of the Judeo-Christian notion of fairness in penal justice, neither has the secularization process diminished the significance of faith-based rehabilitation within penal institutions. This is because faith plays a powerful role in the development of personality. This role can be both positive, and negative. Within the prison settings, the strength of one's religious convictions of right and wrong is capable of engendering a wide range of empowerment factors enumerated above. For example, a convict who believes that he or she has been unjustly convicted for a crime that he or she has not committed in the first place, may consider the unjust conviction as a "struggle" that the Heavens has put on his or her way to test his or her strength of faith, a premise that has both Judeo-Christian, or Islamic confessional reciprocity to their articulation. The story of Prophet Job in the Bible and the Qur'an is the case in point. The Prophet Job (in the Qur'an is known as Ayyub) is portrayed as a fortuitous man who was living in good health with much wealth, high social standing and respect among his people. The Satan, being the trickster that he is goes to the Heavens challenging the Almighty that if Job were to face a series of calamities, he would not be as faithful as in the time of prosperity and good fortunes. The Almighty, we are told, accepts the challenge and starts sending all kind of unexpected calamities upon Job, but Job never flinches in his deep love for, and humility and submission to, the Almighty to the effect that Satan admits that Job's faith was true faith and not due to his good fortunes. Upon

Satan's admitting this fact, the Almighty returns Job's good health and fortune back to him once again.

The morale of this and similar stories of the Bible and the Qur'an is that whatever comes our way, be it good or bad, it has a rationale to its unfolding. Those of true faith, never give in to despair, never question Almighty's eternal wisdom by complaining to Heavens, but cling on to their righteous deeds as they try to not succumb to lowly inclinations and immoral deeds in order to weather the storm. Applied to the adverse impacts of incarceration that we discussed in previous chapters, this teaching of the faith is capable of enhancing, rather than weakening, the resolve of the faithful convict. Instead of giving in to the criminogenic pulls of the subculture of crime and violence that permeates prison settings, the faithful may resist them through various means that faith-based rehabilitation programs have availed for their adherents.

Within the prison setting, the faith is also capable of engendering congregational solidarity with the like-minded cohorts regardless of denominational differences. Unlike various race and ethnicity based gangs that use penal institutions for perpetuating criminal endeavors, thus one of the main structural reasons for the perpetuation of prison subculture of violence, faith-based networks are capable of functioning as bulwarks against proliferation of criminal gangs in American penitentiaries. The same applies during post-conviction release especially if the ex-convict believes that there are prospects for his or her positively re-incorporated into the ambits of main social and economic life. On the other hand, prison-bound conversion to Islam is also capable of negatively radicalizing convert's view about American society thus propagating anti-American sentiments leading to terrorism. This has been one of the main concerns of the prison administrators in relation to the radicalization of Muslim converts within prison settings since 9/11 terrorism events in the USA. The causality between prison-bound conversion to Islam and political radicalization leading to terrorism is very hard to assess at this juncture. However, vigilance is the name of the game.

Who Converts to Islam and Why?

Islam is a major monotheistic religion in the line of Abraham, the other two being Judaism and Christianity. Religions in the line of Abraham are in their core similar to one another believing in an Omnipotent, Omniscient and Omnipresent Universal God. The very act of identifying with such a divine being is capable of engendering internal peace and tranquility within prisons' overwhelmingly depressing atmosphere, as reported by some of the studies that we have cited above. This Universal God is Omnipotent beyond our wildest imagination expressed in the Bible and especially in the Qur'an as, for example, in ii:21-29. In these verses Allah is represented as The One Who is the Everlasting who has created the earth (*al-ard*) and the heavens (*as-samawat*) and everything in between including the human kind. Muslim faithful, like their Judeo-Christian counterparts, believe wholeheartedly that that those who earnestly repent and refrain from resorting to crime and violence are redeemable in the proverbial eye of Allah, thus should positively be reincorporated in society once released from prison. Because a good number of prison-bound converts to Islam are from inner-city African-American neighborhoods, it is very likely that they consider incarceration of the Black males as an unjust process. Thus conversion to Islam gives these inmates a new uplifting identity and purpose in life. The prison-bound Muslim Mosque assumes a powerful place in the formation of this new identity considering the fact that historically speaking, Muslim mosques have a rich tradition of involvement in the affairs of the community, education and family. The Black Muslim Mosque, like its Christian and Jewish counterparts (i.e., the Black Christian Church and Black Jewish Synagogue) of the past, has produced influential orators, educators, community leaders to represent the voice of its Black constituents. For example, The One Million Men March organized by the Nation of Islam under the leadership of its controversial leader, the Reverend Louis Farrakhan—it took place in Washington, D.C., in 1995—is a good indication of the ability of the Nation of Islam in mass mobilization abilities that has its prison-bound constituency.

Islam is also gaining foot among African-Americans who are economically viable, and are positively adjusted to the wherewithal of the American free market economy, but are becoming increasingly alarmed with the overtly materialistic and immoral aspects of the social relationships manifested as, for example, in the deleterious impacts of high rates of teenage pregnancy, out of wedlock births, addiction to, and pushing of, illicit dugs that engenders the so-called black on black violence. The Black Male Disappearance syndrome to which reference has already been in previous chapters, not only has led to the disappearance of legitimate role models, but has created a strategic power vacuum in the inner-city black neighborhoods that is being filled by the gang-pimp-drug-pusher trio. It is this trio that comprises an emerging male power-bloc in the inner-city neighborhoods that the Nation of Islam is trying to dislodge from inner city ghettoes, barrios and slums based on its literature to that effect.

The common consensus among those African-Americans who have been attracted to Islam is that these negative aspects of life have adversely affected the quality of social and legal relationships between the White and Black America. In contrast to the overtly materialistic aspect of social relationship in a post-modern America, the faith of Islam actively promotes a balanced and virtuous way of life, based on hard and honest work advising the believers to share the fruits of their economic and communal successes and fortunes with one another, as well as with their fellow humankind with an eye to the overall betterment of the communal life. The faith also stresses on the moral aspect of conduct at home and society at large by actively promoting abstinence from illicit sex (both premarital and extramarital), abstinence from consumption of illicit drugs and of alcoholic beverages, gambling and other vice type of activities. Family and community next to moral conduct are in the center of the faith's advocacy for a better life. Respect for parents is of paramount importance, so is the love and affection for offspring. Of special significance is the place of the teachers at the school and of elders in the community. Neither of the two groups attracted to Black Islam seem content with the operational dynamics of the American criminal justice system and especially with the manner in which law and justice is applied to African-American community in general and to economically challenged minority groups in particular.

In sum, religions in the line of Abraham encourage believers to help one another especially in times of hardship. The believers are also duty bound to encourage each other for the commission of good deeds and enjoinment from committing wrongs. In their eschatological essence, religions in the line of Abraham posits the notion of salvation within the righteous disposition of the believers saying, that it is the purity of one's thoughts and deeds that endear one to God and not the spurious attributes of wealth, race, gender, or class. In sum, this book's view of faith-based rehabilitation is one that transcends religious denominations concerning Judaism, Christianity and Islam; in this model, truism in faith is not a matter of ritualism *per se*, but one in which the faithful relates to the self, community and public at large through a regime of just and righteous conduct. This said, there is no doubt that there are important inter- and intra-denominational difference between the three religions in the line of Abraham. In the same manner that there are Islamic fundamentalist circles within the penal settings that are avowedly anti-Semite and/ or anti-Christian, there are similarly Jewish and Christian fundamentalist circles who consider Islam a false religion bent on destroying Western civilization. In this day and age of Internet-based pseudo-intellectualism, one can find a plethora of arguments as to why one religion is the expression of ultimate "truth," while others are nothing but "falsehood."

The author of this book however, adheres to advocacy of faith-based rehabilitation that emphasizes the epistemic similarities between the three rather than the differences between the three; by building ecumenical bridge and dialogue with other faith-based organizations that work in American penal settings to rehabilitate inmates, a more positive prison-bound as well as post-release integration can be achieved as against those schools of thought that portray Islam anti-Semitic and/or anti-Judeo-Christian values. The idea that a monotheistic world religion such as Islam is the sole cause of international terrorism and unbridled violence is antithetical to the core teachings of religions in the line of Abraham. This does not mean, nor is it this book argument that religions are immune to radicalization for the purpose of enticing people to terrorism. The point is that religions, including Islam, are subjected to a wide range of interpretive nuances some of which can be abused for unscrupulous manipulation. From this perspective, some penal institutions may indeed have become suitable grounds for religious radicalization; this radicalism may lead to certain inmate's post-release engagement in international terrorism. Thus prison administrators have to be vigilant against the abuse of the faith-based organizations and especially of radical Islam. However, it is an historical fact that American faith-based organizations have also utilized Judeo-Christian dogmas and rituals for penance-based rehabilitation purposes within both state and federal penal settings.

The question is can Islam perform similar rehabilitative functions? Although life in American penal settings, be it of the state or of the federal jurisdiction, has never been fully conducive to their stated Judeo-Christian ideals of rehabilitation so as to enable ex-convicts to reintegrate into American society's main socioeconomic structures upon release, they have nonetheless evolved from one of colonial primitiveness to their present total institutional status; as explored in this book in some details, faith-based rehabilitation has consistently been considered as a natural instrument for consciousness-building among inmates. This is because Anglo-American penal philosophy, following its Judeo-Christian epitome that the faithful must refrain from crime commission, seeks various ways to correct convicts so as to deter/reduce recidivism. Can Islam be utilized for such purposes? The thrust of this book is a guarded positive response to this important question for various reasons that this book has articulated.

Legal Justice in the Land of Opportunity

What this book considers as true legal or penal justice in a society that prides itself as being the land of opportunity is premised on the ideal of reaching the stage at which one's possessive-individualism is not allowed to enhance at the expense of mass poverty, misery and loss of human dignity. This implies that material success in America, the Land of Opportunity, should ideally depend on equal opportunity to access social, economic and legal opportunities that this land of opportunity should ideally strive to avail to all, regardless of race, gender and ethnicity. The other is the structural and procedural factors that function in a way so as to enable the highest number of participants the positive and just utilization of such opportunities. This formula is not Marxian, but it is a modern Islamic Social Just perspective in that it does not deny the central role of private property, nor does it advocate for public control of the means of production, but argues that America as the Land of Opportunity has to provide equal opportunities for all. The motto of this modern Islamic Social Justice is simple yet coherent and achievable: the limit of one's success in America is not the sky *per se*, but the length of the ladder by means of which one attempts to ascend. This ladder is created by innumerable visible or invisible nets of social organizations and structures at both local and national levels that link the individual to the larger community and its social institutions.

Islam on Balanced-Proportionality in Thought and Conduct

The thrust of the Islamic Social Justice view as to what causes societies to fall victim to socioeconomic as well as moral decay has a lot to do with what the faith has characterized as deterioration in the principle of balanced-proportionality in thought and conduct. Accordingly, an ideal disciplined life is one that is built on the principle proportionality that one has to balance between various factors that play a role in our daily life, be it personal or communal. This disciplined-proportionality, formulated in the Qur'an as that which balances between the two extremes (*khayral umura owsatiha*), is a factor that has its very *raison d'être* in Islam's view of Cosmological Order (*Nizamil-khilqat*) of which the humankind is an important constituent. Reading different verses of the Qur'an, one gets this distinct impression that Allah, as the Creator par excellence, has created the cosmos with a balanced-proportionality (*al-mizan*) that permeates in all aspects of cosmic as well as human affairs; this balanced-proportionality reflects, among others, Allah's most judicious sense of benevolence that is discernable from every living entity from the highest among the celestial heavens to the most infinitesimal lower organism in a droplet of rain. For example, the Qur'an in lxxviii: 1–40 is adamant that every event, every act of creation and deed including the creation of humankind has been planned by the Heavens for a purpose; life be of cosmic or human nature, is maintained through this proportionality that is both just and dignified. Islam, like its Judeo-Christian counterparts, encourages faithful to refrain from any form of extremism in thought as well as in conduct. Crime, not withstanding its form and/or amount of social harm that inflicts, upsets this balanced order on the one hand. On the other hand, any form of injustice violates the cosmological proportionality. Therefore Muslims, like their Jewish and Christian counterparts, are duty bound to refrain from acts that upsets this balance, no matter where they are and under what adverse conditions they reside, be it in penal institutions or in ghettoes, barrios and slums. In other words, the thrust of the principle of balanced-proportionality is that the faithful ought to refrain from unbridled violence and immoral acts even under conditions that are harsh. Desistance against hard and/or criminogneic conditions is a sign of a believer's strength of *taqwaa*, a term from the Qur'an that can be translated as moral strength and dignity.

Although discipline is a prime anti-criminogenic factor that ideally is inculcated in the family as previously mentioned. However, its continual maintenance is contingent upon other factors such as faith in Islam's teachings in regards to moral conduct, and just disposition towards self and others. Accordingly, a person of true faith is duty bound to follow the route of high morality, self-perpetuating justice, social conscience, good mannerism, and patience; he or she is by necessity, a person who would abide by the society's rules and regulations including those that pertain to incarceration. The family occupies a central place among both immigrant as well as African-American Muslim communities. This importance stems from the fact that the faith of Islam has historically portrayed family as the most important primary social institution in the confines of which Islam's core values are inculcated. These core values include, among others, love and respect for parents. In the Qur'an much stress is placed on the family characterized as the provider of legitimate goods, discipline and authority. The Qur'an also alludes to a cooperation between the parents as providers for household members, and charges both parents with the responsibility for maintaining emotionally fulfilling and nurturing family environment. Notwithstanding the fact that a strictly sexual division of labor has existed in Islamic world in the past, Muslim Americans believe by and large that it is only in such a disciplined and yet nurturing home environment that the parents would be able to inculcate in their offspring values such as (1) respect for self, siblings, parents, grand parents and other members of the society; (2) a conscientious fear of social disrepute preventing the offspring from engaging in deviant, delinquent, or criminal behaviors, and (3) appreciation of the importance of education, positive involvement in the social affairs of the community. In addition, offspring brought up in such a positive family environment, learn about, and appreciates the importance of, legitimate authority. Once these factors are adequately inculcated in the offspring, these moral and social values enable the youths to better appreciate the repercussions of engagement in deviant or delinquent acts by defying parental authority at home or that of other authority figures at society at large.

Three questions are raised: (1) Are the African-American youth offenders disproportionately involved in delinquency and/or serious crime in comparison to other racial and ethnic youths leading to such high incarceration rates? (2) Are the African-American youth offenders victims of a racist juvenile justice systems in many States leading to such high incarceration rates? (3) Is this the result of disproportionate confinement strategies applied to minority, and, especially, to the African-American, youth offenders? Insofar as the first question is concerned, from various self-report studies, it has been ascertained that African-American juveniles' rate of offending behavior is consistent with other racial and ethnic minorities despite the picture depicted by official data as, for instance, the Uniform Crime Report which shows a much higher arrest rates for both adult and minority offending population throughout large urban centers in the US. However, we have already documented in this study the disproportional incarceration of both the African-American male and juvenile offenders at state correctional institutions. It is logical to argue that the disproportional incarceration of the African-American adult males influences the present disproportional incarceration of the juvenile African-American offenders. The reasons for this relationship can be envisioned as a number of plausible scenarios as follows: (a) It is plausible to argue that the black youths in the inner city are subjected to a lesser amount of legitimate male authority at home and in the community, a situation that increases their chances of entanglement with the criminogenic environment of the inner city, an environment that is conducive to status offenses (truancy, curfew violations, foul language), or delinquency; (b) due to lesser an/or less effective supervision, black youth in the inner city are more vulnerable to the criminogenic pulls of the street at an early age; (c) the gradual disappearance of the adult males deprives the youngsters of the much needed legitimate role model at home and in the community.

In so far as the second question is concerned, it is noteworthy that the lack of adult supervision—created through various structural ailments of ghetto life as well as disproportionate incarceration—having its both short- and long-term adverse impacts on inner-city juveniles, has prompted William Wilbanks to argue that the charge of racism, which has been leveled against both the adult and juvenile justice systems in the US, is but a "myth".[1] The validity of the charge, however, depends, to some extent, on what one means by the term racism: if it is meant to represent a whole sale and institutionalized racism that permeates both the adult and juvenile justice systems in fifty states, it is very difficult to document the existence of such an overwhelming nefarious force systematically working throughout both juvenile and adult systems. However, if it is meant to represent situational racism, as pointed out by Michael J. Lynch and E. Britt Patterson[2] then it is a more realistic phenomenon whose discriminatory impacts, prevailing in both adult and juvenile systems, can be assessed. Lynch and Patterson reject Wilbanks' assertion that race-based discrimination is a myth observing:

> Wilbanks conceptualizes racial discrimination as an 'all or nothing phenomenon' in which there is only one possible outcome: either (1) there is discrimination throughout the system (there is systematic bias, or DT), or (2) there is no systematic race bias across all decision making points in all jurisdictions (or NDT). There is, however, an alternative to this 'all or nothing' approach. This view which we call the stage-based racial discrimination thesis (or SRDT), claims that racial discrimination is systematic to the extent that it affects certain parts of the decision making process in a somewhat consistent (systematic) manner across jurisdiction. In short, all decision may not be biased, but certain decisions may be consistently biased. This bias may be related to offender characteristics, or a combination of offender/victim characteristics.[3]

The premise of Lynch and Patterson is realistic in the face of the US Constitutional checks and balances which have been put into daily operational effect in State adult and juvenile systems from mid 1950s to the present. In the same manner that one could hardly substantiate the claim that all judges, prosecutors, police, social workers and correctional officers are racist, neither could one substantiate the opposite namely that racism in the American criminal justice system is a "myth." The reality is that next to decent, conscientious, highly professional judges, prosecutors, lawyers, social workers, and police and correctional officers in the American adult and juvenile justice system, there are also racist and corrupt ones who give a bad name to this noble profession.

---

1 Wilbanks, W., *The Myth of a Racist Criminal Justice System*, Brooks/Cole, 1987.

2 Lynch, M.J., and Patterson, E.B., "Racial Discrimination in the Criminal Justice System: Evidence from Four Jurisdictions" in Brian E. MacLean and Dragan Milovanovic (eds.), *Racism, Empiricism, and Criminal Justice*, (Collective Press, 1990).

3 Lynch and Patterson, "Racial Discrimination in the Criminal Justice System: Evidence from Four Jurisdictions" p. 105 cited in Richard C. Monk (ed), *Taking Sides: Clashing Views on Controversial Issues in Crime and Criminology*, third edn, Guilford, CT, The Dushkin Publishing Group, Inc., 1993, pp. 104–109.

In so far as the third question is concerned, in a 1998 study commissioned by the Office of Juvenile Justice and Delinquency Prevention (OJJDP from now on), Patricia Devine, Kathleen Coolbaugh, and Susan Jenkins observed that:

> The 1988 amendment to the Juvenile Justice and Delinquency Prevention (JJDP) Act of 1974 (Pub. L. 93-415, 42 U.S.C. 5601 *et seq*.) Required that States participating in the JJDP's Act's Part B Formula Grants program address the disproportionate confinement of minority juveniles in secure facilities. Specifically, this provision required State plans to assess the level of such confinement and implement strategies to reduce disproportionate minority representation where it is found to exist.[4]

Thus, youth crime is caused by a combination of socioeconomic factors However, next to parents, and government, there is the educational system that plays a significant role in the propagation, enhancement and internalization of a set of basic values that the institution of family is expected to inculcate in the offspring. Return to Islam's redemptive power proposal is, nonetheless, very difficult to make operational within the American criminal justice system because it runs against the manner in which the system has been structured within the functional ideals of modern capitalism and market economy. In previous chapters these ideals were discussed in some details. It suffices to state at this juncture that those who end up in prison have already been rendered ineffective to succeed in accordance to these functional ideals of the American market economy. Thus, American penitentiaries, as shown in this book have become a natural setting for the adumbration of the Islamic call for a return to the ideal of a Judeo-Christian notion of basic justice within an Islamic garb. One reason for this plausibility has to do with what one might call the redemptive power of the religions in the line of Abraham (Judaism, Christianity and Islam), some of whose characteristics this book has articulated.

In sum, Muslim faithful in American penal institutions, like their Judeo-Christian counterparts, seem to believe that that those who earnestly repent and refrain from resorting to crime and violence are redeemable in the proverbial eye of Allah, thus should positively be reincorporated in society once released from prison. Because a good number of prison-bound converts to Islam are from inner-city African-American neighborhoods, it is very likely that they consider incarceration of the Black males as an unjust process. Thus conversion to Islam gives these inmates a new uplifting identity and purpose in life. The prison-bound Muslim Mosque assumes a powerful place in the formation of this new identity considering the fact that historically speaking, Muslim mosques have a rich tradition of involvement in the affairs of the community, education and

---

4   Devine, P., Coolbaugh, K., and Jenkins, S., (December, 1998), "Disproportionate Minority Confinement: Lessons Learned From Five States", The U.S. Department of Justices, Juvenile Justice Bulletin, p. 1.

family. The Black Muslim Mosque, like its Christian and Jewish counterparts (i.e., the Black Christian Church and Black Jewish Synagogue) of the past, has produced influential orators, educators, community leaders to represent the voice of its Black constituents. For example, The One Million Men March organized by the Nation of Islam under the leadership of its controversial leader, the Reverend Louis Farrakhan–it took place in Washington, D.C., in 1995– is a good indication of the ability of the Nation of Islam in mass mobilization abilities that has its prison-bound constituency.

It is noteworthy that from 1960s to present the African-American communities have gone through a tumultuous stratification process with all of its social, economic and political implications. Within half a century after the rise of the Civil Rights Era, American social and political scene is now becoming more receptive of the idea that American race relationship is still problematic despite positive changes that have taken place since 1950s. For example, there are a small number of Black politicians running for various offices throughout the nation, next to other Black success stories pertaining to academics, business, civic and religious leaders. However, we also witness the deleterious and criminogenic impacts of the widening gap between the haves and the have-nots in this country, a process that has its parallelism in the Black stratification process from 1960s to present. Next to a relatively small Black upper and middle class, there is a wide Black working class a good segment of which have fallen victim to the negative impacts of the post-industrialization of the US economy, a tumultuous social and economic differentiation processes that American society went through during the last four decades of the 20th century. The post-industrialization is a term that economists utilize in explaining how US economy lost its unrivaled position in manufacturing industries that it had gained during post WWII. During this period, the US manufacturing industries provided a wide range of employment opportunities for both highly skilled and semi-skilled labor force. This labor market allowed for the development of a large industrial labor force earning a competitive wage with fringe benefits. In the 1970s American manufacturing industries started losing their technical, managerial and marketing edge to a number of rising economies in Europe and South East Asia. Instead, the US economy started becoming more and more dependent on the service sector thanks to the revolution that took place in the electronic computing and information technology.

Unlike the past, cooption in a post-industrialized service sector required both baccalaureate and post-baccalaureate education. Next to education, success also depended on factors such as discipline, ability to plan and manage one's time and resources in a highly competitive service sector market. Thus the issue of success in post-industrialized US economy became more and more dependent on educational and technical adaptation to the requisites of the service industry. These were of social structural as well as social process nature. The first relates to patterned social relationships that comprise the totality of the realms of action, and the latter to the overall socialization processes that determine the level of success and /or failure. For example, the American educational system is a vast and complex structure that provides both the quality and quantity of education for American society from early childhood to late adulthood. Success in any level of education depends on a wide range of abilities that the educational system requires from individuals at the same time that it tries to inculcate and/or enhance in its clientele. However, American educational system is by and large a middle-class institution run by those who largely belong to middle-class strata. In addition, the bulk of the American educational structure (e.g. educational curricula, testing system, notion of IQ and the manner of its determination, extracurricular activities, language structure and utilization etc.) is biased towards those who adhere to middle-class values and norms of conduct. Thus, youngsters who go through middle-class socialization norms, ethos and world views, start their education with an already inbuilt advantage in comparison to those who do not belong to the middle class strata.

Post-industrialization in conjunction with the loss of skilled labor market in the steel and manufacturing industries led to the rise of the phenomenon of underclass among poor inner-city white as well as African-American and Hispanics communities. Thus a large segments of the Black youths residing in the nation's sprawling metropolitan inner-cities and ghettoes became much more vulnerable to the negative impacts of life there because next to the wide range of socially disorganizing factors prevailing in the inner-cities, the lack of legitimate Black role model (the father-husband duo) further added to the weight and impacts of underclass and its criminogenic impacts. This premise, of course, does not mean an automatic and wholesale and inevitable road to early delinquency thus to full-blown criminality for African-American youths thanks to the combined and positive role of the Black mother, Black churches, Black synagogues and now Black mosques in the life of the African-American communities. However, the gradual disappearance of the adult male at home is exposing the Black youth to a higher chance and level of vulnerability to early experimentation with sex, alcohol and illicit drugs, droppings out of high school, as well as involvement with delinquent and criminal gangs, all ingredients that may lead to an early onset of criminality.

This book also discussed several dimensions of Islam's challenge to American socioeconomic structures arguing that America could indeed become a land of opportunity for a new trend of Islamic thinking that transcends race-based reading of Islam, a reading that has its rationale in a modern school of thought that proposes that Islam, like its Jewish and Christian counterparts, is a faith in the line of Abraham whose core teachings is for justice and social progress within mainstream American society and economy; it is this reading of Islam that should be the epistemological base of the post 9/11 faith-based rehabilitation in American penal institutions. Thus, instead of asking for legal segregation, those who profess their faith in Islam should promote an Islam which is not antagonistic to American ideals of democracy and social and economic progress upon which social justice and equity could be institutionalized for the largest amount of common good. One would hope that under the Presidency of Mr. Barack Obama, a more constructive and respectful engagement with Islam will enable America to become a more equitable society for all, including Black America that has contributed its sweat and blood to America from the time that the first slave galleys dropped anchor on the port of entries along North Atlantic shores up to this day, Inshallah.

Index